Object-Oriented Programming

Fundamentals and Applications

Probal Sengupta
Bidyut Baran Chaudhuri

Computer Vision & Pattern Recognition (CVPR) Unit
Indian Statistical Institute, Calcutta

Prentice-Hall of India Private Limited

NEW DELHI - 110 001

1998

Rs. 150.00

OBJECT-ORIENTED PROGRAMMING: Fundamentals and Applications
by Probal Sengupta and Bidyut Baran Chaudhuri

ISBN-81-203-1258-9

The export rights of this book are vested solely with the publisher.

Published by Asoke K. Ghosh, Prentice-Hall of India Private Limited, M-97, Connaught Circus, New Delhi-110001 and Printed by Syndicate Binders, B-167, Okhla Industrial Area, Phase I, New Delhi-110020.

Contents

Preface

In recent years, object-oriented programming (OOP) and object-oriented analysis and design (OOA&D) have assumed great importance in the computer science community. Although object-oriented programming is not a new concept, the renewed interest in the field has been primarily triggered by the advent of the C++ language.

A number of books are now available that describe the syntax of the C++ language and aspects of programming using C++. Many of these books are good supplementary reading material for some version of a commercial C++ compiler environment (usually for popular PC-specific application development systems like Visual C++, Borland C++, etc.). Such a system usually comes with some form of a container class library and/or an 'object-based' library for programming under some 'Graphical Users' Interface' (GUI) like MS-Windows. Many of these books therefore include chapters on GUI programming (MS-Windows programming), based upon how to develop (Windows) programs in the application development environment under discussion.

On the more academic side, a large number of papers, monographs, and reference books on object-oriented analysis and design concepts on the one hand and formal semantics of OOPLs on the other, are also available. While some of the books on OOA&D are extremely well written, most of them do not go into the details of OOP except as case studies. Unfortunately, we have found, on several occasions, that persons supposedly well-read in aspects of OOA&D have very poor knowledge of OOP. We believe that this is because a surprisingly few number of books deal with OOP concepts in reasonable depth. Reading this book could possibly enhance the capacity to appreciate the contents of the above-mentioned books.

The papers and other references on OOP proper deal mostly with semantic and formal aspects of different OOPL. An understanding of these highly theoretical concepts is apparently not an essential prerequisite for achieving good object-oriented programming skills.

As mentioned above, there is a real dearth of books entirely devoted to OOP, which contain the theoretical and practical principles upon which OOP is based, although most books on C++ include the term "object-oriented programming" in their titles. In our opinion, an understanding of these concepts is essential for building efficient program modules in C++ or any other OOPL.

Our book is not intended to serve as yet another handbook on C++. We feel that it is worth the effort to provide a good insight into the paradigm through an exposure of the essential concepts of object-oriented programming in the light of a popular OOPL like C++. Therefore, we have consciously attempted to avoid this becoming a book on the C++ language only. The syntactic aspects of C++ have been introduced only through a single chapter. We assume that the readers of this book have developed basic skills of programming, preferably in a development platform based upon the C language. Most of the aspects of C++ are introduced either as modifications of similar constructs of C or as constructs specific to C++ that provide it the flavour of an object-oriented programming language (OOPL).

This book is also meant to provide a good understanding of the *design philosophy* behind the container class libraries and the GUI libraries, which are provided with most commercial C++ development systems. The motivation behind this is our belief that a workman using some tool cannot reach beyond a certain level of excellence unless he becomes conscious of the prudence that led to the development of the tool. Here we particularly refer to the so-called "visual tools" that are being designed by many commercial development environments. These tools have no doubt made (Windows) programming easy. Major portions of the program can automatically be generated through these tools and should, in the ideal case, leave the programmer only with the concerns that are specific to the problem at hand. Unfortunately, a generation of programmers have already passed through the formative years of their careers using such tools but with no good reading material that explains the design philosophy behind the tools. Most of these programmers therefore have inevitably been confined to mediocre levels. An attempt to redeem the situation is a strong enough motivation for us.

Probal Sengupta
Bidyut Baran Chaudhuri

Acknowledgements

In writing this book, a number of individuals have rendered their helpful suggestions, comments and encouragement; for them we would like to express our grateful thanks. At the outset, we express our gratitude to Sabyasachi Basu of Agniroth Inc., CA, for introducing us, for the first time, to the intriguing world of C++ and object-oriented programming.

We wholeheartedly acknowledge the contribution of all our students—M. Tech students and research scholars of Indian Statistical Institute, Calcutta as well as those who obliged us by attending various lecture sessions on OOP conducted at different places.

In terms of encouragement, we are immensely thankful to Aditya Bagchi and Partha Paramanic—our colleagues who managed to find time out of their busy schedules to attend our lecture sessions and offered their valuable advice in shaping the contents of this book. At times, they have cheerfully taken up the arduous job of proof reading some portions of the manuscript. A similar gratitude is due also to Tamaltaru De for his contribution in producing and correcting some of the code fragments. Thanks are also due to Anil Shukla and Niladri Shekhar Das who helped us with typing of the manuscript.

Finally, we thank our wives for bearing with us for one and a half years of coming home late at night as we were involved in the preparation of the manuscript.

Probal Sengupta
Bidyut Baran Chaudhuri

1
Introduction

If a survey to locate some of the most used jargons by the software community in the 1990s is carried out undoubtedly, 'OOP' (or OOPS as some of them love to use, fascinated by the sonic burst uttering the term produces) would occupy one of the top slots. Strangely enough, a similar survey for a period about a decade ago would scarcely come up with the term at all. The meteoric rise in the usage of the term OOP, or more precisely, of the adjective 'object-oriented', has woven a mystic fog around it. What is OOP? What does one mean while attributing the adjective 'object-oriented' to anything? This book may clear some of the mystic aura associated with the term, and may also answer some of these questions. Let us begin by briefly tracing the evolution of programming languages with the idea of finding out why Object-Oriented Programming (OOP) as a discipline, and Object-Oriented Programming Languages (OOPL) as tools have gained sudden prominence.

THE PREHISTORY OF OBJECT-ORIENTED PROGRAMMING LANGUAGES

Using an electronic computer for computing is a relatively new discipline, barely dating back to the early 1950s. The capabilities of the electronic computer as a computing machine have increased phenomenally in the subsequent years. The power of a computer is felt by the user community through well-designed and implemented software, and the effectiveness of any good software depends upon the programs that it is constituted of and the data structures that these programs use to store information.

The Old Stone Age

Since the earliest days of computing, programmers have looked for better ways of feeding computers with the most appropriate set of instructions to carry out a task in the best possible manner. The earliest computers had to be programmed by directly loading their memories with machine level instructions. The mechanism soon proved to be cumbersome and inelegant—the translation of a computation idea to (machine level) instructions and figuring out from a set of instructions what computation they were designed to perform, was extremely

1

difficult. Adding to the problem was, and still is, the fact that computers manufactured by different vendors as well as different models by the same vendor, have different sets of machine instructions.

The New Stone Age

The first refinement was proposed in the form of assembly languages. Using an assembly language, a programmer can 'represent' a computation using textual mnemonics to represent instructions and data (i.e., memory locations). Special software called assemblers can translate such a representation, i.e. an assembly language program, into a set of machine level instructions. In spite of the advantage of being able to represent a program using textual mnemonics, assembly language programs for a reasonably complex problem are difficult to arrive at from the domain, and equally difficult to comprehend. Such a program remains 'machine dependent'—the program written for a certain model of a certain make of computer may not be portable to another machine of a different make or model.

FROM PREHISTORY TO HISTORY

The Ancient Age

High level languages like FORTRAN, C, and COBOL solve to a large extent, the problem of machine dependence. At the same time, these languages propose standardized data types and instructions that may be woven together through the language syntax into a more readable program code. A compiler for the language translates such a program code to machine instructions. Many high level languages are 'general purpose', that is, their selection is not dependent on the domain application that is being programmed for. Sometimes however, a language is more tuned towards a particular application domain. For example, COBOL is more useful for the business application domain than say, the scientific application domain. Even with the general purpose languages, a particular language may be specifically designed to make programming simpler if a particular design philosophy and/or application domain is assumed. For example, scientific applications that require a lot of formula evaluations might be suitably programmed in FORTRAN.

The Middle Ages

The evolution of high level languages has been a continuous process. The earliest languages were not sufficiently 'structured'. As a result, programs written in these languages and the data used in them could not be modularized easily. The need for structured programs was increasingly felt even in the early days of programming, with the result that a number of structured programming languages like ALGOL, Pascal, and C were proposed in the ensuing years.

The Modern Age

Structuredness is only one aspect of modular design. When a project is very large, it is natural to expect that the number of modules constituting the project would also increase appreciably. A situation may result where the management of the modules themselves becomes a serious design burden. The quest for finding a solution to this aspect has led to the growing popularity of object-oriented programming in the recent years.

There is nothing new with the underlying principles of Object Oriented Programming (OOP). Most of the key concepts of OOP like the *abstraction specialization syndrome, data encapsulation, and polymorphism* are aspects of modular thinking process of human beings that have been employed ever since the dawn of knowledge. Good designers and programmers, by and large, have always used various facets of OOP in their designs and programs. Even Smalltalk-80, the earliest general purpose object-oriented programming language (OOPL—a language that provides with syntactic features that makes OOP easier), is more than a decade and a half old. However, the renewed interest in OOP has, without doubt, been triggered by the growing popularity of the C++ language.

The Birth of C++

The invention of the C++ language has almost universally been attributed to Bjarne Stroustroup. However, like most things that are good and well accepted, C++ did not 'happen' in a day. In a recently written book, Stroustroup has traced the design and evolution of C++ since 1979. It began with the motivation to provide the facilities for program organization—as in the then popular simulation language called Simula—with C's efficiency and flexibility for systems programming. The first C++ manual followed in early 1984 with a published book on the C++ programming language by Stroustroup in late 1985. It was this book that really provided the impetus that drove C++ to its present popularity.

The recent hype for OOP that began with the OOPSLA conference (September 1986) was initially centred around a rejuvenated Smalltalk. However, people soon discovered that in spite of being a more 'proper' OOPL, Smalltalk offered less freedom as compared to C++ and required a major stage of syntax learning. C++, on the other hand, was intentionally designed with the purpose of extending the syntax of C. The learning curve for C++ is therefore minimal, especially for programmers with a C background. Moreover, almost all the programming freedom associated with C is supported in C++. Understandably, in the recent years, C++ has materialized as the OOPL icon. Hordes of material—papers, books, monograms, etc., have already been written on C++. There are journals specifically devoted to aspects of C++ programming and C++ specific conferences are periodically held in different places around the globe.

C++ Learns to Walk

A major boost to C++ programming, especially in the academic environment, was provided by the GNU version of the C++ compiler (release 1.13), a relatively clean version of a UNIX-based C++ compiler which is available as a 'free' software downloadable from the Internet.

One of the earliest PC versions of a C++ compiler was the Zortech C++, first released in June 1988. The first Borland C++ development environment for PCs was made available in May 1988. While this was not the first C++ development system from Borland (there were earlier Turbo C++ editions), it provided, for the first time, the capability to programme MS-Windows through C++. The development system included a container class library and a rudimentary class library for MS-Windows programming. About the same time, several 'third party' vendors came up with better and more compact C++ class libraries for containers, and MS-Windows programming that could be used to augment the capabilities of the existing C++ development systems like Zortech C++, Borland C++, etc.

C++ Comes of Age

Surprisingly enough, Microsoft joined in the fray relatively late. The first Microsoft C++ release (Visual C++) came in as late as March 1992. However, since then, Microsoft has remained a frontline player, along with Borland, in the C++ development system for PCs. What has come as a boon to programmers as a result of the switch of Microsoft's attention to C++, is the availability of an enormous amount of technical literature made available through the *Microsoft Technical Journal*.

Amidst the quest for the leader's spot in C++ by the well-known compiler vendors for different operating system environments, some amount of chaos prevailed due to a lack of standardization of either the language syntax or the class libraries available in the market. Thankfully, right minded groups sat together to resolve the issues, and at present, there is at least some standardization of the language and its compilers through the ANSI specifications. At the same time, there have been attempts to standardize class libraries, resulting in a *Standard Template Library* (STL) being proposed and accepted as a standard for the same.

Peers and Siblings of C++

The trend of augmenting the syntax of a popular language to incorporate some object-oriented features was not restricted to C++. Borland tried the same with Turbo Pascal from version 5.5 onwards (1986), which continued through several versions of Turbo Pascal and Borland Pascal, finally being formalized in a new language called Delphi (1994). Microsoft on their part, came up with an easy to programme object-oriented version of BASIC in their Visual Basic product (1992). The race is on with many other languages. For example, the later versions of the database manipulating language Visual Foxpro offers object-oriented features. It is quite possible that in the years to come, we shall see several versions of object-FORTRAN, object-PROLOG (some versions of the same already exist), etc.

The Newborn Baby in the OOPL Family

The latest in the fray till the writing of this book that has generated almost an equal amount of hype as C++, is the language Java. This language is being portrayed as something similar to C++ except that the freedom in C++ of not to encapsulate certain things, have been taken away in Java. Java is also the contemporary standard for passing 'active' material through the network. This feature of Java provides the power to a site designer for the Internet to send 'Java applets' that generate portions of a multimedia document *in situ* (i.e., at the client machine) at the net browser end. With its popularity growing at the same rate as the Internet, it is possible that Java may really become the first programming language of the entirely new computing environment of the 21st century that is surely going to be based around the Internet.

Contradictions of the Modern Age

The tremendous speed of development of the OOP paradigm in the last 10 years has unfortunately, taken its toll in a different manner. In their attempt to retain market superiority through providing more advanced tools and better features, the manufacturers never seems to have given the ever growing programming community a chance to have come to terms with the advanced underlying concepts. As a result, a large percentage of the programmer population was compelled to switch to newer tools even before they got a chance to have the design philosophy of these tools sink into their brains.

Added to this was the subtle marketing hype of the vendors that somehow spread the message that suddenly, with the arrival of the mostly 'visual' tools, programming has ceased to be the pain that it used to be in the yesteryears. "Just press the proper keys and choose the proper attributes and you have your program 'generated' for you," is the message that most unsuspecting programmers are increasingly getting.

The irony of the situation is that the statement quoted above is, to some extent, true. It is now possible to proceed blindfolded to a much greater distance than ever before. However, it certainly does not imply that one can make a long journey through a difficult terrain completely blindfolded. In other words, it is simply not possible to get the best out of a tool without at least a realization of the philosophy behind the working of the tool. It would become amply clear from reading this book that it is designed precisely to act as an aid in the realization process.

ORGANIZATION OF THE BOOK

Besides **Chapter 1,** the book consists of five chapters.

Chapter 2 deals with the fundamental concepts of object-oriented programming. The idea is to provide a thorough understanding of the object-oriented paradigm from a need-driven viewpoint. The necessity of OOP is traced to the complex and distributed nature of the software development process in the present days where the average code 'size' of projects is going up like never before. The abstraction/specialization process is identified as a viable design technique. It is shown through an exposure to key OOP concepts like *encapsulation, inheritance* and *polymorphism*, (with C++ examples) how close and to what degree of easiness we can incorporate abstraction and specialization in programming through an OOPL.

Chapter 3—Although it is not our intention to make this book a reference material for the C++ language, we have chosen C++ as the OOPL vehicle to present different concepts. It was therefore imperative that we provide a short chapter on C++. This chapter serves that purpose. C++ is first looked at as a language that is a superset of C. Next, some of the newly introduced constructs in C++ that are specific to OOP, are discussed with examples.

Chapter 4 essentially deals with the philosophy behind design and implementation of container classes and effective use and reuse of the same. A lengthy pre-discussion on preliminary concepts of data types and data structures is provided to gradually orient the reader into the domain of container classes.

Chapter 5 is meant to explain the design philosophy of object-based libraries for GUI programming platforms. MS-Windows application development has mostly been considered. Aspects of the message driven paradigm that is found in Windows and most GUIs have been explained and encapsulation of the same in a message handling class has been discussed. Also covered are 'menus', 'controls' 'dialog boxes' and 'device context'.

Chapter 6, the final chapter of the book, discusses some advanced OOP concepts, especially in the context of creating graphics based applications. Elements of the *document-view paradigm* that attempts to delineate modeling and user-interface aspects of such applications, have been covered. Design and development of Computer Aided Design (CAD) software under GUI (MS-Windows) or non-GUI environments, has been discussed in the light of the document-view paradigm. The effectiveness of geometric modeling for internal representation of drawing primitives and actual generation of pictures from them, has been taken up. Abstract 'event-driven' simulation as yet another aspect of CAD software development, has also been touched.

WHO SHOULD READ THIS BOOK

In this book, we have primarily targeted those readers who have a reasonable proficiency in programming in a C language based environment and now want to graduate into object-oriented programming using C++, with minimum effort. A typical reader would therefore be, either a university student of computer science, or a programmer working with the software industry. It is difficult to define what we mean by *a reasonable proficiency in programming*. We expect that such a person has working knowledge of some of the fundamental algorithms with some idea about program complexity. (S)he has either gone through a course on data structures or has developed data structure knowledge by other means. (S)he is willing and is capable to browse through code fragments to understand the finer aspects of concepts and in doing so, can 'port' ideas to other application areas. Finally, (s)he must have been exposed to enough programs, as developer, to maintain or study them, so as to be able to appreciate the skills for writing 'large' programs.

Clearly, our prerequisite for readership of this book is a tall order. However, our advice to everybody with a motivation towards learning OOPL concepts is to have at least a fast glance through this book. Skills mentioned above are quite often at a nascent state in the minds of persons, sometimes quite unknowing to the person h(er)imself, waiting to be triggered by the slight push of insight from any material at hand. As authors, we would be happiest if this book can act as such a 'push' for at least one reader.

This book should not be read as one describing a particular object-oriented programming language like C++. Rather, it should be used as a companion in the initial days of experimenting with actual programming. Throughout the book, we would use the notation *OO* to represent the prefix *object-oriented*. The prefix may be used with *P* (*programming*), *PL* (*programming language*) or *A & D* (*analysis and design*).

POINTS TO REMEMBER

- This is *not* a beginners' book on programming, algorithms and data structures, and Windows programming.

- This book is *not* one covering all aspects of C/C++ or any other programming language, OOPL or otherwise.

- Similarly, this book does *not* cover aspects of *any* commercial C++ development platforms and/or third party sub-systems.

- This book is *not* meant to be the first book to learn about Windows programming.

- This book does *not* provide any ready-made code to be included, compiled, linked or otherwise. The code fragments provided as examples are only for the purpose of illustration, and the authors do not guarantee that they are completely free from syntax and/or run-time errors.

- Keeping in mind the above mentioned points, the reader should supplement reading this book with at least a few of the following materials:

  1. Book(s) on algorithms, data structures, program design, etc.

  2. Book(s) on aspects of Software Engineering and Design.

  3. Book(s) or manuals or help files of C++, preferably covering the intricacies of the C++ development system intended to be used.

4. Book(s) on MS-Windows programming, preferably some that deal with classical Windows programming on C using Microsoft Software Development Kit (MS-Windows SDK) and others dealing with the visual tool accompanying the C++ development system intended to be used.

SOME MYTHS SHATTERED

- Object-oriented programming is extremely difficult, or conversely, nothing that deserves writing a book solely on the subject.

- *Any* program developed in C++ is necessarily an object-oriented program.

- A program developed in a so called non-OOPL can never be object-oriented, not even to a limited extent.

- OOP in C++ is all about renaming `struct`-s as `class`-es, using access specifiers `private protected` and `public` judiciously and introducing some member functions.

- At most, OOP is all about inheriting a class from another and so on.

- If one does not understand the polymorphism aspect of OOP, (s)he can still be considered knowledgeable of OOP, albeit to a limited extent.

- In C++, `virtual` class member functions are no different from other member functions and therefore, using the `virtual` directive has no bearing upon the program.

- Windows programming (at least the more complex ones) can be done only through using some visual tool or the other.

2

The Fundamentals of Object-Oriented Programming

With the growing popularity of some object-oriented programming languages (OOPLs) like C++, Delphi, etc., in the recent years, the discipline of object-oriented programming (OOP) has experienced renewed interest. An increasing number of applications are now being developed in some OOPL environment or the other.

Most commercially available compilers and development platforms for these languages (especially C++) come equipped with object-oriented libraries (also called *class* libraries) to make programming 'easier'. There has also been a rapid proliferation of 'third-party' object libraries, mostly for C++.

However, in spite of the wide availability of such advanced tools, the real power of the object-oriented paradigm has not been exploited by programmers to even a fraction of its possible extent. From about half a decade of experience in teaching object-oriented programming and design, as well as being involved in design and development of quite a few commercial software packages, we have arrived at the following conclusion.

While 'object-orientedness' is perhaps the most natural aspect of rational human thinking, translating the same to proper constructs in an OOPL appears to be less natural. Possibly, the fact that the 'popular' languages of the yesteryears did not have well defined object-oriented features have resulted in the apparent mind block. Coupled with this is the fact that C++, currently the most popular OOPL, is in a way a superset of the language C. Somehow, the following myths seem to have spread among the software development community:

- Since C++ is an OOPL, *any* program developed in C++ is necessarily an object-oriented program.

- Conversely, any program developed in a so-called non-OOPL can never be object-oriented, not even to a limited extent.

One major purpose of this text is to break both the above myths. In our belief, a reasonable starting point might be through understanding the object-oriented paradigm from a need-driven viewpoint.

THE NECESSITY FOR OBJECT-ORIENTED PROGRAMMING

The necessity of object-oriented programming is more strongly felt when the overall software project at hand is 'large'. The largeness we refer to here does not pertain only to the amount of coding required. In fact, a project requiring relatively less amount of coding effort could as well be considered large under certain circumstances. By large projects, we mean those which have several of the following features.

- There is a requirement for an involved design phase in the project. A 'design team' interacts with the principal—persons or groups who lay down the specifications of the requirements of the software. Individual members of the design team are considered 'experts' in various fields— system analysis and design, user interface design, data structure design, domain experts in the relevant problem domain, marketing, management, etc. Thus, every expert of the design team *need not be 'a programming knowledgeable person'*.

- The design phase is not 'static'. Generally, the design does not get 'frozen' at an early period in the life-cycle of the project, so that the 'coding' team is left with the responsibility of implementing a relatively fixed design. Rather, the specifications, and hence the design go on changing dynamically almost throughout the life-cycle of the project. Moreover, the changes in design generally occur in a most unpredictable manner.

- As a result of separate design and coding groups (a few individuals definitely may belong to both the groups, but that is not assumed to be the general rule), there is a constant flow of information between the groups—specifications (code 'specs') from the design group to the coding group, and implementation reports and/or feedback in the reverse order.

- Often the coding group consists of various teams entrusted with the implementation of specific sub-modules of the overall program. It is quite possible that some of the teams are remotely located from each other (for example, one team in Calcutta, India, and another in San Francisco, USA) with less scope for interaction.

- Services of freelancers and/or third-party libraries are sometimes employed in order to off-load some amount of programming effort.

- 'Proper documentation' is necessary at every stage of development.

It is quite obvious that a 'large' software project has certain problems resulting out of the largeness. Let us review some of these problems.

Too Much Design Detail at Every Level

The 'inevitable' changes in design must percolate down to the individual programmers who would carry out the changes. In the process of the flow of information, many people get unnecessarily flooded with design details that are not exactly relevant for or required by them. Let us take an example.

Assume that for some project at hand, the design process has come up with the concept of *Triangle*s. It was decided that a triangle would be represented by a collection of three *Point*s. Assume also that the coding effort concerned with `Points` and `Triangles` has been delegated to team-A.

Now, suddenly, the principal wants to bring 3-dimensional figures under the purview of the project. However, it is decided that triangles would still be considered as 2-dimensional figures. The project manager decides to delegate the job of including 3-D figures to a new team-B. Under such circumstances, usually team-A would be informed about the design changes and asked to incorporate the third dimension in `Point`. Moreover, all teams that 'generate' triangles must be informed so as to ensure that every time a triangle is generated, the third dimension be given a pre-defined value (say 0). Otherwise, if the values of the third dimension are kept undefined, a large number of computations might produce weird results. Therefore, even the minor change described above might ultimately lead to a situation where many teams, every team in the worst case, must assimilate the change, possibly by modifying already generated code in many places.

Re-compilation of Many Modules Needed

We have shown how even a slight change in specifications might lead to source level changes in many places. This automatically implies two things—first that the previous version of the source must be available and second, that after the changes, the new source must be compiled. The first requirement may as well fail for third party libraries which do not come with source codes. The second requirement unnecessarily adds up to time and cost overruns.

Low Code-Sharing

The underlying reasons why the problems listed above are associated with large projects not designed and implemented using object-oriented principles, may be summarized through a single statement: *The systems incorporate lower 'code sharing'*. What is meant here is that in a non-object-oriented design/ implementation, two related data items with many similarities but which are different in some aspects, are treated as two entirely separate items. Hence, a lot of similar behavioural descriptions for the items have to be implemented separately. Also, and this is more important than the previous aspect, a similar type of 'abstract' behaviour of closely related objects cannot be unified into a single referable concept.

OOP and the Abstraction-Specialization Syndrome

As a matter of fact, in principle, OOP is all about 'abstraction' (unification) of ideas at one level and appropriate 'specialization' at another. It may be appropriate to clarify the quoted terms, especially abstraction, in the context of OOP.

Abstraction defined through an example

By abstraction, we mean identifying *different but similar* behaviour of related entities (objects) through a 'name' (also called a 'handle'). Although one basic idea behind abstraction is to break down a complex description in terms of less complex ones, the term is sometimes extended to the domain where we attempt to 'reason' about behaviours of objects through abstract concepts related to them.

One of our favourite examples is one from school-level biology, where the concept of an *Animal Kingdom* is introduced in a hierarchical fashion. It is classified further and further till every animal species known to humankind occupies a leaf position in the hierarchy. Of course, in high school (or, for that matter, at any level of education), it is impossible that the entire hierarchy be actually studied in detail. What is done in most cases is that further details of a group of animals related at some level of the hierarchy, are restricted to some relevant examples. For example, one might stop further description of the animal class called 'Mammal' after stating that the female animals in this class 'suckle their babies', and provide some examples—lions, elephants, deer, whales, humans, and so on.

Consider the phrase 'suckle their babies' in the above description of mammals. It merely abstracts a mammalian behaviour. One need not invoke the details of how every mammalian species suckle their babies to unify suckling as a concept. Nor does one need such details to reason out that any mammalian baby meets (at least a part of) its food requirement from its mother's milk. One could, of course, be interested in more details of a particular mammal, say elephant, and describe in detail or provide 'specialized' description of how an elephant mother suckles its baby. However, that would in no way affect the previously carried out abstract reasoning.

Consider a more common statement often made about animals—"all animals *eat* ..." Clearly, the verb *eat* here represents an abstract behaviour about animals. In all probability, neither the speaker nor the listener of the above statement is concerned about the ingestion habit of the countless number of animals that exist on planet earth. Nevertheless, the statement never fails to register a profound fact about life. Figure 2.1, represents a possible mental picture triggered by the above statement.

Abstraction-specialization in programming

We can cite examples of the abstraction-specialization syndrome even from programming. Consider the problem of 'swapping' the contents of the i-th and j-th contents of an array. Even the most novice programmer knows that the above can be done using a third temporary variable with three assignment statements. Note that the knowledge is independent of the type of the variables in question. Thus, *swapping* is an abstract behaviour with all types of variables that can be stored in an array.

Another example could be from graphics—of drawing and moving around pictures of geometrical shapes on a display screen.

Fig. 2.1 A possible mental picture triggered by the statement "all animals *eat*".

The key steps for moving an object from one position on the display to another can be abstractly described as:

- Erase object (at present position).
- Re-position object.
- Draw object (at new position).

Note that the above description is absolutely independent of the specialized tasks of erasing, re-positioning and drawing of a particular object, and, therefore, the mentioned tasks are abstract behaviours of objects identified by behaviour names (erase, re-position and draw).

Most programmers should have realized by now that if object-orientedness is all about abstraction and specialization during the design phase, nothing new is being introduced as a concept. However, OOP using an OOPL goes slightly beyond that. OOPLs actually permit the same abstract code to be dynamically shared among related 'objects'. A discussion on object-oriented programming using an OOPL should therefore describe how this dynamic code sharing can be achieved using the OOPL. As a matter of fact, with such a code sharing, most of the problems listed at the beginning of the present section are automatically solved.

A THREE-STEP INTRODUCTION TO 'OBJECT'

This section provides a hurried tour through the essentials of object-oriented design and programming, beginning with a three-step introduction to 'object'.

   Programming in a procedural programming language (like FORTRAN, Pascal, C, etc.), treats 'data' as the central concept. The *semantics* (meaning) of a data item in a program pertains to some salient feature of the supposedly real-life problem that the program is intended to solve. It is known that down at the bare machine level, any data item is basically a string of bits in the computer's memory. However, depending upon the level from which one looks at a data item, it has a certain innate classification. For example, at the assembly language layer there are Bytes, Words, Double-Words, etc., while at the layer of a high-level programming language, one would rather use concepts like real (float), integer, char, etc.

Data Abstraction

The innate classification of data is the basis of data *abstraction*. It is quite obvious that the human mind is trained to split complex concepts into simpler ones for the purpose of better understanding. The same principles also hold for visualizing data. As an example, let us conceive of the data item representing a Triangle. A possible 'natural' way to classify the data for a triangle is to declare it to be *containing* three *identical sub-items* representing the three vertices. A vertex is, after all, a Point in the XY plane (assuming 2-D geometry) and every Point is a pair (x, y) of real (i.e. float) numbers.

   In older programming languages like FORTRAN-IV, an abstraction of the above type requires considerable amount of data jugglery on part of the programmer. With Pascal or C, a less painful way of abstracting the above data item for a triangle is to use constructs like record (Pascal), struct (C) and array. For example, in C (actually in a slightly modified and extended syntax of C++), a straightforward abstraction for the above would be:

```
struct Point { float x, y; };
struct Triangle { struct Point vertices[3]; };
```

Procedural Abstraction

The human mind is trained to classify bigger jobs into smaller ones. Good programming is all about how to break down complex programming requirements into simpler sub-programs—*functions*, *procedures*, etc. The key to procedural abstraction in conventional Von-Neumann architecture computers lies in the fact that the *code* in such an architecture can be *shared*—if a similar job has to be repeated, possibly under different data definitions, a single sub-program may be made to perform all possible task instances of the job in a parametric manner. For example, consider a complex problem where we need to compute the perimeter of a large number of Triangles at different task instances. The intelligent way to do this is to suppose that a sub-program (to be called *function* henceforth, irrespective of the language referred to) is defined to calculate the perimeter of a Triangle passed to the function as a parameter. Next, for each task instance, the triangle whose perimeter is desired, is passed to the function for the required computation. In C, the code for the function computing the perimeter of a Triangle is:

```
float perimeter(struct Triangle t)
{
  return  (length(t.vertices[0],t.vertices[1]) +
          length(t.vertices[1],t.vertices[2]) +
          length(t.vertices[2],t.vertices[0]) );
}

float length(struct Point p,  struct Point q)
{
  return  (sqrt((p.x-q.x)*(p.x-q.x)+(p.y-q.y)*(p.y-q.y)));
}
```

Observe that in the above code, the perimeter function calls another function length to compute the Euclidean distance between two points fed to it as its two parameters. Observe also that the function length, in turn, calls the C library function sqrt to compute the square root of a number. Indeed, in a real program solving complex problems, there would, in general, be several functions calling each other. Sometimes, a function may call itself, a phenomenon generally known as *recursion* in computer terminology.

Combined Data and Procedural Abstraction—Object

On many occasions, a data type and a function *go together*, in the sense that the function is dedicated to perform computations that are meaningful only for a particular data type. For example, the perimeter function given above is meaningful only for Triangles. In a similar manner, there may be other functions that may go together with the Triangle data type. For example, the function centroid given below could be another function that goes together with the Triangle data:

```
Point centroid(struct Triangle t)
{
  Point p;
  p.x = (t.vertices[0].x+t.vertices[1].x+t.vertices[2].x)/3;
  p.y = (t.vertices[0].y+t.vertices[1].y+t.vertices[2].y)/3;
  return (p);
}
```

Let us now consider the abstract entity consisting of a described data type and all functions that go together with the data type (and relevant for the problem domain). Clearly, such an entity conforms more closely to objects in real life, and consequently, we would call this abstract entity an **object**. Objects, just as the ones conceived of by human beings, are not simply a bundle of data—classified, but ultimately detailed down to a few numbers and/or character strings. Objects are livelier entities. Some objects can do certain things (this may not be clear at present) and certain things can be done upon them, meaning thereby, that specific units of code carry out specific activities associated with a *class* of objects. These associated codes are called *methods* or *member functions* of the class of objects in OO parlance. In the offered view, an object is an *instance* of its class and an object class *encapsulates* (see below) the behavioural properties or methods relevant for any instance of the class. As an example, the Triangle class may have perimeter as a method. Similarly, we may have a centroid method for the Triangle class, or even conceive of another one—draw, that draws the outlines of a Triangle object on some 2-D drawing surface.

In classical procedural programming, attention is first focused on the code and then shifts to the data associated with the code. Thus, one talks about the 'perimeter function that takes a Triangle as a parameter'. In OOP, the central focus is on the objects. The code associated with an object class— the methods—is considered to be much more tightly coupled. In an OOP environment, one would therefore talk about the 'perimeter method of the Triangle class'.

Note that up to the present point, we have really not achieved anything fantastic, except for a tighter coupling between an object and its behaviour through methods in the object's class. Nevertheless, it is quite apparent that the OOP concept is nothing extraordinary. Through OOPLs, we can not perform something that cannot be performed through non-OOPLs. OOP is simply a new discipline, based upon a combined data and code abstraction that will, as we shall see later, help solve a class of programming and associated problems in a less tedious manner than usual.

ESSENTIALS OF OBJECT-ORIENTED PROGRAMMING

The key concept of OOP is the 'object', a term we have already explained. There are three facets of OOP, namely **Encapsulation, Inheritance** and **Polymorphism**. The last mentioned is the most important one. However, to achieve the same, the others are necessary.

Encapsulation

We have already introduced the idea of combining data and code that go together with the data as a single concept called object. Encapsulation essentially deals with this unification. As a programming discipline, encapsulation is nothing new. Good programmers always strive to achieve the same in their programs.

In OOPLs however, encapsulation is more involved, being an inherent feature of the language itself and the primary launching pad to achieve the benefits of OO programming.

What is meant by encapsulation?

Simply speaking, encapsulation in an OOPL means the following:

- The definition or declaration of a class of objects consists of two parts—declaration of *data* (also called *member data*) and declaration of *code* that goes together with the object, also called *methods* or *member functions*. Usually, access to both member data and member functions (accessibility is not automatic) are carried through member selection operators like . or →(C++).

  The term *member* is sometimes used to refer to the union of member data and member functions of an object as declared in its class. However, it would be appropriate to explain here that the semantics of membership of data and methods of an object are slightly different. Different objects of a class (i.e., different instances of a class) may (and generally would) have different values for any member data declared in the class. However, all the objects of a class share identical behavioural properties. In other words, all objects of a class 'share' the method codes of the class[1] in C++, whence the member is also shared among all the objects of the class.

- Certain aspects, normally the member data items of an object, are not 'visible' from everywhere in the program, meaning thereby that it is not possible to 'resolve' into (through operators like . or →) the object to access these aspects. Certain other aspects, on the other hand, may be visible from everywhere. There may also be partial visibility, as described (after inheritance).

- A member function of an object has free access to all the member data introduced in its declaration. Member data inherited (see later) from other objects may or may not be visible, depending upon the programming language and values of special switches meant for the purpose. If accessible, a member data need not be resolved within the body of a member function. They are within automatic scope, as in the target of a with statement of Pascal.

- A member function of an object is a static bunch of code. However, at run-time, it runs *in the environment of an instance of the object*. Thus, the run-time semantics of a member function of an object depends upon the instance of the object through which the invocation of the same has taken place.

---

[1] A possible exception case is where a data member of a class is declared static.

An example in C++

Possibly, the best way to clarify our statements above is to actually declare an object in the syntax of an OOPL—C++. We take up our original example of the point and the triangle.

```
class Point {
private:
  float xCoord,yCoord;

public:
      Point();
      ~Point();
  void setX(float newX);
  void setY(float newY);
  float x();
  float y();
  float length(Point otherPoint);
};

class Triangle {
protected:
  Point vertices[3];

public:
      Triangle(Point a,  Point b,  Point c);
      Triangle();
      ~Triangle();
  Point *vertex(int which);
  float perimeter();
  Point *centroid();
};
```

In C++, the keyword class declares a description of an object[2]. Note that within the scope of the declaration, not only have we declared the data items in the usual manner, but have also declared the member functions.

Note also that all the member functions have one parameter less than the corresponding non-OOPL version, the missing parameter being a pointer to the object itself.

The keywords public, protected and private are directive switches controlling visibility—private and protected directives make the declarations following it invisible from the external world, while public makes them visible. The difference between private and protected will be considered later.

Observe that as per tradition, we have made the data items of the Point and the Triangle objects invisible, but have kept the member functions visible. Thus, we needed two extra functions each for setting and reading the

---

[2]The same can also be done with struct. The reader may refer to Chapter 3 for more detail.

values of the member data. The member function `perimeter` and `centroid`[3] of `Triangle` have one parameter less than the corresponding non-OOPL declarations.

Member function implementation

Let us consider the body of one typical member function, say `perimeter` of `Triangle`, denoted and defined as `Triangle::perimeter()`.

```
float  Triangle::perimeter()
{
  return  vertices[0].length(vertices[1])  +
          vertices[1].length(vertices[2])  +
          vertices[2].length(vertices[1]);
}
```

A statement accessing member data as well as member functions

Observe the strange construct `vertices[0].length(vertices[1])`. This is a typical statement involving access to member data as well as member functions of an object. Since `vertices` is a member data of `Triangle` object, it is visible within the scope of the member function of our interest, i.e. `Triangle::perimeter()`. The construct `vertices[0].length(...)` invokes the `length` member function of the `Point` object represented by `vertices[0]`.

Object binding of a member function

Looking at the declaration of `Point`, we find that this function requires a `Point` as its parameter, which is duly sent here as `vertices[1])`. There remains a final question. The `vertices` referred to in the above function refers to the `vertices` of *which instance* of `Triangle` at run-time? It entirely depends upon how this function has been invoked at run time.

Consider the declaration:

```
Triangle t1, t2, *t;
```

Here, `t1` and `t2` are `Triangle`s, while `t` is a pointer to a `Triangle`.

Thus, because `t1` is a `Triangle`, the statement `t1.perimeter()` would invoke the member function `Triangle::perimeter` and within the *scope* of the invocation, the `vertices` data item would refer to the `vertices` of `t1`.

The same would happen with the statements `t=&t1;` and `t →perimeter();`. However, for `t2.perimeter();` the `vertices` data item of `t2` would be referred to.

The invisible self-referencing pointer `this`

A possible question at this point could be: 'How does the member function

---

[3]The return value here is a *pointer* to a `Point` class of objects rather than simply an instance of `Point` for convenience only.

come to know the instance which has caused its latest invocation?' Although at the lowest level this is basically an implementation dependent feature, usually, an *invisible* parameter representing the instance of the object making the invocation (or a pointer thereof, as in C++) is passed to the function. The compiler ensures that all the references to the member variables in the scope of a member function are actually directed to those of the invisible parameter. Some programming languages permit (but discourage) reference of the invisible parameter through special constructs (for example, this in C++).

Implementation of `Point::length()`

With our acquired knowledge, let us see how `Point::length(...)` can be implemented.

```
float Point::length(Point otherPoint)
{
  return sqrt((xCoord-otherPoint.x())*(xCoord-otherPoint.x())+
          (yCoord-otherPoint.y())*(yCoord-otherPoint.y()));
}
```

Note that while the member data xCoord, yCoord of the this parameter may be directly referred, those of the explicit parameter otherPoint may not be directly referred.

Constructors and Destructors

Readers must have observed a few strange-looking functions declared within the scope of Point and Triangle above.

In C++, a function with the same name as the object is its **constructor**, and one with the name which is a tilde ~ followed by the object name is its **destructor**. Constructors and destructors are essential aspects of OOP and hence OOPLs, as described below.

The constructor(s) and the destructor make it possible to make objects behave as 'first class data types' for the compiler. First class 'privileged' data types are those data types about which the compiler has special or inherent knowledge, thus making it possible for one to do many things with such data types. In most programming languages, the built-in data types are the only first class data types. However, in OOPLs, the programmer is also permitted to create new first class data, or rather, make newly created data behave somewhat like first class ones (mostly through the polymorphism facet of such languages).

Constructor

The starting point of making 'objects' behave as first class data types is through the constructor. A constructor is a special member function of *object* meant to register the creation of a new instance of an object. All necessary housekeeping, most of which a standard user would not even be aware of, associated with registering an instance of an object as a first class data, is carried out by the constructor. Minimally, housekeeping involves arranging for allocation of memory appropriate for the object being constructed. However, in OOPLs, the constructor acts as the primary formulation upon which polymorphism is based.

Languages like C++ permit the user to add additional code to do other things that the object designer feels must be done during the construction of an object (for example, initialization of member variables, construction of dynamic member objects, etc.).

An object is 'created' the moment it comes into extent. Global and static variables are created right at the time of loading of the program. Automatic or local variables are created during function invocation, while dynamic variables are created by the user through special constructs/functions with pointers.

In C++, multiple constructors having different parameter lists are permissible. Refer to Chapter 3, or better still, a C++ manual for guide to how to arrange for invoking different constructors for construction of different instances of an object.

Destructor

The destructor of an object un-does what the constructor does. Usually, *object* has one non-parametric destructor. It is invoked whenever an instance of the *object* goes out of extent.

Inheritance

The next most important facet of OOP is object inheritance. All OOPLs permit definitions of objects inherited from another (and sometimes multiple) objects. Both member data and member functions may be inherited. The inheritance mechanism imposes a modifiable *is-a* hierarchy on objects.

Inheritance defined

Generally, as with most OOPLs including C++, the inheritance mechanism has the following characteristics:

- An inherited object incorporates *all* data items of the object (or objects in case of OOPLs allowing multiple inheritance) inherited from (*parent object*), with identical definition.

- An inherited object class may declare additional data items for itself, which in turn would be inherited by object classes derived from it.

- An inherited object class inherits all member functions of the parent object class *by name* (or declaration). However, it may choose to redefine the implementation of such member functions. Two possibilities exist:

    - No change in implementation of a member function of the parent is required. The function is simply not re-declared. An invocation of the function through an instance of the inherited class results in the invocation of the parent's function.

    - The inherited object class may choose to re-implement a member function of the parent. The function is re-declared and re-implemented.

- Thus, in the former case, a limited 'code sharing' is achieved. The member function provides an abstraction that is not further specialized by the inherited class.

- In the latter case, however, the inherited class provides an alternative definition (and hence specialization) of the re-implemented function.

- The inherited class may declare and implement member functions of its own. These functions are inherited by offsprings of the *object* in question, but is undefined for its parents. This feature permits proper specialization—that of introducing a totally new object behaviour—in the inherited class.

Some more classes for the example problem

In light of our already declared object, we would like to declare a few more object classes.

1. A `TriangularLamina` class that represents a triangular shaped lamina of some real material (specified by a code). We are interested in computing the weight of such a lamina, apart from its perimeter and centroid.

2. A `TriangularFrame` class representing a triangular frame of some material. Here also we would like to compute the weight of the frame.

3. A `HoledTriangularLamina` class to represent a triangular lamina with a circular hole of variable diameter drilled somewhere on the surface of the lamina. Perimeter here is defined as a sum of the outer perimeter of the triangle, as well as the circumference of the hole. Here also, we are interested in computing the weight and perimeter of the object.

Clearly, a `HoledTriangularLamina` is a specialization of `TriangularLamina`, and may be inherited from it.

As for the `TriangularLamina` and `TriangularFrame` classes, though they have a few things in common, it is difficult to identify one being more general than the other. Such situations are sometimes unavoidable in OOP, and there are a few thumb rules to handle such cases in OO design.

As of now, we have chosen one that is frequently resorted to—arbitrarily making `TriangularFrame` the child class of `TriangularLamina`. However, this choice would be a temporary one. Later in this chapter, we would provide a better hierarchical description. Thus, `TriangularLamina` has two children—`HoledTriangularLamina` and `TriangularFrame`. Let us declare the `TriangularLamina` object class in C++.

The `TriangularLamina` class

```
class TriangularLamina public Triangle {
protected:
  int     materialCode;

public:
        TriangularLamina(Point a, Point b, Point c, int m);
        TriangularLamina();
        ~TriangularLamina();
  float weight();
};
```

Observe that we have used a particular construct to inform the compiler that the parent of `TriangularLamina` is `Triangle`. The directive `public` in the first line of declaration is another mechanism for altering visibility— `public` keeps visibility unchanged from the parent.

We have used only one member data to represent material code. The data for the vertices are acquired from `Triangle`. The `perimeter` and `centroid` member functions are also acquired without change, since we have not declared them here. However, we have declared a new function `weight` for computing the weight of a lamina.

The `TriangularFrame` and `HoledTriangularLamina` classes

Next, we declare the `TriangularFrame` and `HoledTriangularLamina` classes.

```
class TriangularFrame public TriangularLamina {
public:
        TriangularFrame(Point a, Point b, Point c, int m);
        TriangularFrame();
        ~TriangularFrame();
  float weight();
};
```

```
class HoledTriangularLamina public TriangularLamina {
protected:
  Point holePosition;
  float holeDiameter;

public:
        TriangularLamina (Point a, Point b, Point c,
                          Point hole, float d, int m);
        TriangularLamina();
        ~TriangularLamina();
  float perimeter();
  Point *centroid();
  float weight();
};
```

Observe that in `TriangularFrame`, we have *not added a single member data* or *member function*. However, we have redefined `weight` to indicate that this object computes weight differently from a triangular lamina.

For `HoledTriangularLamina`, on the other hand, we have not only added new data items to take care of the hole, but have shown intentions to redefine the perimeter, centroid and weight computing member functions, some of which had been acquired all the way from `Triangle`.

A few points may be made in light of the inheritance mechanism.

A short discussion on member visibility

First, the question of visibility of member entities. Usually, all member data of the parent are visible from any member function of the offspring.

Some languages like C++ allow this to be switch selectable. In C++, the directive `protected` makes all following declared items visible to the immediate descendants. However, the inherited class may 'turn-off' the visibility for its own descendants (refer to C++ manuals for further details of the phenomenon).

A short discussion on constructor invocation

The next point of discussion is about the constructor(s) and the destructor of the inherited class.

The thumb rule is that the constructor of the offspring invokes the (one) constructor of the parent in a recursive manner *before* invoking its own special constructing functions.

This way, during creation, just before an instance of a class gets its special definitions, all definitions that it acquires through inheritance are already fully described. Hence, the only knowledge the (constructor of) derived object needs is about its parent's constructor.

In case multiple constructors are permitted in an object class (as in C++), the language permits the user to pinpoint the constructor of the parent to invoke in each of a class's constructors.

The scenario is similar for the destructor except that the destruction process of the parent is carried out recursively *after* the destruction process specific for the offspring.

Pointers to Objects

The ensuing discussion in this and the following sub-section is meant for a build-up towards polymorphism.

Most OOPLs have the concept of associating pointer variables with objects. The 'semantics' of pointers to objects in such cases is obtained as a straightforward and intuitive extension over the non-OOP scenario.

A *pointer* p to a class O acts as the *l-value* of a memory chunk representing an *instance* of O.

Upon *de-referencing* p, not only do we lead to the data items of the instance of O pointed at by p, but also all the member functions of O come into scope.

If the data items of the object are totally encapsulated, the data chunk obtained by de-referencing a pointer variable pointing to an object instance would not be meaningful, and indeed, may not be accessible at all. Normally, if an attempt to access an encapsulated item of an object is made, the compiler flags an error indicating visibility conflict. However, all the 'public' items of the pointed object instance, usually all the necessary member functions, may be accessed through pointer de-reference.

We have already introduced the notion of the invisible parameter (called `this` in C++) in every member function of a class, that identifies the instance in whose scope the function has been invoked. In C++, the `this` parameter is actually a pointer to an instance of the class. Within the scope of the member function, the self-pointing parameter, therefore, has well-defined semantics. It points to the object instance, which was used to invoke the function.

Now, consider the following declaration:

```
TriangularLamina *t;
```

Assume that somehow, `t` is made to point at some instance of the `TriangularLamina` class. In that case:

- A reference `t->materialCode` would flag a compiler error as the `materialCode` member variable has been encapsulated.

- The construct `t->perimeter()` would correctly invoke the `perimeter` function of `TriangularLamina`, which is again inherited from (and therefore same as) the `perimeter` member function of `Triangle`.

- Within the body of the `perimeter` function invoked as in the above call, the `this` parameter would have the same value as `t`. However, its semantics *would be of a pointer to a* `Triangle` *class and **not** of a pointer to a* `TriangularLamina` *class* (this is C++ specific, but nevertheless highlights an important point). The emphasized text in the previous sentence is a crucial point to note before taking up polymorphism.

Assignment of an Object to Another Object

Every imperative programming language has some 'assignment' operator, for example, := in Pascal, = in FORTRAN and C/C++, etc. Assignment of *values*, which may result out of evaluating *expressions*, is the primary 'side-effect' creating operation in these languages. Assignment normally reduces to a bit-by-bit copy from one memory location (may be a temporary one, holding the evaluated value of an expression) to another, the latter being represented by the variable it is assigned to.

For certain 'built-in' data types, many programming languages incorporate implicit *type-conversions*, when the type of the source (expression) is different from that of the destination variable. However, for complex user-defined data types, most of these languages permit assignment only from one variable to another of *the same type*.

In the presence of the inheritance concept in OOPLs, the principles governing the assignment of one object to another become somewhat difficult.

Most OOPLs do not permit assignment of a totally unrelated object to another. However, they define principles for assignment between objects belonging to the same hierarchy.

In C++, for an assignment of the type

```
o1  =  o2
```

where o1 and o2 are instances of object classes O1 and O2, respectively, and = is the assignment operator, the following cases are to be considered:

- When O1 and O2 are mutually unrelated, i.e., neither O1 is ancestor class of O2, nor vice versa. In this case, C++ (as also most OOPLs) treats o1 and o2 as normal unrelated objects, and declares the assignment operation to be *illegal*.

- When O1 is an ancestor class of O2. This case is considered *legal*.

- When O2 is an ancestor of O1. This case is considered *illegal* due to pragmatic reasons.

In the OOP definition of hierarchy, every descendant object has same or more number of member variables than any ancestor. Conversely, an ancestor object has same or less number of member variables as any descendant. In the type of assignment discussed here, some member variables of o1 might remain undefined after the assignment. To prevent such an event from happening, the languages are designed to reject the assignment construct.

Note that by similar reasoning, the previous case may, at worst, lead to loss of information, but no undefined values get introduced through assignment.

Assignment of pointers

The semantics of assignment described above is extended to incorporate pointers to object classes. This is in spite of the fact that all pointers are (usually) of the same size, and the question of losing information or adding improper information does not arise.

If pO1 and pO2 are pointers to classes O1 and O2 respectively, and the assignment statement pO1 = pO2 is legal, then either O1 and O2 are identical classes, or O1 is an ancestor of O2. Thus, at run-time, if any pointer (to object O, say) is pointing at a valid instance of a class, the pointed class is either an instance *of* O or an instance of a descendant of O}.

Polymorphism

Of the three facets of OOP, we have already discussed two of them, namely, encapsulation and inheritance. We have stressed earlier that the third facet, i.e. 'polymorphism' is actually the most important one, to the extent that OOP can essentially be thought to be centred around this key concept. However, in our opinion, rather than providing with a description of the same arbitrarily, let us make an attempt to arrive at it logically through an example problem.

The problem description

Consider that a person has an *assorted* collection of objects of types TriangularLamina, TriangularFrame or HoledTriangularLamina (but of course, *not* Triangles—they do not exist). He is interested in computing the *total weight* of the collection. Subsequently, he intends to include other objects to his collection, but is sure that they would be some specialization of Triangles only. However, by the time he would be aware of the newer object type, many of the programmers involved in the original project would not be available, and there is a possibility that some of the source modules (not the header files) of the original program may also be lost during this time. It is decided that there would be at most, MAX_ENTITY number of objects in the collection. Also, a global variable collectionSize holds the actual number of articles in the collection.

A solution approach

It should be clear from the above description of the problem that, notwithstanding its smallness in size, many aspects of large scale software development scenario have been intentionally introduced. A real life solution to the above problem is quite obvious.

With an initial value 0.0 for variable (conceived mentally or on a note pad) totalWeight, bring out objects one by one from the collection and add up the respective weights to totalWeight. In the end, totalWeight contains the value of the total weight of the collection.

In programming implementation of the problem, we must consider three key aspects:

1. How to represent the assorted collection of objects? We must remember that the objects in the collection are *heterogeneous* in nature, i.e. the nature of individual objects of the collection is only known at run-time.

2. Being objects, every individual item in the collection knows how to compute its own weight. But unless we check every object for its type, how do we know which weight computing function to invoke for the presently picked out object.

3. How do we take care of future extendibility of the system even without the benefit of the previous source code? As we shall see later, this aspect is very closely related to the previous aspect considered above and shall be taken up together.

A short discussion on heterogeneous containers

Data structural constructs meant primarily to store other data items are generally termed as 'containers' in computer science, particularly in OOP parlance. In courses on algorithms, data structures, etc. we learn about various types of data structures and containers. An entire chapter (Chapter 4) of this book is devoted to design and usage of containers. In that chapter, we shall draw clear distinctions between containers as objects and data structural elements used to implement them.

For the time being, we remain *as unclear as most text books* on data structures and choose *array* as the container (actually data structure) for our problem. Now, by definition, all entries in an array must have an identical memory requirement. In the given problem this is not ensured, as our items could be of different object types and hence of different sizes. However, we know that all pointers are of identical size. Thus, instead of making our collection an array of objects, we make it an *array of pointers to objects*. We assume that we would be given the array representing the above-mentioned collection with the pointers properly pointing to instances of objects.

The first question is how do we *declare* the array representing the container. It is an array of pointers to *what*? This question is easily answered considering the principles of assignment of pointers to objects. The pointers in our array could be pointers to some *common ancestor of all possible classes whose instance may be included in our collection*. In the given problem, the Triangle class has been clearly marked for this role. Thus we may declare:

```
Triangle *myCollection[MAX_ENTITY];
```

Note that while the array actually contains pointers to Triangle, as per our declaration, *none of the pointers would actually ever point to an instance of* Triangle. This apparently strange phenomenon is typical of OOP philosophy, and arises directly due to the inheritance concept of OOP.

From the above discussion, it is clear that implementation of heterogeneous containers is not difficult with OOPLs. The first implementation aspect noted previously has thus been taken care of.

A short discussion on run-time binding of data to code

We shall now take up the second key implementation aspect considered above. We shall see that the feature of OOPLs that solves this problem takes care of the last aspect also.

Most conventional (non-OOPL) programmers would have solved the problem mentioned in the following manner: First, a tag member variable would be included for every object of the collection. In the given problem, it is easily done by declaring it only for the Triangle class, as in that case, it is inherited by all descendant object classes whose instances are ultimately candidates for our collection. We also declare and implement a member function int getTag() to read out the value of the tag. During invoking the weight computing function, the tag is first checked, and accordingly, the appropriate function chosen.

A naive implementation

Our implementation (code fragment) in C++ would be:

```
// Let 't' be the next object from the collection
   switch (t->getTag()) {
   case TRIANGULAR_LAMINA: totalWeight +=
                           ((TriangularLamina *)t)->weight();
      break;
```

```
    case TRIANGULAR_FRAME: totalWeight +=
                          ((TriangularFrame *)t)->weight();
        break;
    case HOLED_LAMINA: totalWeight +=
                          ((HoledTriangularLamina *)t)->weight();
        break;
}
```

In the above code, the construct (XX *) is the usual *pointer typecasting* mechanism meant to force the compiler to believe that t following the cast is a pointer to XX, irrespective of what it actually points to.

> **Important:** Pointer typecasting, as in the above examples, is an essential operation in OOP. The typecasting is known as *dynamic*. The actual types of the pointer and the cast pointer could be widely different. However, the cast pointer is known to point to an instance of a derived class of the class to which the original pointer is declared to point. In version-1 of C++ language (whose syntax we mostly follow), the typecasting is normally done as above. However, in the current version-2 of C++, the suggested operator is dynamic_cast<...>, where the ellipsis should be substituted by the actual pointer type. (see Chapter 3 for more details.)

While the above code fragment works, it is not the one best suggested in OOP. It is *naive* because it definitely goes against the philosophies of OOP as follows:

- The construct totalWeight += ((XX *)t)->weight() is common across the three cases, and hence could be reused.
- Supposing a new class is later on inducted into the system and the above fragment of *source code* is not available, we would *not* be able to incorporate the extension unless we re-implement the code from scratch.

A less naive solution

An observant reader may point out and suggest the following:

- Do away with the tag.
- Do away with the switch statement.
- Introduce a member function float weight() for Triangle and implement it in an appropriate manner.
- Replace the entire switch statement by totalWeight += t-> weight();. After all, the only part where the three cases differ is at the type cast.

The new code fragment is:

```
totalWeight += t->weight();
```

Indeed, for many languages, the suggestions are most appropriate and complete. However, with languages with C++, a few changes need to be made.

Nevertheless, if for arguments sake, the above suggestions are complete, we can easily conclude that it automatically solves the third key aspect of our implementation! Indeed, the new code has *no* construct that is dependent on the actual *class* of the object and hence, if new classes are inducted, the code does not get affected. In fact, it need not be recompiled!!

It has been our experience in almost every introductory session on OOP conducted by us, that at this juncture, most listeners raise some version of the query: *How does a compiled code come to know about the newly introduced data type?* We have to reassure them that nothing magical is happening here and that we would explain it in more detail at the appropriate place. For the moment, let us consider the requirements in the semantics of the language to achieve the above, i.e. *binding of code to data of an object at run-time.* This is precisely what is needed to get correct results in the less naive solution.

We shall resume our discussion on the problem at hand after a discussion on polymorphism and virtual functions carried out in the next section.

POLYMORPHISM AND VIRTUAL FUNCTIONS

We had promised earlier to arrive at the concept of polymorphism in a natural manner through an example. In our analysis of the example problem in the previous section, we have reached a point where we have talked about run-time binding of data with code. As a matter of fact, in OOP parlance, polymorphism is nothing but this run-time binding.

In languages like C++, this is achieved through *virtual* functions, i.e. virtual functions in C++ have capabilities of run-time binding or, as it is also known as, 'late binding'. Simply speaking, it can be explained as follows.

Let C be a base class which has a function f() that is virtual. Let there be descendant classes X, Y, Z, ... of C, some of which at least re-implement the virtual function f(). Let pC be a pointer to C. Thus pC can, at run-time, actually point to an instance of C or any of its descendants (X, Y, Z).

In the given scenario, the construct pC->f() would execute the implementation of f() for that class whose instance pC is actually pointing to. Thus, the run-time behaviour of the construct pC->f(), though externally (*morph* = external) unchanged, would lead to multiple (*poly-*) and particularized behaviour. This is precisely what is meant by the term polymorphism in OOP parlance.

Note that with respect to the construct pC->f(), the behaviour f() is basically an abstraction identified by a name, f() here. One way of looking at the construct is performing the abstract behaviour f() on whatever object pC is pointing at.

Thus, in OOP parlance, the following terms are semantically similar and quite often used interchangeably:

- Run-time or late binding.
- Virtual functions.
- Polymorphic behaviour.
- Abstract behaviour.

Although the interchangeability of the above terms are valid for OOP as a whole, we would like to point out that there are OOPLs which do not have any concept of non-run-time binding at all. All member functions for such languages are, therefore, virtual.

Virtual Function Implementation

An understanding of this sub-section is not essential to the understanding of OOP. Nevertheless, the following material describing how virtual functions are implemented in most compilers often leads to a better awareness of them. At least, the importance of constructors (and destructors) gets reiterated.

Assume the working process of a C++ compiler when it comes across a statement p = t->perimeter() where t is of type Triangle*. Compilers generally translate a function call statement into a sub-routine CALL instruction in the machine language of the target machine. A necessary parameter of the CALL instruction is a target address of the first instruction of the subroutine.

Thus, a compiler would quite naturally translate the function invocation statement t->perimeter() to a CALL statement with a target address Triangle::perimeter(). This binding of the target address of the CALL instruction is *fixed* at compile time and *may not be changed during run-time.*

Observe that though t can point to any instance of any class same or derived from Triangle, the invocation t->perimeter() *always* leads to Triangle::perimeter(). Even if t is pointing to an instance of HoledTriangularLamina (whose perimeter calculation is quite different from that of Triangle), the invocation t->perimeter() would compute the perimeter, assuming that t is actually pointing to an instance of a Triangle.

Binding of target of function invocation statements to actual addresses is known as static binding. Most non-object programming languages have statically bound functions. In fact, unless specially directed, member functions of even C++ are statically bound.

We have already concluded that in order to have polymorphism, we require to bind targets of function invocations to actual addresses at run-time, i.e. to have *dynamic* binding of functions. While in some OOPLs, all member functions of all object classes are dynamically bound, in C++, the keyword virtual is required against a member function to notify to the compiler an intention to bind the function dynamically.

'Position Invariance' of virtual functions—VFT

Once a function is declared virtual in a class in C++, all the descendant classes inherit the function as virtual. From this, we may conclude that the *position* of a virtual function (in a list of virtual functions) is invariant down a class hierarchy.

To further explain what we mean, let us suppose we list the virtual functions of a class (say C) in order of their declaration as follows.

1. All virtual functions declared for the first time in C are positioned in order of declaration *after* all inherited virtual functions.

2. All inherited virtual functions of C have the same position in the list as the parent class of C.

With the above assumptions, every virtual function of a class may be mapped to a unique position number in a table of virtual functions. Besides, the position number of a particular virtual function (say f()), remains invariant down a hierarchy of classes.

In C++ implementations, the table in question is usually referred to as the *Virtual Function Table* or VFT. Let us use the notation #f to denote the position number of f() in the VFTs of the class where it was first declared, and its descendant classes. Corresponding to every class C, with at least one virtual function (inherited or newly declared), the entry at position #f in the VFT of C contains the address of the function C::f(), inherited or overloaded.

C++ implementation of virtual functions

A C++ compiler translates any function invocation for a virtual function through a construct like pC->f() (where pC is a pointer to C) to an *indirect* CALL to the base address of the VFT *of* the class pointed at by pC at run-time, offsetted by #f.

An indirect CALL instruction has a data address as a parameter and causes a subroutine reference to a location whose address is contained in the location pointed at by the parameter to CALL.

The target address for a virtual function is only partially committed at compile time—the compiler only qualifies #f, the offset, into the VFT. At run-time, the base address of the VFT is referred to in the CALL instruction in a dynamic manner and as a result, dynamic invocation of a virtual function is achieved.

The pseudo-codes corresponding to the construct pC->f() (pC declared as a pointer to C), where f is either not virtual or virtual, are as follows:

Where f() is not a virtual function

```
CALL  C::f()
```

Where f() is a virtual function

```
base <- VFT of what pC points to, dynamically determined
CALL [base + #f]; Here #f is statically known.
```

Fixing VFT addresses at run-time

A final question remains: How are VFT base addresses determined at run-time?

As a matter of fact, C++ language specifications are silent on this question beyond a certain limit. What is clarified is that in some way, every instance of a class having a VFT must be somehow bound to the VFT. In other words, there must be some pieces of code specifically meant for this binding.

As already stated, we reiterate that (in C++) one part of code (for a particular class) that a class instance most definitely passes through, is the *constructor* of the class. This is because during running of the program, the creation of every instance of every class must be filtered through the constructor.

In our discussion about constructors, we had mentioned that the constructor carries some work other than just memory allocation. We may now mention that one of the duties of the so-called 'hidden code' of a constructor, is to associate a class's instance to its VFT. The manner in which the association is achieved is, however, fully compiler dependent.

THE EXAMPLE PROBLEM SOLVED USING VIRTUAL FUNCTIONS

The discussions in the previous section should now make it clear that if member functions like `perimeter()` are declared `virtual` for all classes in the hierarchy headed by `Triangle`, invocations of the type `t->perimeter()` would have run-time binding.

Suppose that at some instant, `t` points to an instance of `HoledTriangularLamina`. During creation, the constructor of `HoledTriangularLamina` has bound the instance to the VFT of the class. The compiler translates the statement `t->perimeter()` to an indirect CALL through the VFT of class of the instance pointed to by `t`. Since `t` at the instant of interest is pointing to an instance of `HoledTriangularLamina`, the resulting run-time binding would cause an invocation of the function `HoledTriangularLamina::perimeter()`, and *not* `Triangle::perimeter()`, although `t` has been declared to be a pointer to `Triangle`.

Let us turn our attention back to our problem at hand—computing the total weight of a collection of `Triangle` like objects.

Declaring `weight()` as 'pure' virtual in `Triangle`

First, we must introduce a `virtual` member function `weight()` in the `Triangle` class.

The implementation of this member function in `Triangle` is not essential, since we assume that our collection has no instance of `Triangles`. Such cases are quite common where an object class simply acts as an artefact to head a class hierarchy, and acts as a point from where one or more virtual functions are first declared. The declared virtual function(s) simply act as name handles to abstract behaviours. For example, the virtual function `weight()` in class `Triangle` acts as the handle to the weight calculation behaviour of triangles.

Quite often (as here), a virtual function declared as above has no meaningful implementation for the class in question. In our example, since there is no concept of weight calculation of a `Triangle` object, it is meaningless to talk about the implementation of `Triangle::weight()`.

In C++, one can implement such a virtual function as *pure* virtual function—one that has a null body (observe the declaration of a pure virtual function in the example code).

Abstract Classes

In C++ terminology, a class with at least one pure virtual function is known as an *abstract class*. The compiler ensures that no instance of an abstract class is ever created. An abstract class can have other abstract classes derived from it. However, no abstract class may be derived from a non-abstract (or 'real' class). In our example, not only is the class `Triangle` abstract, the class `MaterialTriangle` inherited from it (see below), is also abstract.

A Better Class Hierarchy for the Problem

The reader would perhaps remember our promise for a better description of the `Triangle` class hierarchy.

The question at that time was whether to declare `TriangularLamina` as a parent class of `TriangularFrame`, or vice versa. At that point of time, we arbitrarily chose the former. Our problem was that though the two above mentioned classes represent 'material' triangles, i.e. both have valid material codes, the codes are used with different meanings in calculating their weights.

As many readers had pointed out, if the sole reason behind making `TriangularLamina` a parent class of `TriangularFrame`, or vice versa, is to incorporate the material code data member, a better and more logical description should have some class (say, `MaterialTriangle`) heading both the above classes. Of course, the class `MaterialTriangle` is derived from `Triangle`, and is itself an abstract class.

Thus, we redefine our class hierarchy as:

```
class Point {
private:
  float xCoord, yCoord;

public:
    Point();
    ~Point();
  void setX(float newX);
  void setY(float newY);
  float x();
  float y();
  float length(Point otherPoint);
};

class Triangle {
protected:
```

```
    Point vertices[3];

public:
      Triangle(Point  a,  Point  b,  Point  c);
      Triangle();
      ~Triangle();
  Point  *vertex(int which);
  virtual  float  perimeter();
  virtual  Point  *centroid();
  virtual  float  weight() = 0;  // Note the syntax for a PURE
                                 // virtual function.
};

class MaterialTriangle public Triangle {
protected:
  int    materialCode;

public:
      MaterialTriangle(Point a,  Point b,  Point c,  int m);
      MaterialTriangle();
      ~MaterialTriangle();
// We do not overload weight. So it remains pure, and thus,
//}; this is an abstract class.


class TriangularLamina public MaterialTriangle {
public:
      TriangularLamina(Point a,  Point b,  Point c,  int m);
      TriangularLamina();
      ~TriangularLamina();
  float weight(); // Once virtual always virtual
};

class TriangularFrame public MaterialTriangle {
public:
      TriangularFrame(Point a,  Point b,  Point c,  int m);
      TriangularFrame();
      ~TriangularFrame();
  float weight(); // Once virtual always virtual
};

class HoledTriangularLamina public TriangularLamina {
protected:
  Point holePosition;
  float holeDiameter;

public:
      TriangularLamina(Point  a,  Point  b,  Point  c,
                       Point hole,  float  d,  int m);
      TriangularLamina();
      ~TriangularLamina();
  float perimeter(); // Re-defining perimeter
  Point *centroid(); // and also centroid
  float weight(); // and, of course, weight
};
```

In Fig. 2.2, we have given a pictorial description of the class hierarchy.

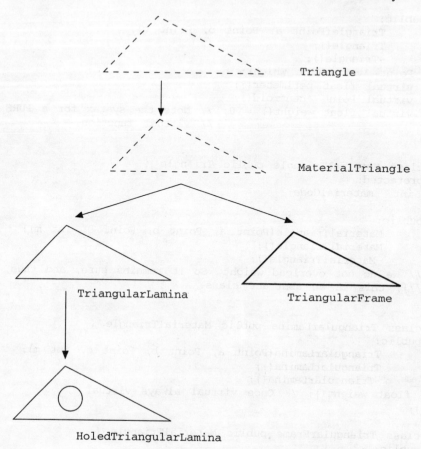

Fig. 2.2   A pictorial representation of the class hierarchy of the example problem.

The Final Solution to the Example Problem

Finally, let our collection (called `myCollection`) be an array of pointers to triangles, where the current size of the bag is found in variable `collectionSize`. Thus:

```
Triangle *myCollection[MAX_ENTITY];
```

Hence, the weight calculation function can be written as

```
float weightOfCollection() // Assuming myCollection to be global.
{
  float totalWeight=0;
  for (int i=0; i<collectionSize; i++)
   totalWeight += myCollection[i]->weight();
  return totalWeight;
}
```

Note that the weight collection routine has no reference to the actual object type pointed at by the i-th pointer, so long as it is some descendant of Triangle. Actually, even the source code for the above function need not be available. With only the object module being present (and of course header files to clarify what is actually contained in the object module), the overall software may arbitrarily extend the Triangle class hierarchy.

So long as it is ensured that only instances of Triangle derived classes are contained in myCollection and that each new class in the hierarchy implements its own specialized version of the weight() function (or inherit the implementation of its parent class), the global weight calculation function would work perfectly.

A Variation in the Problem Specification

Let us introduce a small but interesting variation in the problem specification.

In the original specification, it was assumed that there are at most, MAX_ENTITY number of objects in the collection and that the global variable collectionSize holds the actual number of articles in the collection. Let us now remove the above restrictions. First, there is no defined upper bound in the number of articles in the collection. Secondly, the actual number of articles in the collection is not stored in any separate variable.

The 'link' of a linked list for the example problem

Most readers would recognize that the extended specification is ideally solved through implementation of the collection as a dynamic structure like the linked list. The immediate question that arises is how to declare a 'link' of such a linked list, given the heterogeneity of the items. As before, we may conclude that the best way is to store pointers to Triangles in the 'data' part of the link. With that, declaration of the collection and a modified implementation of the weight calculation function is as follows:

```
struct LinkNode {
  Triangle    *data;
  LinkNode    *next;
};

LinkNode      *myList; // Head of the linked list representing
                       // the bag.

// Assumptions:  //If myList is NULL, collection is empty.
                 //If the next field of the current link is NULL,
                 //the current node is the last node.

float weightOfList() // Assuming myList to be global.
{
 float totalWeight=0;
 for (int LinkNode *lNode = myList; lNode != NULL; lNode = lNode->next)
   totalWeight += lNode->data->weight();
 return totalWeight;
}
```

A `ListMover` class for our linked list

Note that in the body of the above function, the internal details of implementation of the linked list—members `data` and `next`, were freely used to refer to the current triangle and the next link, respectively. A proper encapsulated implementation should hide these details. We may therefore have:

```
struct LinkNode {  // As before.
  Triangle    *data;
  LinkNode    *next;

  LinkNode(Triangle *t, LinkNode *n) // A constructor for easy creation.
    { data = t; next = n;  }
};

class TriangleList {
  LinkNode      *head; // Head of the linked list.
public:

  TriangleList() { head = NULL;  }
  // Constructor, initializing the linked list.
  ~Triangle();
// Destructor, whose implementation we shall not discuss now.

  void add(Triangle *t) // To add a triangle at head
    { head = new LinkNode(t, head);  }

friend class ListMover;
// This is to make life in the ListMover class easy.
} *myTriangleList;

class ListMover {
  TriangleList *tList;
  LinkNode      *currentNode;

public:

  Triangle    *current() { return currentNode ? currentNode->
data : NULL;  }
  Triangle    *init() { currentNode = tList->head; return current(); }
  Triangle    *next()
    { currentNode = currentNode ? currentNode->next : NULL;
return current();  }
  int         endReached() { return currentNode == NULL;  }

  ListMover(TriangleList *tl) { tList = tl; init();  }
};

float weightOfTriangleList()
// assuming myTriangleList to be global.
{
  float totalWeight=0;
  for (ListMover l(myTriangleList); !l->endReached(); l->next())
    totalWeight += l->current()->weight();
  return totalWeight;
}
```

A class declared as a `friend` of a class C can directly access even the private members of C.

Obviously, the new implementation of the weight calculation function is sufficiently detached and quite independent of the details of the implementation of the `TriangleList` class or its `friend ListMover` class. As a matter of fact, either or both of the above classes may be re-implemented (keeping the member interface fixed) without affecting the `weightOfTriangleList()` function in any way.

A look at the above `TriangleList` class from an abstract point of view leads to certain revelations. First, the primary purpose of the said class is to hold or contain instances of other interrelated classes—derived classes of the `Triangle` class in this case. Secondly, as already observed, implementation and reasoning about such a class may be carried out quite independent of the details of the contained classes. Indeed, it is quite possible to talk about such 'container' classes for containing instances of *any* class, so long as they are abstracted in an appropriate base class. In a later chapter, we shall inspect this aspect of object-oriented programming in greater detail.

CONCLUSION

In this chapter, we have tried to provide a bird's eyeview of what has come to be known as *object-oriented programming*. We have defined the term 'object' in this regard and have, through a step-by-step introduction, arrived at the central concept of OOP, i.e., *polymorphism*. Polymorphism is achieved in C++ primarily through `virtual` functions.

Somehow, at the end of the day, many exponents of OOP miss this key issue. They lay unnecessary emphasis on the encapsulation and inheritance aspects of OOP while playing only lip service to the most useful aspect of OOP, namely, the 'abstraction-specialization' syndrome achieved through true polymorphism.

There is another tendency of new learners of the C++ language to identify *all* types of function overloading with polymorphism. Function overloading in C++ allows functions with same names but different parameter types/ return values, to be declared in the same environment. Non-virtual function inheritance is also an instance of function overloading. However, unless the overloaded function is virtual, *it can not be used as a name bound to an abstract concept across an object hierarchy*. The emphasis on the last part of the above sentence is intentional. Our sincere advice to the reader is to go through this chapter again till the above realization is properly in place.

PROBLEMS

1. OOP *gurus* generally advise C++ programmers to declare functions as virtual in a miserly manner. However, whenever a function clearly represents an abstract behaviour, there should be no hesitation in declaring them as virtual. Can you elaborate upon the prudence behind the advice?

2. Declare and implement the class `Point3D` that represents a point in a three-dimensional rectangular co-ordinate system, as a specialization of the class `Point`.

3. Given the present declaration of the `Triangle` class, can it be directly extended to the domain where the vertices of triangles are actually points in 3-dimensional space, i.e., vertices could as well be `Point3D`-s? If not, what modifications do you suggest in the `Triangle` class for the purpose?

4. A new type of triangular object is conceived of as follows. It is basically a triangular frame, but the mid-points of the three sides are joined to each other by wires of a material different from the material of the frame. By definition, the perimeter and centroid are unchanged from corresponding definitions of `Triangle`. Declare and implement the class for the object.

5. Write a function to compute the overall centre of gravity of a collection of (original, two-dimensional) `Triangle` like objects. The collection size upper bound is not known.

6. Write a function to enumerate (simply print the coordinate values) all those vertex points that are common to at least two distinct `Triangle` like objects in an arbitrarily size collection of such objects.

3

A Brief Survey of C++ as an Object-Oriented Programming Language

In this chapter, we take a look at the language syntax of C++, especially at those aspects that facilitate object-oriented programming. Even till the writing of this book, the language specification of C++ has not stabilized. Starting from version 2.0 of C++ language specifications, some newer facilities have been incorporated. The two most important of these are *multiple inheritance* and `templates`. The former feature allows a class in C++ to be derived from more than one class. However, this aspect has been avoided throughout this book, as in the authors' opinion and experience, programming and abstraction advantages of having multiple inheritance facility is far outweighed by the confusion in programming discipline and reasoning caused thereby. Templates, on the other hand, are less problematic for relatively disciplined programmers, and also reduce the scope of certain programming errors. However, use of templates leads to less transparent codes. We have, nevertheless, provided a cursory description of the two aspects at the end of the chapter. They have not been taken up in any other portion of the book.

We would like to reiterate once more that the chapter should *not* be read as a reference manual either for the C++ language, or for any compiler of the language. The reader is encouraged to read books, manuals, and help files specifically meant for the purpose. The language specification of C++ is a superset of the specification of C. Virtually every construct that is legal for C (ANSI C) is legal and of identical semantics in C++. However, C++ provides more generality in declaration than C, even in aspects of the language that may not be specific to the object-oriented framework. Let us take up some of these aspects.

NON-OOP SPECIFIC SYNTAX EXTENSIONS IN C++

Single Line Comments

Over and above the comment envelope symbols /* and */ of C, C++ allows a single line commenting mechanism through a 'double-slash' (//) construct. Everything on a line to the right of a // construct is disregarded by the compiler. In this book, // comments have been used quite liberally.

Local Variable Declaration within Function Scope

In C, local variables—both automatic and static—must be declared before the first line of code. This restriction has been removed in C++. Variables can be declared anywhere within the body of a function. Indeed, the extended scope rules of local variables range from the point of its declaration till the end of the scope of the region where it has been declared. This allows declaration of more than one variable with the same name within the scope of a function, provided they do not clash in their respective scopes. There is, however, one restriction in the above declaration principles. No local variable may be declared with initialization within the scope of a region of code that may be bypassed. For example, no variables may be declared within the scope of the target of a switch statement. The reason for this is not difficult to comprehend. Automatic variables have to be 'created' (constructed) on the stack at the point where it is declared and destroyed at the end of the scope. For example:

```
int i = 10; // Let us call this variable 'outer i'.

if ( i > 5) { // Note this brace.
int i = 5; // This 'inner i' has a scope and extent till the
// closing brace matching the opening brace immediately above.
// All references to i here refers to inner i.

} // inner i has scope and extent upto here
// outer i back in scope. Still has value 10

// However, in the case below, the compiler would flag error.
switch (i) { // Scope of newVar declared below starts here.
 case 0: int newVar = 20; // newVar declared with initialization.
 // But this code may be bypassed.

 break;
 case 1:
  // newVar is still in scope here,
  // but code may bypass initialization upto here.
} // end of switch.
```

Function Declaration

Function declaration syntax in C++ is almost the same as that of ANSI C as shown below. However, there are a few points of difference. One of them is the strong type checking feature of C++ discussed below.

The second point of difference is that in C++, a function declaration may specify *default* values for one or more of its parameters. A parameter is indicated as a default parameter by assigning a constant value (using the = operator) to it. In the declaration of a function with several parameters, there should not be a default parameter to the left of a non-default one. In other words, parameters must be marked default from right to left. A C++ compiler may get confused (and hence flag error), if it encounters different declarations of the same function mentioning default parameters, even if the values these parameters are defaulted to are identical.

In C, only the name of the function is its identifier. In C++, the entire function declaration statement—the function name and the parameter list (only the type list) together constitutes its identity or signature. Two declared functions are identical only if their signatures are identical.

From the above descriptions, it is clear that whenever a C++ compiler encounters a function declaration (including its mandatory use as the header of the code implementing the function) or a function invocation, it checks for its signature in the symbol table. It is liable to get confused if in a function invocation, the signature of the invocation statement matches with more than one declaration signatures with default parameters and built-in typecasting taken into account. Most C++ compilers flag error in such cases.

```
int func0(int param1, float param2); // Full declaration.

int func0(int, float);
// Declaration identical to above. Parameter names omitted.

int func0(float, float, int);
// Different function from above because although
// names are same, signatures are different.

int func1(int param1, float param2 = 1.5, int = 0);
// Two default parameters.

int func2(int = 1, float, int = 0);
// ILLEGAL Default parameter left of non-default.

int func0(float, int, int); // Consider this declaration

// and invocation:
//    ...       func0(5, 6, 7)
// The compiler gets confused as to which function func0 to call—
// the last one, or the second one declared above.
```

Stronger Type Checking

C++ enforced pre-declaration of functions before use. Except with explicitly defined variable argument list (through ellipsis, i.e., ...), the actual parameters passed during a function call *must* match in type and number with the declared function header. This rigidity of syntax is mostly beneficial. Some flexibility is, however, allowed through the use of default parameters. Explicit mention of default parameters is optional. If not mentioned, the compiler is expected to generate a parameter having the default value for it in the function declaration.

Some examples may be in order. Consider the function declarations (the legal ones only) in the previous sub-section.

```
// LEGAL function invocations:
//----------------------------
// func0(5, 10.5) — Calls first func0
// func1(1, 10) — Calls func1 with actual arguments 1, 10.0 and 0
// func1(1)      — Same as above

// ILLEGAL function invocations:
//----------------------------
// func0()          --- No signature of func0 provides for zero arguments
// func0(5, 10.5, 0, 6)    --- Neither with four arguments
// func1(1, "Some String")  --- Type mismatch in second parameter
// func0(5, 6, 7)       --- Compiler confused between two signatures
```

l-Value or Reference Variables

One major innovation in C++ over C and quite often a serious source of confusion, is allowing variables to be declared as 'l-value' (or reference) variables. Just as the prefix symbol* is used to denote a pointer variable during declaration, the symbol & is earmarked in C++ to denote an l-value variable. For example, in the declaration:

```
SomeType    instanceVar, *pointerVar, &referenceVar;
```

the declared variables in order are an instance of SomeType, a pointer to SomeType and an l-value (or reference) variable of SomeType, respectively. Needless to say, any of the formal parameters of a function, as well as its return value could be of l-value type.

There is a certain amount of confusion observed among C++ programmers, upon first encountering an l-value variable. This is primarily because of the closeness between l-value and pointer variable semantics while being different at the level of syntactic representation. The actual 'value' stored in an l-value variable is a pointer of the appropriate type. However, unlike pointer variables, an l-value variable need not be de-referenced to access the actual variable pointed at. The latter behaviour of an l-value variable makes it closer to a non-pointer variable at the syntax level. Let us assume the declaration below and some examples that follow:

```
SomeType,          instanceVar, *pointerVar, &referenceVar;
```

- The constructs pointerVar = &instanceVar and referenceVar = instanceVar achieve the same purpose—ensure that constructs *pointerVar and referenceVar act as aliases of instanceVar. As a matter of fact, referenceVar can be used in any place where the use of instanceVar is legal, with identical effect.

- Assuming the assignments in the above item, the constructs

```
instanceVar = <expression leading to value of SomeType>,
```

```
*pointerVar = <same expression leading to value of SomeType> and
```

```
referenceVar = <same expression leading to value of SomeType>
```

lead to identical results.

- A reference parameter to a function permits modification of the actual variable passed during the function invocation. Observe the example below:

```
void swap(int& a, int&b) { int temp =a; a = b; b = temp; }

// Say i has value 5 and j has value  10.
// The call swap(i,j) would make
// i to have value 10 and j to have value 5.
```

- Normally, the return value of a function is an *r*-value, i.e. it is not meaningful (nor legal) to modify the value returned by a function. However, if the return value of a function is of a reference type, the same may be used to access and modify the actual variable that it acts as an alias for. This is similar to accessing and modifying the value of a variable through dereferencing a (valid) pointer returned by a function. For example:

```
int globalVar;

int *pointerToGlobal() { return &globalVar; }

int &referenceToGlobal() { return globalVar; } // Observe the body

// Constructs.
//
// a) globalVar = 10;
// b) *(pointerToGlobal()) = 10;
// c) referenceToGlobal () = 10;
//
// have identical results — setting value of globalVar to 10.
```

Operators new and delete

In C++, memory allocation and deallocation through pointers has been formalized in the language syntax through operators new and delete. The operator new is basically a unary operator. However, it takes a set of (within parentheses, comma separated) additional default arguments called *initializers*. The syntax specification of new is:

new *type-name*[*initializer*]

Type-name is the essential argument of the operator new, and determines the type of the variable to be allocated. It could also be an array on any dimensions of a type. However, all specified dimensions, except the first one, must be compile-time constant expressions evaluating positive integral values, while the first dimension could be any integer evaluating expression.

The new operator allocates memory of amount sizeof *type-name* (multiplied by actual dimension limits if specified) on the global heap and on successful allocation, returns a pointer of type *pointer to type-name* as the result of the operation. The resultant pointer points to the dynamically created variable (or the first variable of a dynamically created array) if successful, and NULL otherwise. If *type-name* is a user defined type (say, a class or struct), new invokes the constructor of the class.

For built-in types, the initializer must be an expression of a conforming type within a pair of parentheses. The dynamically created variable is initialized to the specified value. For complicated user defined types, the initializer list is used to select the constructor to be invoked. Absence of any initializer invokes the default constructor. The initializer must not be specified for allocation of arrays. The new operator creates arrays of objects only if the object's class has a default constructor.

Some examples of use of new are:

```
MyType   *myPtr;

myPtr = new MyType; // Invokes default constructor of MyType

myPtr = new MyType(); // Same as above

myPtr = new MyType(0, 1.5);
// Invokes a constructor of appropriate signature

myPtr = new MyType [10];
// Creates an array of 10 instances of MyType

myType = new MyType[2*n];
// No of instances created determined at run-time

myType = new MyType[2*n][10];
// Creates a 2-dim array. First dimension extent determined at
run-time
```

The delete operator undoes what new does. The delete operator takes only one argument, which is pointer to a known type. First the destructor of the instance pointed at by the argument is invoked, followed by deallocation of space occupied by the instance. The argument could also be an array of unspecified size, whence the entire allocated array is deleted.

If the destructor of the class to which the argument to delete is a pointer, is virtual, the actual destructor invoked is determined at run-time, depending upon which class instance the pointer points at. Some examples of use of the delete operator are:

```
delete myPtr;    // Deletes the instance pointed at by myPtr. The
destructor of
                 // MyType is called if the destructor is not virtual.
Otherwise,
                 // the destructor of the class to whose instance myPtr
points
                 // currently, is called.

delete [] myPtr; // Deletes an array of instances of MyType
```

For non-class objects, new and `delete` refer to standard library routines for global operators `::new` and `::delete`, respectively. For an object of class X, the new and `delete` operators refer to operator functions `operator X::new` and `operator X::delete`, respectively. These operators implicitly invoke the global operators unless explicitly overloaded. Overloaded new and `delete` operators in a class are inherited in classes derived from the class.

Like most standard C++ operators, all versions of new and `delete` may also be overloaded. The new operator takes a `size_t` type argument indicating memory requirement and returns a `void *` pointer pointing to the memory allocated for the object. Operator `delete` takes a `void *` as the argument and deallocates it. Overloading of new and `delete` operators allows the programmer to incorporate his own memory management scheme.

The Typecasting Operator

The language specification of C allows for casting between some standard built-in data types. Most often, the casting is automatic, i.e. the code for typecasting is automatically inserted by the compiler. However, the programmer may also explicitly cast between types using the following construct:

`(<A type name>) <An instance of a different type>`

Pointers to defined types can also be cast similarly.

It is not difficult to conceive of the typecasting construct as a unary operator. Indeed, in C++, typecasting is considered as an operator. Thus, the construct
`(<A type name>) <An instance of a different type>`

is treated as `::operator <A type name> (<An instance of a different type>)`

The scheme is most interesting in the context of classes, where,

the construct `(<A type name>) <An instance of a class X>` is treated as `<An instance of a class X>.operator <A type name> ()`.

In all these cases, the operator results in `<Value of type name>`.

Upto the older version of C++, casting between two pointers of any class was freely permitted. The newer version of C++ prohibits casting between user defined types. However, since casting from a baser class pointer to a derived class pointer has a special significance in the context of OOP, the newer version of C++ has introduced a new operator `dynamic_cast` that takes the casted type as the first argument in angular brackets and the pointer to be casted as a regular argument.

Some examples are:

```
class X {
  int      code;
  .
  .
public:
  .
  operator int () { return code; }
};

class Y : public X {
  .
  .
  .
public:
  void localToY(); // Some member function not declared in X.
};

int func0(int, float);

int func0(float);

X     x, *px;
  .
  .
func0(10, 20); // Compiler casts second parameter to float.
  .
  .
func0( (int) 10.0 ); // Programmer has given explicit typecast.
  .
  .
func0( x ); // LEGAL  Same as ... func0( (float) (int) x ), or
            // ... func0( (float) (x.operator int()) );
  .
  .
  .
  .
((Y *) px)->localToY();
// Legal in older version, but illegal in newer version.
// Observe the parenthesizing to beat operator precedence.
  .
  .
( dynamic_cast<Y *> px)->localToY(); // In the newer version of C++.
```

Operator Overloading

One of the exquisite features of C++ is operator overloading. The following C++ operators may be overloaded:

```
+        -        *        /        %        ^
!        =        <        >        +=       -=
^=       &=       |=       <<       >>       <<=
<=       >=       &&       ||       ++       --
(    )   [    ]   new      delete   &        |
~        *=       /=       %=       >>=      ==
!=       ->       ->*
```

Thus, all operators except . (struct, class or union member),.* (pointer to member), : : (scope resolution) and ? : (conditional), may be overloaded. If an operator can be used as either a unary or a binary operator, each may be overloaded separately. An operator may be overloaded using either a nonstatic member function or a global function that is a friend of a class. A global function must have at least one parameter that is of class type or a reference to class type. If a unary operator is overloaded using a member function, it takes no arguments; If it takes one argument, it is overloaded using a global function. If a binary operator is overloaded using a member function, it takes one argument; and if it is overloaded using a global function, it takes two arguments.

The keyword operator followed by the operator symbol name is known as the *operator function name*, and acts like a normal function name in the redefinition of the operator. An operator function called with arguments behaves like an operator working on its operands in an expression. However, a redefined operator function cannot alter the number of arguments, precedence and associativity rules that apply to normal operator usage.

Consider, for example, the binary addition operator +. The following operator overloading function definition is a valid one:

```
MyType3 operator + (MyType1, MyType2);
// Only one parameter of function.
```

With declarations:

```
MyType1    v1;
Mytype2    v2;
MyType3    v3;
```

The expressions v3 = v1 + v2; and v3 = v1.operator + (v2); have identical behaviours and invoke the operator function declared above.

Unary operator functions take one parameter. For a given overloaded operator function for the operator @ (say) with argument of some type X, the expressions @x and x@, where x is an instance of X, have identical effects and is interpreted as operator @ (x). For example, the overloaded operator function for the pre- or post-decrement operator could be:

```
MyType2 operator -- (Mytype1)
```

The expressions v2 = --v1 and v2 = v1-- have identical semantics.

Overloading operators as class member functions would be discussed at the appropriate place.

Inline Functions

C++ provides the keyword inline as a function qualifier. An inline function behaves more like a macro—the compiler places a new copy of the inline function in each place it is called. Inserting of inline functions eliminates the overhead of function call at the expense of slightly increasing the size of the run-time module of the program.

Unlike macros which are 'expanded' by the pre-processor, inline functions are processed by the compiler itself. This allows for type checking of arguments passed to the function against the types of its formal parameters. Thus, inline functions are free from many of the side-effects that macros have.

Another distinct macro-like behaviour of inline functions is that they can be expanded in header files that are to be included in different source files to be linked together later. As a matter of fact, it is prudent to define inline functions in header files only so that the compiler becomes aware of the existence of an inline function before the same is called anywhere.

Inline functions are expected to be of short length. The inline specifier is merely a hint to the compiler to treat the specified function as an inline one. However, if the expansion is not feasible or the function is not small enough, the compiler may choose to ignore the specifier and treat it as a normal function.

An example of an inline function could be:

```
inline int max(int a, int b) { return a > b ? a : b; }
```

This behaves similar to the macro

```
#define max(a, b) ( (a) > (b) ) ? (a) : (b)
```

except that type checking takes place in the former.

Inline functions must preferably be defined in header files. This is because since they are treated as macros by the compiler, there is no harm in them being defined in multiple modules of a program. On the other hand, unless they are defined in header files, it is likely that the compiler would not become aware of their inline nature at the proper juncture. Class member functions can also be inline ones.

EXTENSIONS TO C SYNTAX IN C++ TO PROVIDE OBJECT-ORIENTED PROGRAMMING FACILITIES

C++ offers extension to the standard C type declaration system to provide declaration of user-specified classes of objects. Each class type represents a unique set of objects and the operations and conversions available to create, manipulate and destroy such objects. Classes may be *derived* or *inherited* from one (single inheritance) or more (multiple inheritance, not discussed here) *base* classes with well-defined principles of inheritance.

Class Declaration

The syntax for class declaration is:

```
<class-key> <class-name>  < optional : <base-list>> { <members> }
```

The zone within the braces enclosing the members of a class is defined to be the *primary scope* of the class. The *class-key* could be any one from class, struct or union. If *base-list* is omitted, the class is a *base class*, i.e. it is not derived from any class. Otherwise, *base-list* is a list of comma-separated pairs (*base-class-name, optional-access-specifier*). In the single inheritance scenario described here, declarations with at most one such pair would be considered. The class *base-class-name* in that case is the base class for the declared class. In most of our subsequent discussions in this chapter and elsewhere, we shall refer to the class mentioned as *base-class-name* as the *parent class* of the class in question.

The *class-name* is an identifier unique within its scope. The name may be omitted in untagged structures, although this is rarely done in standard C++ programs. The *members* represent an optional sequential list of *member data* and *member functions*. The member data are the ones declared for the class over and above the member data inherited from the parent class. The member functions are the function prototypes declared within the primary scope of the class without a friend specifier. As with normal functions, more than one member function of a class can have the same name, so long as their signatures are different.

The declarations, i.e. the prototypes of functions relevant in the scope of the parent class, are inherited by the descendant class. If a function with identical signature to one in the parent class (except possibly omitting the virtual specifier, if present) is declared in a class; the function is said to have been *overloaded*. An overloaded member function is a promise by the designer of a class to re-implement it for the class.

Scope of a Class and the Scope Resolution Operator ::

The global name of a member (data or function) m of a class X is X::m — :: being the (class) scope resolution operator. Member functions declared in a class can be defined (i.e., implemented) like any normal function, except that the global name of the function must be used as the header. For example,

```
class X {
      .
      .
    MyType1 someMember(MyType1, MyType2);
// A member function declaration.
      .
      .
};
      .
```

```
MyType1 X::someMember(MyType1, MyType2)
// Global header in function definition.
{
       .
// The extended scope
       .
// of class X.
}
```

The zone covering the body of a member function definition of class X is the extended scope of class X.

Member Functions of a Class

Member functions of a class (the no-static ones, to be precise) operate on a class type object with which they are called. Let X be a class with a member function f(), and x and xptr be an instance of X and a pointer to X, respectively. The construct x.f() executes X::f() in the environment of x, while xptr->f() executes X::f() in the environment of *xptr. During execution, a member function of a class X comes to know about the object x, in whose environment it is executing, through an invisible argument of type X* which points to x.

The Keyword This

In C++, the pointer to an object over which a member function works, can also be referred directly through the keyword this. In any case, all references to members (data and function) in the extended scopes of a class are treated by the compiler as having a prefix this->. Thus, the internal ramification of a construct like x.f() is:

$X::f(\&x)$

where the non-explicit entities have been shown emphasized.

Class Member Visibility—the private, protected and public Access Specifiers

Any member of a class may have three types of visibility, indicated by three types of *access specifier* keywords—private, protected and public. The use of these specifiers is discussed below. Members of a class with private visibilities are accessible (visible) only from the extended scopes of the class. Members of a class with protected visibilities are accessible from the extended scopes of the class or classes derived from it. Members with public visibilities are accessible from everywhere. It is clear therefore, that in terms of visibility, private is less visible than protected, which in turn, is less visible than public.

The visibility of a member of a class depends upon the access specifier (i.e. visibility directive—one from the above three keywords followed by a colon) immediately preceding it. For classes declared with the `class` keyword, the compiler assumes a `private:` directive immediately after the opening brace beginning the class's immediate scope. For classes declared with the `struct` keyword, a `public:` directive is assumed at the same place.

Example:

```
class X {
      int       i;      // X::i is private by default,
      char      ch;     // so is X::ch.

public:

      int j;    // next two are public.
      int k;

protected :
      int l;    // X::l is protected.
};

struct Y {
      int i;    // Y::i is public by default.

private :

      int j;    // Y::j is private.

public :

      int k;    //Y::k is public.
};
```

The access specifiers can be listed and grouped in any convenient sequence. A little typing effort can be saved by declaring all the private members together, and so on.

Use of directives in further controlling of visibility is discussed later, in the context of inheritance.

Friends of a Class

Non-member functions and other classes may be declared as friends of a class. Such entities are provided with the privilege to access private members of a class. Friends must be declared within the declaration scope of the class with the special declaration directive `friend`. All member functions of a `friend` class to a given class acquire the privilege to access private members of the latter.

Friendship is not commutative, i.e. if class B has been declared as a friend in class A, member functions of B can access even private members of A, but not vice versa. Friendship is also not inherited. Consider the following examples:

```
class X {
private:
   int privateOfX;
   .
   .
   void privilegedClassMember();
   .
   .
};

class Y : public X {
   .
   .
   void privilegedMember();
   void notPrivilegedMember();

   void privilegedClassMember(); // Overloaded from X.
   .
   .
};

void globalPrivilegedFunction();

class SomeClass {
private:
   int somePrivateData;
   .
   .

   void someFunction();
   friend class X; // All members of X have access to private members.
   friend int Y::privilegedMember(); // A friend function.
   friend void globalPrivilegedFunction(); // Another friend function.
};

void X::privilegedClassMember()
{
   SomeClass sc;
   .
   sc.somePrivateData = 0; // Legal.
}

void Y::privilegedMember()
{
   SomeClass sc;
   .
   sc.somePrivateData = 0; // Also Legal.
}
```

```
void Y::notPrivilegedMember()
{
    SomeClass sc;

        .
        .

    sc.somePrivateData = 0; // Illegal Compiler flags error.
}

void globalPrivilegedFunction()
{
    SomeClass sc;

        .
        .

    sc.somePrivateData = 0; // Legal again.
}


void SomeClass::someFunction()
{
    X xInstance;

        .
        .

    xInstance.privateOfX = 0;
        // Illegal! Friendship is not commutative. So,
        // SomeClass is NOT automatically a friend of X.
}

void Y::privilegedClassMember()
{
    SomeClass sc;

        .
        .

    sc.somePrivateData = 0; // Illegal Friendship is NOT inherited.
}
```

The ability to declare friend functions allows considerable compactness of code. However, it is not good OOP practice to declare friends arbitrarily. The feature should definitely not be used as *an excuse* for bad encapsulation discipline in C++ programs.

Pointers to Class Members

The type modifiers for indicating a pointer to a class member in a declaration is X::*, where X is the class name. The operators .* and ->* are used to dereference a pointer to a member through an instance of a class and a pointer to an instance of a class, respectively. Consider the following examples:

```
class SomeClass {

        .
        .

public:
    int      someData, anotherData;
```

```
MyType someMember(MyType1, MyType2); // A member function declaration.
        .
        .
        .
};

SomeClass    scInstance, // A global instance.
             *pSomeClass = scInstance;
             // A global pointer properly initialized.

int SomeClass::*pInt_1
    // Declaring a pointer to an 'int' member data of SomeClass.
            = &SomeClass::someData;
    // and initializing it to 'someData'
        .
        .
        .
  scInstance.*pInt_1 = 10; // Same as scInstance.someData = 10
  pSomeClass->*pInt_1 = 10; // Same as pSomeClass->someData = 10
        .
        .
        .
  pInt_1 = &SomeClass::anotherData;
  // Re-initializing pInt_1 to 'anotherData'.
        .
        .
        .
  scInstance.*pInt_1 = 10; // Same as scInstance.anotherData = 10.
  pSomeClass->*pInt_1 = 10; // Same as pSomeClass->anotherData = 10
        .
        .
        .
typedef MyType (SomeType::*FUNC) (MyType1, MyType2);
// Type defining a pointer to a
// member function of SomeClass of appropriate signature.
        .
        .
        .
FUNC pFunc = SomeClass::someMember;
        .
        .
        .
  (scInstance.*pFunc)(.....); // Same as scInstance.someMember(....)
  (pSomeClass->*pFunc)(.....); // Same as pSomeClass->someMember(....)
// Parenthesis around the left sub-structure above required because
// . and ->* have lower precedence than function call operator '()'.
```

Inline Member Functions

Class member functions can also be defined inline. There are two ways to do this. The first implicit and the most commonly used mechanism is to define the body of the function along with its declaration in the primary scope of the class. An alternative explicit way is to define the function outside the primary scope of the class, but with the `inline` directive, as with normal inline functions. As with the latter, an explicit inline function is best defined in a header file, preferably the same one in which the class has been declared.

Example:

```
class X {
private:
  int data_1, data_2;
     .
     .
public:
  int getData_1() { return data_1; } // An explicit inline member
function.
  int getData_2();
     .
     .
};
     .
     .
inline X::getData_2()  // Explicitly defined inline function in same
                       // header file
                       // as above class declaration.
{
  return data_2;
}
```

Header and Implementation Files

In this sub-section, we are not actually talking about any syntax extension in C++, but rather about certain aspects of programming discipline.

The declaration of a class—the member data and member functions, is an interface between the implementation of the behaviour of a class and a user of the class. In most reasonably sized C++ programming projects, the team responsible for the implementation of a class is different from the teams benefiting from the class (the users of the class). Usually, therefore, a number of source modules (files) need to be aware of the interface, i.e., the declaration of a class and not be bothered about its implementation. The customary way to achieve this is to carry out the declaration of a class in a *header* file—an .h file. The implementation of the class, i.e., the definition of the member functions of the class (and possibly some auxiliary data/functions required for the definitions), are put in one (usually) or more *source* files, i.e., .cpp (or .cc, etc., as the case may be with the compiler being used) files.

Pointer to a Class

A variable which is a pointer to some data type in C is one that holds an address value of some instance of the data type. The data type could range from language-defined simple type to a user-defined complex one. Subject to some model specificity allowed by some compilers for some hardwares, all pointer variables are of the same size, i.e. they occupy the same amount of memory space, irrespective of the type of the data they point to. However, a pointer expression (an expression that evaluates a value which is a pointer to some instance or none of some data type) in C can be assigned only to a pointer variable of the same type as the expression. For example (in C):

```
struct SomeStruct { ... };

struct SomeStruct *pStruct; /* A pointer to SomeStruct. */
int             *pInt;  /* A pointer to an integer. */
    .
    .
  pInt = pStruct; /* Illegal. */

  pInt += 5; /* Legal. pInt points to 5 ints 'ahead' of where it was
pointing. */

  pInt = (int *) pStruct; /* Legal. Pointer typecasting to go around
the problem. */
```

The situation becomes a little more complicated in C++, where a class may be inherited from another class.

In C++, a variable declared as a base class pointer can point to (store the address of) an instance of a derived class. In other words, an expression that evaluates to a pointer to a derived (or same) class can be assigned to a pointer to a base class. For example (in C++):

```
class Base { ... };

class DerivedImmediate : public Base { ... };

class DerivedFurther_1 : public DerivedImmediate { ... };

class DerivedFurther_2 : public DerivedImmediate { ... };

Base              *basePointer;

DerivedImmediate  *diPointer;

DerivedFurther_1  *df1Pointer;

DerivedFurther_2  *df2Pointer;
    .
    .
basePointer = df2Pointer; // Legal.

  diPointer = (new DerivedFurther_1 [10]) + 5; // diPointer points to
    // sixth instance of dynamically created array of DerivedFurther_1.

  df1Pointer = basePointer + 10; // Illegal Right side is of type Base*
                // and Base is not derived from DerivedFurther_1.
```

```
df1Pointer = (DerivedFurther_1 *) (BasePointer) + 10;
// basePointer is known to point to an array of DerivedFurther_1
// and hence typecasted

df1Pointer = dynamic_cast<DerivedFurther_1 *>BasePointer +10;
// Same as above in new syntax

df2Pointer = df1Pointer; // Illegal.
 // The respective types have no base-child
df1Pointer = df2Pointer; // relationship. No point typecasting.
```

Constructors and Destructors

Constructions and destructions are special member functions that determine how the objects of a class are created, initialized, copied, and destroyed. Although these functions have many of the characteristics of normal member functions—one may declare and define them within the class, or declare them within the class and define them outside—they have some unique features:

1. They do not have return value declarations (not even void).

2. They cannot be inherited. However, a derived class constructor(s) and destructor can call the base class constructor(s) and destructor, respectively.

3. Constructors can have default arguments or use member initialization lists, just like most C++ functions.

4. Destructors (but not constructors) can be virtual.

5. Their addresses cannot be extracted.

6. In many compiler environments, constructors and destructors can be generated implicitly by the compiler if they have not been explicitly defined. On many occasions, they are invoked without explicit calls in other parts of the program. Constructors or destructors generated by the compiler are usually public.

7. Constructors may not be called explicitly like the way a normal function is called. However, destructors may be called by using their fully qualified name. For example:

```
     .
     .
     .
  X *p;
     .
     .
     .
  p->X::~X();     // Legal call of destructor.
  X::X();         // Illegal Direct call of constructor not
                  // allowed.
```

8. The compiler automatically calls constructors and destructors when defining and destroying objects. Construction of global and static objects takes place at start-up time, even before main() is called. Destruction of global and static objects takes place at wind-up time, i.e., after the program exit()s. Automatic as well as implied temporary objects are constructed on the fly when they come into scope, and destroyed when they are no longer in scope. For example:

```
operator + ( X & leftOper, X &rightOper) { ... }
    .
    .
    .
X xInstance; // Global object. Constructed at start-up time.
    .
    .
    .
void someFunction(..., X & xParam /* Constructed before function call.
                               */, ...)
{
    X localX1, localX2, localSumX;
// Constructed just after function invocation.
    .
    .
    .
localSumX = localX1 + localX2 + xParam;
    // At least one temporary X object
    // created to hold 'partial' sum.
    .
    .
    .
}
```

9. An object with a constructor or destructor cannot be used as a member of a union.

If a class has one or more constructors, one of them is invoked each time an instance of the class is defined. Constructors create the instance and initialize it. Destructors reverse the process by destroying the class objects created by constructors.

Constructor

Constructors are distinguished from all other member functions in having the same name as the class they belong to. When an object of that class is created or is being copied, the appropriate constructor is called implicitly.

A class X constructor cannot take X as an argument. However, a constructor can accept a reference to its own class as a parameter, and when it does so, it is called the *copy constructor*. A constructor that accepts no parameters is called the *default constructor*. If no user-defined constructor exists for a class, most C++ compilers generate a default constructor. On a declaration such as X x, the default constructor is used.

Like all functions, constructors can have default arguments. However, this may lead to ambiguity in calling constructors.

Example:

```
class X {
public:
    X();
    X(int i = 0)
};

main ()
{
    X firstX(10);      // No problem, X::X(int) is invoked.
    X two;             // Illegal. Ambiguous whether to call
                       X::X() or X::X(int = 0).



}
```

The copy constructor for a class, i.e. one that can be called with a single argument of type reference to the class, is invoked when copying a class object. This typically happens during initialization of an object by another instance of the same class. Most C++ compilers generate a copy constructor for class if one is needed and none is defined.

Like normal member functions, constructors can be overloaded, allowing objects to be created, depending on the values being used ʿ initialization.

Example:

```
class X    {
    int       intMember;
    double    doubleMember;

public:
    X(int i)    { intMember = i; }
    X(double d) { doubleMember = d; }
};

.
.
main ()
{
    X one(10);     // invokes X::X(int).
    X one(3.14);   // invokes X::X(double).



}
```

For an inherited class, a base class constructor is invoked before the derived class constructor. If the base class has more than one constructor, the one that is invoked may be made explicit by inserting a parameterized call to the appropriate base class constructor between the derived class constructor's header and its body.

Example:

```
class Base {
    .
    .
    .
public:
    Base(int); // One constructor.
    Base(char *, int); // Another constructor.
    .
    .
    .
}

class Derived: public Base {
    .
    .
    float memberFloat;
    Derived(int i, float f) : Base(i          // Directing to first
                                             // constructor of Base.
                { memberFloat = f; }         // Then initializing
                                             // local member(s).
    Derived(char , int , float );
    .
    .
}

Derived::Derived(char *s, int length, float f)
    : Base(s, length) // Directing to second constructor of Base.
{
    memberFloat = f;
}
```

If no constructor of the base class is explicitly mentioned, the default constructor of the base class is invoked.

Destructor

The destructor for a class is called to free members of an object before the object is itself destroyed. The destructor is a member function whose name is that of the class preceded by a tilde (~). A destructor cannot accept any parameters, nor will it have a return type or value declared.

```
class X {
public:
    ~X();       //Destructor for class X.
};
```

If a destructor is not explicitly defined for a class, the compiler generates one. A destructor is called implicitly when a variable goes out of its declared scope. Destructors for the local variables are called when the block they are declared in is no longer active. In the case of global variables, destructors are called as part of the exit procedure after the main function. When pointers to objects go out of scope, a destructor is not implicitly called. This means that the delete operator must be called explicitly to destroy such an object. Destructors are called in the exact opposite order from which their corresponding constructors are called.

Base and Derived Class Access

In the declaration of a derived class D, the parent base class B (say) is listed with an access specifier as in:

```
class D : <access modifier> B { <members> }
```

Clearly, D can directly access only the public and protected members of its base class B. But, what will be the access attributes of the inherited members as viewed by D? This is determined by the access modifiers before the base class name at the time of declaration. The access modifier also has one out of `public,` `protected`, or `private` visibilities.

The access modifier does not alter the access attributes of base class members as viewed by the base class, but can alter the access attributes of base members as viewed by the derived class. The default visibility is `private` if the derived class is declared using a `class` declaration and `public` if it is declared using a `struct` declaration.

The derived class inherits access attributes from a base class as follows:

`public` base class	`public` members of the base class are `public` members of the derived class. `protected` members of the base class are `protected` members of the derived class. `private` members of the base class remain `private` to the base class.
`protected` base class	Both `public` and `protected` members of the base class are `protected` members of the derived class. `private` members of the base class remain `private` to the base class.
`private` base class	Both `public` and `protected` members of the base class are `private` members of the derived class. `private` members of the base class remain `private` to the base class.

In all the above cases, the access modifier can only *reduce* (or keep unaltered) the visibilities of the members inherited from the base class.

The effect of access specifiers in the base list can be adjusted by using a qualified name in the public or protected declarations in the derived class.

Example:

```
struct S : C { .... }      // Default for struct is public C.
struct T : private D { .... } // Override default for D.
class X {
    int a;      // Private by default.
public :

    int b, c,
    int funcInX(void);
};
```

```
class Z : public X { .... };  // Visibilities of X's members
                              // unchanged in Z.

class Y : private X { // The private modifier is unnecessary
                      // as default for class is private X.

// a, b, c and are now private in Y

    int d;              // Private by default, NOTE: a is not
                        // accessible in Y.

public:
    X::c;               // c was private, now it is public.
    int e;
    int funcInY(void);
    int funcInX(void); // Overloaded from X.
// This function has access to
//   i) "adjusted-to-public" member c,
//  ii) "private-to-X" members b and X::funcInX()
//iii) Y's s own private and public members: d, e, and funcInY()
//  However, this function cannot access the "private-to-B" member, a
};

int funcExternal(Y& y);        // external to X and Y.
// This function can use only the public names a, e, and funcInY().
```

Inheritance

A (derived) class may be inherited from a (single parent, since we restrict ourselves from discussing multiple inheritance) base class through the following construct:

```
class D : <access modifier> B { <members> }
```

Here, D is the class derived or inherited from the parent or base class B. The importance of the access modifier directive was discussed earlier.

Subject to some of the restrictions to be discussed later, the following holds true:

1. The derived class inherits all member data of the parent class with identical semantics.

2. Visibility of the inherited data is determined by its visibility in the parent class, moderated by the access modifier in the declaration of the derived class. Under no circumstances can the visibility of a data member of the parent class be increased in the derived class. However, irrespective of its visibility, the data members of the parent class are always 'present' in the derived class.

3. The derived class can declare further data members.

4. All member functions of the parent class are inherited by name (actually,

by signature). If a member function of the parent class is not declared explicitly in the derived class, it is inherited with unmodified semantics.

5. A member function of the parent class may be re-declared in the derived class. This action called *overloading* for non-`virtual` member functions, is a promise by the implementor of the derived class to provide modified semantics for the function in the scope of the derived class.

6. A `virtual` member function can also be re-declared in the derived class with or without the `virtual` directive. In any case, the *overridden* function as it is called, remains virtual.

7. Further member functions, `virtual` or otherwise, may be declared in the derived class.

***Examples*:**

```
class TopMost { // This class is not derived from any other class.

    int     dataTop_1;

protected:

    float   dataTop_2;

public:

    TopMost(); // A Constructor — the Default constructor
        virtual ~TopMost();    // The destructor, declared virtual.

    void    nonVirtualFunction_1(int n)   { dataTop_1 = n; }
    // A non-virtual function implemented inline.

    int     nonVirtualFunction_2(float, int);
    // Another non-virtual function.

    virtual void virtualFunction_3() { dataTop_1 = 0; }
    // A virtual function.
    // Defined inline but compiler ensures outline implementation.

    virtual int virtualFunction_4(float); // Another virtual function.

    virtual float virtualFunction_5() = 0; // A pure virtual function.

    //Thus TopMost is an abstract class.

};

class ChildOfTop1 : public TopMost { // This class is inherited
                                     // from TopMost.
protected:
    int     dataChild1_1; // A newly introduced data.
```

```
public:

    ChildOfTop1() : TopMost()
// Constructor, calls parent class constructor.
        { dataTop_2 = 2.0; }
// Variable dataTop_2 is visible from this class.

// Destructor not declared and hence introduced by compiler.

    int     nonVirtualFunction_2(float, int); // Re-defined.

  void virtualFunction_3() { nonVirtualFunction_1(2); }
  // Same as dataTop_1 = 2,
  // however must go around private nature of member dataTop_1.
  // Function is virtual through inheritance, overridden for this class.

// Non-virtual function nonVirtualFunction_1(int), and
// Virtual function virtualFunction_4(float) inherited without change.

// Pure virtual function virtualFunction_5() inherited as such.
// So this class remains an abstract class.

  virtual void newVirtualFunction_1();
// A newly introduced virtual function.
};

class ChildOfTop2 : public TopMost {
// This class is inherited from TopMost.
// No member data declared.
// The only data members are those inherited.
public:     ·
    ChildOfTop2() : TopMost()
// Constructor, calls parent class constructor.
        { dataTop_2 = 1.0; }
// Variable dataTop_2 is visible from this class.

    ~ChildOfTop2() {} // Destructor, virtual through inheritance.

  int     nonVirtualFunction_2(float, int); // Redefined function

  void virtualFunction_3() { nonVirtualFunction_1(3); }
  // Same as dataTop_1 = 3,
  // however must go around private nature of member dataTop_1.
  // Function is virtual through inheritance, overridden for this class.

// Non-virtual function nonVirtualFunction_1(int), and
// Virtual function virtualFunction_4(float) inherited without change.

  float virtualFunction_5() { return dataTop_2; }
  // Pure virtual function overridden in this class. So this class
  // is no longer an abstract class.

  virtual void newVirtualFunction_1();
  // A newly introduced virtual function
  // Although of same signature as one declared in ChildOfTop1, bears no
```

```
    // inheritance relation with it.
};

class ChildOfChild1 : public ChildOfTop1 {
public:
// Inherits everything from ChildOfTop1 except that
// it overrides the pure virtual function.

    float virtualFunction_5() { return 2.0 * dataTop_2; }
    // So this class is no longer an abstract class.

    ChildOfChild1() : ChildOfTop() {} // Constructor. Directs to
    // default constructor of ChildOfTop and then does nothing.
};
```

Virtual Functions

Virtual functions allow derived classes to provide different versions of a base class function. The keyword `virtual` is used as a directive to the compiler to treat the function as virtual. Like non-virtual functions, a virtual member function of a base class may be re-declared in the derived class, an act known as *overriding* of the function. So long as the signature of the function declaration in the derived class matches with that of a virtual function of a base class, the `virtual` keyword is not necessary, i.e., a *function declared virtual in a base class remains virtual in classes derived from it.* However, like non-virtual functions, a class may inherit a virtual function from its parent class.

Unlike non-virtual functions, virtual functions lead to *dynamic* or *late* or *run-time* binding between the object through which it is invoked and its invocation. In other words, in a construct like

```
pointerToBaseClass->someVirtualFunctionInBase(...)
```

the address of sub-routine call is reserved till run-time. It is determined by the class of the object `pointerToBaseClass` which is actually pointing to at the time of execution of the code. Recall that a pointer to a base class can actually point to an instance of a derived class through legal assignment(s) to it. Hence, it is not possible to fully resolve the called subroutine's address at compilation time.

Examples: (Consider the class declaration in the previous sub-section):

```
    TopMost          *pTopMost;
    ChildOfTop1      *pChild1;
    ChildOfTop2      *pChild2;
    ChildOfChild     *pGrandChild;

    pGrandChild  = new ChildOfChild;
    pChild2      = new ChildOfTop2;

    pChild1 = pGrandChild; // Perfectly legal assignment.
```

```
pChild1->nonVirtualFunction(10.0, 5);
// Invokes ChildOfTop1::nonVirtualFunction(), which is presumably
// O.K.,
// since it has not been re-defined in ChildOfChild.

// But,
pTopMost = pGrandChild; // Legal assignment too.
pTopMost->nonVirtualFunction(10.0, 5);
// Invokes TopMost::nonVirtualFunction(),
// which is presumably WRONG, since
// it has been re-defined in ChildOfTop1, inherited by ChildOfChild.

// However (with no further assignments on the above pointers),
pChild1->virtualFunction_5(); // and,
pTopMost->virtualFunction_5(); // and also
pGrandChild->virtualFunction_5(); // all have the identical effect of
// calling ChildOfChild::virtualFunction_5().

// Similarly,
pTopMost = pChild2; // Even this is a legal assignment,
pChild2->virtualFunction_5();   // and
pTopMost->virtualFunction_5(); // have the identical effect of
// calling ChildOfTop2::virtualFunction_5().

// See below for a discussion on virtual destructors.

// Destruction. With no further assignments on the pointers,
delete pTopMost; // destroys the ChildOfTop2 object pointed at,
// while
delete pChild1; // destroys the ChildOfChild object
// because, the destructor was declared virtual in TopMost.
```

A destructor can also be virtual. Declaring the destructor determines the way the delete operator works. The construct delete pointer invokes the destructor of the class to which pointer has been declared to point (say, X). However, if X is a base class, at run-time, pointer may be pointing to an instance of a class derived from X. Unless the destructor ~X() is virtual, delete pointer still leads to an invocation of ~X(). However, if ~X() is virtual, the destructors of the classes automatically become virtual and the construct delete pointer leads to the destructor of the class to whose instance pointer is pointing at the instant of invocation of the operator.

Abstract Classes and Pure *Virtual Functions*

The essential aspect of OOP is abstraction of behaviour(s) over an hierarchy of classes. This key concept is achievable in C++ through virtual functions. Quite often, a number of relatively independent class sub-hierarchies have to be unified at an abstract conceptual base class level. The unified abstract concepts in such cases are initiated through virtual functions in the base class. Quite often, as a result of the forceful conceptual unification, the base class through which the unification is achieved does not have a real world semantics. In other words, one or more of the unifying concepts initiated through virtual functions in the base class are meaningless for the class itself. C++ permits such functions to be declared as *pure* virtual functions. The syntactic mechanism prescribed for the operation is to declare the virtual function(s) and equate them with zero (= 0) . The construct = 0 is known as a *pure specifier.* For example:

```
class X {
        .

        .

public:

    virtual void onePureVirtualFunction() = 0;
    // A pure virtual function.
    virtual int anotherPureVirtualFunction(int, float) = 0;
    // Another one.
        .

        .
};
```

If a pure virtual function is inherited, i.e. not overridden in a derived class, it remains pure. The destructor, if virtual, cannot be pure.

An *abstract class* is one which has at least one pure virtual function, inherited or declared fresh in the class. An abstract class can be used only as a base class for other classes, i.e. no 'non-abstract' class can have an abstract derived class. No instances of an abstract class can be created. An abstract class cannot be used as an argument or a function return type. However, it is perfectly legal to declare pointers to abstract classes.

Static Member Data and Static Member Functions

The storage class specifier static is used in class declarations of static data and function members. Such members have certain distinct properties from non-static members. With non-static members, a distinct copy exists for each object in its class. With static members on the other hand, only one copy exists, and it can be accessed without reference to any particular object in its class. Thus, if x is a static member of class X, it can be referenced as X::x, even if objects of class X have not been created yet. It is also possible to access x using the normal member access operators. For example, if y is an object of class X and yPtr is a pointer to class X, y.x and yPtr->x can be both used anywhere, although the expressions y and, more particularly, yPtr are not evaluated yet. In particular, a static member function can be called with or without the special member function syntax:

```
class X {
    .
    .
    int     nonStaticInt; // A non-static member.

    static int x; // Static member data.
    static void staticFunction(); // Static member function.
    static char *myName() { return strcpy(new char [8], "Name: X"); }
    .
    .
    .
};

void X::staticFunction() // Definition of static function.
{
    x++; // Same as X::x++. Quite legal to access static members.
    // nonStaticInt = x; Illegal if present.
    // Cannot access non-static member.
    // (new X)->nonStaticInt = x; is, however, legal.
}
    .
    .
    .
X       y, yPtr = NULL ;
// An instance of X and a pointer to X pointing to nothing.

int X::x = 0; // Static member data may be initialized in global scope.

    // Assuming yPtr is still NULL.
    y.staticFunction(); // Increments static member X::x.
    yPtr->staticFunction();
    // Same effect as above. No error, even though yPtr=NULL.
    X::staticFunction(); // Same as above.
```

Since a static member function can be called with no particular object in mind, it does not have a this pointer. A consequence of this is that a static member function cannot access non-static members without explicitly specifying an object with .or ->. Apart from inline functions, static member functions of global classes have external linkage. Static member functions cannot be virtual functions. It is illegal to have a static and non-static member function with the same name and argument types. The declaration of a static data member in its class declaration is not a definition, so a definition must be provided elsewhere to allocate storage and provide initialization as in int X::x = 0; in the above example.

The main use of static members is to keep track of data common to all objects of a class, such as the number of objects created, or the last used resource from a pool shared by all such objects. Static members are also used to

- reduce the number of visible global names,
- make it obvious which static objects logically belong to which class, and
- permit access control to the names of classes (see myName() function in example).

Overloading Operators as Class Member Functions

Operators can be overloaded as non-static class member functions. A member operator function takes one parameter less in its declarations than an outside class declaration of the same operator. Thus, a unary member operator function takes no parameter, while a binary member operator function takes one argument. The operator function is called through an object—the only object operand in a unary operation and the left hand side object in a binary operation.

Example:

```
class X {
    .
    .
public:
    void operator ++ (); // No parameter for the unary operator ++
    X&   operator *  (X&); // One parameter for binary operator *
    .
    .
};

X x1, x2, pX = & x1, x3;

    x1++; // Same as X::operator ++ (&x1).
    ++x1; // Same as above (till C++ ver 2.0).
    (*pX)++; // Same effect as above.
    pX->operator ++ (); // Same as above.

    x3 = x1 + x2; // Same as x3 = x1.operator *(x2)
                  // OR x3 = X::operator *(&x1, x2).
    x3 = x1 + x2 + x3; // Same as x3 = (x1 + x2) +x3
                       // because * is left associative.
        // Beware!! A temporary instance of X would be constructed.
```

With the exception of the assignment operator (= ( )), all overloaded operator functions of a class X are inherited (may be further overloaded) by classes derived from X.

SOME C++ FEATURES NOT USED IN THIS BOOK

Multiple Inheritance

Most modern C++ compilers support the multiple inheritance feature of the language. In this scheme, a class can actually be derived from more than one class. The parent classes of a class are declared in a comma delimited list in its declaration as is mentioned in the syntax for class declaration, i.e.

```
<class-key> <class-name>  < optional : <base-list>> { <members> }
```

With multiple inheritance, a base class cannot be specified more than once in the `<base-list>` of the derived class declaration. However, a base class may be *indirectly* passed to a derived class Z (say) more than once, where two classes X and Y (say) in the base list of a derived class are in turn ultimately derived from the same class B (say), as in the example below. In the normal case, an object of class Z would have two sub-objects of classes B. In case this causes a problem in a derived class ZV (say), the common parent may be included as a `virtual` base class in XV and YV (say), the parents of ZV.

Example:

```
class X : public B { ... };

class Y : public B { ... };

class Z : public X, public Y { ... }; // OK. But there are two
                                      // sub-objects of B.

class XV : virtual public B { ... }; // B is a virtual base class here.

class YV : virtual public B { ... }; // and also here

class ZV : public XV, public YV { ... }; // OK again. But there
                                         // is only one
                                         // sub-object of B in an
                                         // instance of ZV.
```

Templates

The template feature of C++ is an attempt to provide in the language the capability to declare *generic* or *parameterized* types. Through judicious use of template declarations, a programmer can create a family of functions or classes through single declarations and definitions.

   Template functions behave like macros, except that they actually produce function codes where the parameter and/or local variables may be generic. The advantage of template functions over macros is, that unlike in macros, compile-time type checking can be enforced through template functions. A template function is not an actual function. *Explicit* instances are created on demand when the compiler feels such a requirement. (See the use of the template function max(x, y) in the example below.)

   A class template behaves like a class *generator*. In the declaration of a class, various declaration constructs—member data type, member function return type, member function argument types, etc., may be made generic. Like template functions, template classes are not actual classes. Actual classes are generated by the compiler whenever it comes across instances of a template class definition with fully qualified template. (See the use of the template class Vector in the example below.)

Example:

```
template<class T>   // A template declaration—pre-header of a template
                    // function.
T max(T x, T y) // Header. Note that parameters are generic.
{  return ( x > y ) ? x : y; }
          .
          .

  int  na, nb, nc;
  char ca, cb, cc;
          .

  na = max(nb, nc); // Calls (generated) int max(int, int).

// In actual expansion, the template <class T> can be any type,
// not just a class.

  ca = max(cb, cc); // Calls (generated) int max(char, char).
  na = max(cb, nc);
     // Can't find match for int max(int, char). Compiler error.

          .
          .
```

```
template <class T>
class Vector    { // A Template class.
  T             *data; // Pointer to generic item.
  int           size;  // Fully qualified.

public:

  Vector(int); // Observe it's outline definition later
  ~Vector() { delete [] data; }

  T  itemAt(int at) { return data[at]; }
};

// Note the syntax for outline definition of the constructor
template <class T>
Vector<T>::Vector(int n)
{
  data = new T [ (size = n) ];
}

          .
          .

  Vector<int>     intVector(20); // A Vector of ints, size 20.

  Vector<MyClass> myClassVector(20); // Ditto for class MyClass.
```

Template classes are extremely useful in generating *type-safe* container classes. Many modern compilers provide template-based libraries for containers as well as for other purposes. The concept of a *standard* template-based container library has one of the recent aspects of interest in the C++ programming community. As a matter of fact, some early versions of *Standard Template Library* (STL), are already available commercially. It is expected that in the next few years, most applications would attempt to 'standardize' the design of their data structures through the use of STL.

In spite of the advantages of the template aspect of C++, we would like to make a note of caution to the readers of this book. In our opinion, the template feature was introduced in C++ as an afterthought, presumably to emulate the meta-class feature of Smalltalk. As a result, we feel that its conceptual binding with the other aspects of C++ is not quite seamless. Moreover, debugging into template classes and template functions still remains a nightmare. However, the ability to use standard (and therefore rigourously tested) libraries should reduce the debugging requirement considerably, and allow the programmer to concentrate on other specifics of the design.

Data Structures in Object-Oriented Environment

The classical equation by Niclaus Wirth—**Programs = Data Structures + Algorithms**—is considered axiomatic by most programmers. The important thing to note from the equation is that it lays equal emphasis on data structures and algorithms in writing (good) programs. The term data structures is quite often loosely applied in describing associations of different types of data under a single name, for example, to Pascal and C programmers, a `record` or `struct` respectively, represents a data structure. From the definition of an *object* given in Chapter 2, it is clear that a *class* of an OOPL matches most closely with the conceptual idea of a data structure.

Quite often, the term *data structure* is also used to describe the mechanism through which a number of instances of (presumably) simpler data items are conglomerated into a group. According to this view, well-understood group behaviours are associated with different classes of data structures. It is often possible to reason about the behaviours even without going into the explicit details of how the conglomeration of the different data items was achieved in the class. An emerging field of computer science, called *Software Engineering Principles,* studies such aspects of data structures. In software engineering parlance, such data groups are known as *abstract data types* (ADTs). Insofar as OOP is concerned, an ADT is, in essence, an object class whose basic utility is to associate a group of similar and (presumably) simpler objects. In OOP parlance, ADTs are more commonly known as *container* classes, because the primary role of a container object is to 'contain' or store other objects. Nevertheless, there is a small difference in the emphasis laid on ADTs in software engineering and container classes in OOP.

In software engineering, the idea is to focus on the abstract behaviours of ADTs with less emphasis on the algorithmic environment where an ADT may be put to use. Indeed, through studying the abstract behaviours, a quasi-formal description of the nature of a problem and its solution strategy, that is by and large independent of the coding environment, can be formulated. In OOP on the other hand, containers are treated as full-fledged objects. Behavioural semantics of containers are dealt with in a more stringent manner in OOP—through member functions, virtual or otherwise. However, we must remember that containers are basically ADTs and, therefore, most aspects of studies of their abstract behaviours are equally applicable.

Most C++ program development platforms available commercially, especially the PC-based systems, provide with them a container class library. For more modern of these systems, the container class library is based upon the `template` feature of C++. In the last couple of years, there have been attempts to build a *Standard Template Library* (STL) for C++. Early versions of STL are already available in the market.

In spite of the rapid proliferation of container class usage, there have been very few text books dealing with containers in the context of any OOPL. This has led to a gap in the knowledge of data structures acquired by students of computer science (or software engineers starting off with their careers) and the ADT philosophy incorporated in the design of commercial container classes that would invariably see increasing use in the near future. This chapter is an attempt to bridge the gap.

This chapter consists of four sections covering four aspects of study of containers in OOP environment. First, container classes are viewed as abstract data types (ADTs), taking up certain important pieces of reasoning with ADTs in the process. The reader would, in all probability, find a repetition of ideas normally found in text books on data structure in this section. However, the approach here is to consciously introduce an abstract view of the subject. The 'abstract' behaviour of ADTs are clearly dissociated from aspects of their implementation through *fundamental data structures* (FDSs). Next, the implementational aspects of containers are discussed as a mapping operation from ADTs to FDSs. Even in the earlier part of this section, the reader would find a repetition of ideas from data structure text books, much of which could be avoided. However, we have included them so as to provide a more complete picture of concepts described later. Following this, a few commonly used containers are taken up as case studies and investigated in greater detail. Finally, an important subject of OOP, namely, 'object persistence' (also known as serialization of objects)—a mechanism for storing the logical snapshot of an 'in-memory' data structure onto the secondary memory, is discussed.

Finally, we reiterate that the code fragments introduced in this chapter are provided only for the purpose of illustration.

CONTAINERS AS ABSTRACT DATA TYPES

As we have already discussed, containers in OOP are basically implementational manifestations of ADTs. It is therefore important that we take a deeper look into the 'abstract' behaviour of containers. In this section, certain intrinsic (and hence abstract) properties of different containers will be reasoned about under various heads like access mechanism, orderliness, searching through and enumerating the contents of a container, etc. The term container would be treated as almost synonymous with abstract data type, and vice versa. Cases where one or the other term has been given separate emphasis would be clear from the context.

Access Mechanism of Different Containers

For any container, there are two definite fundamental operations—*adding* a new item to and *extracting* an item destructively out of a container (called *delinking*). Even for these basic operations, there could be different schemes. For example, consider the commonly used container (or ADT) queue, which is characterized by a 'first in first out' (FIFO) access mechanism. The earlier an item is entered into a queue, the earlier it may be brought out, just as in the case of different queues at bus stops, ticket counters, airport security checks, to name a few. Similarly, the container stack has a 'last in first out' (LIFO) access mechanism.

The container array, on the other hand, permits and is especially designed for *random access*. Items may be randomly *inserted* (possibly *overwriting* an existing item) or *read* from an array.

Usually, however, destructive access is discouraged in most containers, except perhaps some specific ones (like stack, queue, etc.). An associated problem of random access is obtaining an *a priori* knowledge of the precise location of the desired item in the container. Often it requires a non-trivial *search* of the container—entire or partial; unconditional or based upon some criteria. The issue of searching of containers is taken up later in this section. Searching is closely related to another important concept—*orderliness* of the items contained in a container. Let us take a closer look at the orderliness aspect of containers.

Orderliness of a Container

Orderliness of a container depends upon whether there is some defined (and hence computable) order in the contained items of a container. Usually, the term order refers to a *total order*. However, with some containers like heap, one might talk of a *partial order*.

Sortable containers

Containers with a total order defined on the contained items are generally known as *sortable* or *sorted* containers. Quite often, a sortable container is not always actually sorted, i.e., the total order on the contained items is not always stipulated. Such containers always support a functionality called *sort* through which the user of the container can enforce a rearrangement of the contents so as to reflect the desired orderliness. This becomes necessary as sorting is a computationally costly process.

When the requirement is such that the container must always remain sorted, a different mechanism called *insertion sort* is used. Here, any new item inserted into the container is 'placed' in such a way that the sorted condition is not violated. If destructive reading or *delinking* is also permitted, the insertion sort process properly rearranges the remaining items whenever an item is delinked from the container. Insertion sort considerably slows down the process of inserting an item into a container. This mechanism may, not therefore, be suitable for applications in which items to be inserted into a container arrive at a high frequency.

There are a number of popular insertion sort based containers like *sorted list, binary search tree,* and *B-tree*. Many of these basic containers provide functionalities specific to certain problem domains. For example, many well-known algorithms are based on the assumption that the associated container is some form of a *binary tree*.

Containers that must be sorted explicitly require, on the other hand, that the user determine, possibly through different logical tests, when to sort the container. It also means that the user may not assume a sorted container every time. Usually, containers supporting this 'sort on demand' feature provide a functionality that reflects whether any modifications (i.e. insertions and/or delinkings) have taken place since the time the container was last sorted. This way, in many cases, considerable overhead may be reduced by avoiding unnecessary sortings.

Sorting a container

Sorting a container is a computationally costly process—a container (with a defined total order) having n items has a sorting time complexity of the order $O(n \log n)$ in the worst case even with the best possible sorting algorithms. For large values of n, the computation time may become prohibitively large. It is, therefore, advisable to avoid frequent sorting of a container with a large number of items.

There are two key steps in the sorting process—first, to compute the *relative order* between a pair of contained items, and second, to *swap* the positions of such a pair. If the contained items are complicated, the time taken to compute the relative order may be quite high. Usually however, the relative order is determined by a small part, known as the *key*, of the items concerned. Swapping of large-sized items may also be time consuming. Often, rather than swapping items directly, references to the items (*pointers* or *addresses*) are actually swapped. In such cases, the sorting process is generally referred to as *indexing*. Indexing logically provides the same functionality as sorting, and is more commonly employed for enforcing orderliness. However, due to tradition, the terms 'sorting' and 'sortable containers' are still used, even though the implementation is actually through indexing.

Hashing and hashed containers

Sometimes, a relatively crude ordering is required at a very fast speed. The technique used then is *hashing*. In hashing, the position of an item in a container is determined as a number called the *hash value* of the item, through simple computations on (a part of) the item. This leads to a very fast positioning of an item in the container. However, there are a few associated problems.

First, since the hash value is a number, any item position in the container must be encodable by a number. This *enforces* the container to be a *linear* one. A linear container is one in which every item (except possibly the first and last under boundary conditions) has associated *preceding* (positionally, not necessarily with respect to the defined total order) and *succeeding* items. Inherent advantages of non-linear containers (`binary search tree` for example) are therefore untenable.

The second problem of hashing is that of *sparseness*. The hash values of the contained items at any instant may not be successive numbers. But there always remains the possibility that a currently unfilled position may be filled later. A hashed container must therefore reserve space for all possible hash values, irrespective of the actual number of contained items. This increases the space requirement of a hashed container.

The third problem of hashing is that of *collision*. It is quite possible that two different items may generate the same hash value. When the first of the above two items is inserted into the container, it presumably finds an empty position and occupies it. However, when an attempt is made to insert the second item, it finds the position already occupied, leading to what is known as *collision*. Every collision increases the time complexity by some amount, small as it may be. Various collision handling and/or prevention schemes that are suitable under different circumstances, have been suggested in the published literature.

In spite of the problems, hashing is a popular technique and hashed containers or `hash tables` are reasonably prevalent. Although finding a *perfect hashing function* for the data set and the problem at hand may be quite difficult, one must always strive to look for such a function.

An important question that may arise is why must a container be ordered at all? Since ordering involves so many problems, why use ordered containers in the first place? The reason is that two of the most basic operations on a container, namely, *searching* and *enumeration*, work best with sorted containers. We now take up the issue of searching an item in a container, after which we shall discuss the topic of enumeration.

Searching an Item in a Container

Searching of a container refers to the operation of finding whether a specified item is currently contained in the container. It is one of the most useful fundamental and basic operations associated with containers. Searching may be carried out as naively as checking the item against every item contained in the container. Obviously, this may require, in the worst case, checking the item against 'all' items in the container. For unordered containers, this naive method often is the only one possible. However, for ordered containers, searching can be performed with a worst case complexity of $O(log\ n)$, using the principles of *binary search*.

For hash tables, the searching process is even faster. In absence of collision, it takes a constant time to compute the hash value of the item being searched and check whether the indicated position is occupied or not. If collisions are expected, the situation is a little more complicated. First, the existing item in the hashed position must be checked against equality. If the test is not successful, some localized naive search must be carried out depending upon the collision handling technique being employed. It is therefore important that the hashing mechanism used should lead to as less collision as possible. Usually, unless one somehow stumbles across a perfect hashing function, a hashing technique that gives less collision increases sparseness.

Enumeration or Iteration of Containers

Suppose we visit the items of a container one by one and exhaustively, in some order (usually in the order of arrangement for ordered containers), perform some pre-assigned job on each visited item, the action is known as *enumeration* or *iteration* of the container. For example, we may like to *print* all the items in a container in some order.

Let us consider the requisites of enumerating a container. First, the container must either be ordered or there must be some way of considering the contained items of the container one by one. Next, there must be some way of defining what exactly must be done with the items as they are visited one by one (in the example above, the action required is *print*).

The concept of enumeration or iteration of a container is sufficiently abstract in the sense that any container may be a potential candidate for enumeration. However, usually, unordered or sequential access containers are not associated with enumeration, though there is no harm in doing so. For example, one rarely asks for the entire contents of a *stack* to be printed. However, there may be rare occasions when such an operation becomes necessary.

The iterator object

For some given container C (say), consider the *container iterator class CI*. The class *CI* has sufficient knowledge about the internal structure of the container, so as to be able to do the following:

- Latch itself on to the `first` item of the container (if any). The functionality is usually known as `restart`.
- Can move on and latch on to the item that is `next` to the currently latched on item where `next` is defined by the order chosen for enumeration. This functionality is also able to flag inability to proceed in case the currently latched on item is the last one in order of enumeration.
- Provide an access to the currently latched on item.

Clearly, *CI* is so closely associated with C, that in C++ based object oriented concepts, *CI* is usually a `friend` of the class of C.

The iteration process

The enumeration functionality of C, usually called `iterate`, can be abstractly defined as follows:

- A functionality for what to do with the enumerated items, known as *iterating function*, is supplied externally. Let the iterating function be f.
- Restart the iterator object of the container.
- Perform f on the currently latched on item.

- Go to the next item if possible (i.e., if there is still some item left to enumerate), else end enumeration.

Let us take a more detailed look at the 'printing' example.

Assume that all the items that may be contained in a container C has an abstract functionality to `print` itself. Consider a (global) function f that can take (a reference to) any 'printable object' as a parameter and print it by using the parameter's `print` functionality. Suppose one now wants to print all items of C. It can be achieved simply by invoking the `iterate` functionality of C with f as parameter. It can be done as follows. The `iterate` functionality of C would carry out the steps shown above. Thus, it would take the items of C one by one and despatch them to f, which in turn would invoke the `print` functionality of the item, thereby printing it.

The need for a separate iterator object

From the above discussions, it may not be clear why a container iterator *has* to be a separate object. Indeed, there is no such extreme necessity. The reason for separating them arises from the central concept of OOP, namely, the abstraction-specialization syndrome.

It may happen—and in any realistic container library it would happen as we shall see shortly—that a container itself is abstract, i.e. it has no physical significance, but is conceived of primarily to capture similarities across a number of containers. For such a container, the concept of iteration or enumeration is still relevant. However, because there is no physical relevance of the container itself, the question of an iterating functionality (now that there is no separate iterating function, the functionality must be incorporated into the container object itself) does not arise. Hence, the abstract concept of iteration cannot be captured at this level. In other words, the iteration concept can *never* be captured abstractly. Thus, for every real container, the concept of iteration will have to be re-introduced, violating the essential foundation of OOP.

Two additional iteration concepts

Along with enumeration, two additional concepts are usually associated as explained below. They can easily be implemented in line of exhaustive enumeration with minor changes in functionality:

- Given a condition C defined over items contained in a container (i.e. for a given item, it either satisfies C or does not), find the 'first' item in the container that satisfies the condition.

- Same as above, except that in this case, find the 'last' item satisfying the condition.

FUNDAMENTAL DATA STRUCTURES FOR CONTAINER IMPLEMENTATION

We have already discussed about different types of containers in an 'abstract' manner. Even without going into the details of how a particular type of container may be implemented in the computer, we could reason out certain behavioural aspects of different container classes and discuss certain issues. In this section, we shall talk about some of the basic tools that human ingenuity vis-a-vis computers has worked out, which may be effectively used to implement containers.

Most conventional books on data structures describe the tools that we refer to here. However, these books also consider the ADTs in the same breath as these tools. Usually, the conceptual difference between the two are not properly stressed. We shall, however, endeavour in this section to clearly bring out the difference. All 'real' tools that directly assume an architectural model (the well-known von Neumann model) of the computer—memory, processor, etc.—shall be referred to as *data structures*. Note that in the entire last section, all discussions carried out never actually referred to any model of computing.

Fundamental Data Structures—A Definition

Some of the *data structures* invented and worked out by various computer scientists have very close links with the computing model we usually consider. Two such data structures are so fundamental, that even a rudimentary exposure to computer programming familiarizes one with them. They are the *vector* and the *linked list*. The two most *fundamental data structures* (FDSs) can be combined in a few trivial manners to produce slightly more complicated structures. We shall refer to these trivial combinations also as FDSs. This way, multidimensional vector, two-way and circularly linked list, binary trees, and vector of pointers are FDSs by definition.

In this section, we shall take a closer look at the more widely used FDSs. Most of the material of this section might appear as rudimentary and repetitive to readers with some insight into data structures. However, we still recommend a study of the chapter for clarifying and formalizing certain issues.

Variables—Static and Dynamic

We begin with the most basic aspect of an *imperative* programming language like Pascal, FORTRAN, and C—that of a *variable*. A variable is simply a *symbolic reference* to a *contiguous block of memory*, which indicates that a variable is definitely an FDS—and, it is indeed so. However, a single variable is so fundamental that it is usually considered separately.

There are four associated aspects of a variable:

1. *Name.* The name of a variable is a *mnemonic* that is used to symbolically refer to it in a computer program. Different languages have different rules of naming a variable. Usually, a variable has a unique name that is a string of a few alphanumeric (plus the underscore character, sometimes) characters. the first character being an alphabetic one.

2. *Type.* Most imperative programming languages (except specially symbolic ones like LISP) permit associating a type with a variable. Through the typing mechanism, the programmer notifies a few facts about the variable to the compiler. These include the *size* of the memory block that one instance

of the variable occupies, whether the variable is a structured one, and if so, what are the associations with the *names* of the sub-units of the variable and at what *offsets* from the top of the memory chunk representing the variable is each sub-unit located.

3. *The l-value.* The *l*-value actually refers to the memory *address* or *location* of the variable. In the commonly assumed, model of a computer, every memory location is coded by a number, meaning thereby, that every location can be represented by a 'value'. The *l*-value of a static variable is a 'compile-time' feature. It is determined by the compiler, *hard coded* in the run-time module and remains fixed throughout the running of the program. Local variables also have partially fixed *l*-values, in the sense that their *l*-values are expressed as fixed offsets from a variable valued *pointer* (usually the stack pointer). Some variables are, however, fully *dynamic*. These variables get created (and destroyed) through explicit commands from the running program. Their *l*-values are therefore not fully known at compile time, and must be 'held' in the program through some other mechanism.

4. *The r-value.* The actual content of the variable at any instant during execution of the program is its *r*-value or simply, *value*. The essence of imperative programming is changing values of different variables in a planned manner.

Vectors and Pointer Variables

Vectors

In many computing problems, multiple instances of a variable of a single type are required to be associated together. The idea is to be able to access any individual instance or enumerate some of the instances with minimum programming steps. The best abstract solution is to have a linearly ordered collection of variable instances, where any individual instance may be referred to simply by mentioning a *number* representing the position of the instance in the order. This facility is offered in most languages through the concept of *vectors* of variables*.

Usually, three things have to be specified (or *declared*) for a vector of variables. First, the name which identifies the vector. Secondly, the *range* of position numbers that may be used with the vector. The position numbers allowed are almost always integral and contiguous (and therefore with a lower and an upper limit on position numbers). Finally, the type of the individual instances must be specified. Remember, all instances have to be of the same type. Languages differ on how the range should be specified. In FORTRAN for example, the lower limit is fixed at 1 and the upper limit must be specified. In C/C++, the case is similar, except that the lower limit is at 0. In Pascal, both the lower and upper limits need to be specified.

---

*We would like to point out here, that usually, books and manuals on programming languages refer to the above concept as *arrays* of variables. However, we shall later use the term *array* for a particular abstract container. To avoid confusion, we shall use the term *vector* for the concept described above.

In most modern languages like Pascal and C/C++, the type of the 'member' instances of a vector may be *any* declared or built-in type. In fact, these languages also permit declaring a vector type, just as they permit declaring a structured type. Indeed, sub-units of a structured variable (or type) could be structured or vector variables (or types) and vice versa. The overall declaration capability for these languages are tremendously rich as a result.

Vector memory layout and instance addressing

A vector variable occupies a contiguous chunk of memory locations. The size of the chunk is the size of individual instance multiplied with the size of the range. The first instance, i.e. the one with lowest position number (or *index*), occupies the topmost locations, and instances with consecutive indices occupy consecutive chunks. Thus, the *l*-value of any instance of the vector can be computed by simple arithmetic. The *l*-value of the vector is the topmost address of the entire chunk, and hence is equal in value to the *l*-value of the instance with the lowest index.

Languages which permit vector types and variables, also offer syntactic constructs to 'refer to' any individual instance of the vector at run time. In Pascal and C/C++ for example, one must give the vector name followed by an integral expression for the index of the instance within brackets ('[' and ']'). The compiler generates code to *compute* at run-time, the *l*-value of the instance being referred to and access it through the computed *l*-value. Thus, here again we have a case where the *l*-value of a variable is not fixed at compile time, even for a static (vector) variable.

Range check with vectors

The facility to access multiple instances of a vector through a single construct, brings in a few other factors into play. One such factor is known as *range check*. What would happen if the expression generating the index of the instance did not fall within the range of the vector indices? Note that it is not possible to predict values of expressions at compile time. If no check is provided, the computed offset into the memory chunk for the vector may actually refer to locations outside the vector. If such an (incorrect) 'instance' is modified, the modification would be extremely difficult to track down and might lead to an unpredictable behaviour of the program. Most compilers therefore allow *range check options* that may be switched on or off. When turned on, the compiler generates code whence every index computation is followed by validity checks of the computed index. A wrong index generates a 'run-time fault', and the program is forced to terminate. Of course, the price paid for range checking is an increase in program size as a result of the extra code and slowing down of execution speed due to time being required to validate the index. Usually, therefore, range check is kept on during the program development stage and turned off in the final version.

In summary, a vector variable represents a chunk of multiple instances of the same type. A particular instance in the chunk may be accessed by specifying an integral offset with the vector name. At the machine level, a vector variable represents the address (i.e. the *l*-value) of the lowest indexed (usually) instance in the chunk. The indexed reference to an instance within the chunk, in turn, represents a variable whose *l*-value is determined at run-time through evaluation of the integer expression for the index.

Pointers

Another mechanism for run-time determination of *l*-value of a variable is possible in certain programming languages through another type of variable generally known as a *pointer*. A pointer is considered as a special type because the respective languages permit *l*-values (or addresses) of other variables (usually of any type, including pointers and vectors) to be stored as their *r*-values. Thus, by suitably modifying its *r*-value, a pointer variable may be made to *point at*, i.e. hold the *l*-value of, another variable. Usually, programming languages impose syntactic restrictions to declare a pointer variable to be a pointer to some type, built-in or user defined. Compilers for these languages flag type violation error when a pointer to a certain type is used to point to a variable of some other type. We shall refer to the type of the variable that a pointer is supposed to point to, as the *pointed type*.

Pointer referencing, dereferencing and dynamic allocation

Two fundamental operations are permitted with pointer variables. The first one involves making the pointer 'point to' an instance of a variable of the pointed type. Actually, most languages supporting pointers permit a pointer variable to point to a vector of the pointed type. This notion makes pointers and vectors somewhat similar, a fact that is laid down clearly in the specifications of the C/C++ languages. The above operation on a pointer is generally known as *referencing* a pointer. We shall investigate the idea of referencing in more detail later. Assuming that a pointer is actually referencing or pointing at an instance of the pointed type, there must be an operation to access the pointed data indirectly through the pointer. The operation in this case is known as *dereferencing* a pointer. Clearly, referencing and *dereferencing* of pointers are inverse operations of one another. Thus, dereferencing the referenced value (i.e. the current *r*-value) of the pointer yields the same data as what the pointer is pointing to. Similarly, referencing a pointer to the variable obtained by dereferencing it, keeps the pointer value unchanged. Let us consider the case in C and C++.

```
int i, *pi; /* 'i' is an int while 'pi' is a pointer to int */

pi = &i; /* pointer referencing—'&' is the referencing operator */

*pi = 5; /* Equivalent to i = 5, given the above referencing.
          '*' is the de-referencing operator */
```

The utility of pointer variables is heightened due to their ability to keep track of dynamic variables. In many programs, the actual memory requirement for variables cannot be determined at development time. The variables that are explicitly declared in the program are allocated space through arrangements made by the compiler. The run-time addresses of these variables are tractable even at compile time. Suppose a programmer cannot determine at development time the maximum size of a vector required under different circumstances in which the program might run. Of course, during a particular execution session, the required size may be obtained through some other means. This is the ideal situation for using dynamic variables.

Most modern languages like Pascal and C/C++ permit dynamic allocation of space for variables at run-time. Usually, the compiler makes arrangements for allocation of a large chunk of memory space for the program in the start-up code. This chunk is generally known as the *global heap*. The run-time support offered by the compiling environment provides a set of functions through which smaller chunks of memory may be allocated from or deallocated to the global heap.

The necessary code fragments of the run-time support for memory allocation (and deallocation) process is generally known as the *heap management* routine. The two fundamental operations allowed by the heap management routines are first, allocation of a required number of *contiguous* memory units (henceforth to be called bytes) and second, freeing an allocated chunk. These operations might involve maintenance of various internal tables by the routines. The programmer usually need not bother about the internal details of these routines.

The allocation routine(s) in general, return a pointer that points to the topmost byte of the allocated chunk. This pointer should be held in some location retrievable by the program—for example, in a variable. Deallocation usually involves passing a pointer value to the relevant heap management routine. The actual number of bytes to be returned back to the heap (for later allocation possibly) is normally calculated by the deallocation routine itself. In C++, dynamic allocation and deallocation is carried out as follows:

```
int *pi; // pi is a pointer to int.

pi = new int[20];    // Allocates 20 int-s on the heap
                     // and makes pi point to it.
                     // 'new' is the allocation operator.

delete [] pi; // Frees memory allocated to pi.
              // 'delete' is the deallocation operator.
```

A dynamically allocated variable may itself be a pointer variable and may be made to point to another chunk of memory allocated on the heap, and so forth. In this way, complicated data structures, threaded with a number of pointers, may easily be constructed dynamically on the global heap. In fact, the proficiency of a good programmer is determined from his or her ability to handle pointers correctly and efficiently. It is quite easy to go wrong with pointers. Since allocation or deallocation errors occur at run-time, the compiler cannot offer support for detecting them. At times, usually in unprotected operating systems like DOS, incorrect pointer operation may lead to overwriting on system code/data area, leading to the machine getting hung. See the following example:

```
int **ppi; /* 'ppi' is a pointer to pointer to int.

ppi = new int*[5]; // Allocates 5 pointers to int on heap.

ppi[1] = new int[20];  // Allocates 20 int-s to second of
                       // the pointers to int pointed at by
                       // ppi. Note the syntactic usage similar
                       // to vector referencing.

ppi[1][6] = 5; // Legal. Expected to work without problem.
*(ppi[1]+6) = 5; // Identical to above.
*(*(ppi+1)+6) = 5; // — ditto —

ppi[2][10] = 20; // Might cause system crash, since pi[2]
                 // has not been made to point at anything.
```

Pointer typecasting

We have seen earlier that in the object-oriented environment, it may happen that the pointer to a parent object class may actually point to an instance of a descendant class. Indeed, this is the starting point of the polymorphic behaviour of objects. However, as a result of this phenomenon, the programmer may face problems with language syntax on certain occasions.

Consider, for example, that pA and pB are pointers to class A and class B, respectively. Also, class A is an ancestor class of class B. Thus, at run-time, it is possible that pA is actually pointing to an instance of class B. Suppose there is a function *f*, which takes a parameter that is a pointer to class B. In our case, since pA is actually pointing to an instance of B, it is a viable candidate for the said parameter of *f*. However, the strong type-checking mechanism of C++ would prevent pA being sent as the parameter of *f*.

It is often possible to know for sure, even at compile time that, at a particular instance, a pointer (say pA here) is definitely going to point to an instance of a different class (class B here). The usual practice in such cases is to force the compiler to ignore the type discrepancy through pointer *typecasting*. Typecasting is a syntactic feature of languages like C/C++, whereby the programmer indicates to the compiler that the result of an expression must be treated as a type different from what it is. For standard data types, this requires that the compiler inserts code to *convert* the data from the previous type to the casted type. For pointers, however, typecasting is treated differently. Recall that for a particular implementation model of the compiler, *all* pointers, regardless of the type it points to (usually) occupy the same amount of memory (for example, four bytes on PC 'large' model). A typecast pointer does not convert any data. The referenced data is simply forced to be an instance of the type which is cast.

In our example, if pA is first typecast to *B, i.e. a pointer to class B before despatching it to function *f* as the parameter, the type-checking mechanism of the compiler would no longer complain. No data conversion would take place, but since pA is *known* to point to an instance of class B, everything would work without any problem.

The most modern specification of C++, however, does not permit arbitrary casting of pointer types, especially if they are pointing to instances of user-defined classes. However, casting a parent pointer to a child class pointer is given a special status through a newly introduced operator called `dynamic_cast`.

The above discussions are exemplified below.

```
class A { // Super class.
  .
  .
  .
};

class B : public A { // B is descendant class of A.
  .
  .
  .
};

void f(B *prm); // Function declaration. Parameter is B *

A *pA;
B b; // b is a valid instance of B.

  pA = &b; // Legal. pA, however, now points to 'b'.

  f(pA); // Compiler error due to strong type checking.

  f( (B *) pA ); // Legal in older version of C++. pA typecasted to B*
  f( dynamic_cast<B *> pA ); // Legal in new version of C++
```

Later in this chapter, pointer typecasting would be extensively used in the implementations of various containers.

Vector pointer duality

From the definition of a pointer (i.e. a variable that holds the *l*-value of a contiguous block of variables of another type), the similarity between a pointer and a vector is evident. In fact, at one level, there is no difference between the two, except that pointers usually point to dynamic variables in the global heap, while vectors are usually associated with static storage (i.e. in the program data segment). Unless specifically blocked through the syntax of the particular language, there is no major problem in letting a vector be allocated dynamically on the heap and a pointer point to a variable in the data segment. Indeed, the C/C++ language family, unlike Pascal-like languages, freely accepts the duality between vectors and pointers, as is amply clear from the examples above.

Vectors of pointers

Another interesting FDS is a vector of pointers which has a few useful properties.

First, usually for an operating environment, all pointers are of identical size, irrespective of the pointed type of the pointer. Thus, the (static) memory requirement for such a vector is independent of the pointed type of the members of the vector and may be determined in the development phase.

Secondly, the actual data to be stored need not reside in the static memory, and may as well be located on the heap. Thus, if the pointed type has large memory requirement (for a large-sized structure for example), the allocation may be easily directed to the global heap. This technique not only frees a lot of static memory, but also helps in cases where some 'actual' data (i.e. not the pointer pointing to the data) has to be moved (or copied) from one offset of the vector to another, as only pointers need be moved (or copied) rather than a big chunk of memory representing the data. This might significantly improve the time complexity of programs. In the example taken up in page 87, the variable ppi is a vector of pointers. The price paid in using vectors of pointers to a data type, rather than simply a vector of the data type, is that every access to an actual data item must be through a pointer dereferencing operation.

Since pointers may be easily typecast, a question that comes into one's mind is whether it is possible to have a vector of pointers such that every pointer element of the vector actually points to data of different types. In case of such a possibility, it can work as an easy mechanism for formulating truly *heterogeneous* data structures—those in which data items of different types are attached. Indeed, such a possibility does exist. However, there is one serious drawback. Suppose, one accesses the data pointed to by the pointer at some offset of the vector. How can one know its type? The question is most important since different data types have different operations relevant for them. Unfortunately, in conventional non-OOPLs, this 'run-time determination of data type' can be achieved only in a roundabout manner. However, in OOPLs, under certain circumstances, there is no necessity for explicit determination of the run-time data type. In such circumstances, the vector of pointers is indeed an easily implemented yet powerful FDS, as will become clear later in this chapter.

To highlight the importance of the vector of pointers FDS, we shall henceforth call it the *Universal Vector.*

Multidimensional Vectors

Many programming languages permit vectors of more than one *dimension* to be declared. A k-dimensional vector permits use of k indices. Each index can have its defined range. In languages like C and C++, the most effective way of looking at a k-dimensional ($k > 1$) vector is to conceive it as a usual one-dimensional vector of type t, where t is actually a $(k-1)$-dimensional vector. This is best explained through an example.

```
int v2i[10][20]; /* v2i is 2-dim vector. First dim range is 10
                    Second dim range is 20. */

/* v2i[5] is a 1-dim vector of int, this being the 6-th member
   of v2i conceived of as being a 10-sized vector of 1-dim
   vector-s of int. Thus:*/

   v2i[5][11] = 10; /* has obvious significance. */
```

The memory layout for such vectors is also clearly defined. In C and C++, the 'row-major' scheme is followed. Here, the overall k-dimensional vector is assumed to be allocated like a contiguous layout of $d1$ elements, where $d1$ is the first dimension, and each element is a $(k-1)$-dimensional vector. The concept can be recursively extended. The actual address of a primitive element of a multidimensional vector can be easily computed if all the actual indices and the ranges of all dimensions except the first are known.

Linked Lists

The next most important FDS is the linked list. A linked list is defined as follows: The central concept of a linked list is a *node*. A node is a structured variable with two fields—the *data* field and the *next* field. The data field holds the actual problem dependent data. The next field is a pointer to a structure of type node, which may either point to another valid node or be a pre-defined pointer constant (usually called NULL or NIL) that the compiler recognizes. The NULL pointer constant is usually compatible with a pointer of any type, and is generally accepted as being one that points to *nothing*. The next field of the last node in a linked list is NULL. The entire list is 'held' by another pointer whose pointed type is node and which may be accessed by a mechanism that does not involve the linked list it holds.

Note: The names *node, head, data, next*, etc., are not sacrosanct, but are generally understood without ambiguity by most computer scientists.

A single 'outside' pointer pointing to a complicated data structure involving few or many pointers is generally known as the *handle* to the data structure. Thus, the *head* is the handle to the linked list it holds.

A few points became clear from the above definition of the linked list:

- The *head* is indeed the handle to the linked list it holds.
- If the *head* is NULL, no list is held by it, i.e. the list held by it is *empty*.
- Dereferencing the *head*, one gets what is called the first *node* of the linked list, from which the *data* for the first *node*, as well as the *next* pointer may be recovered.
- Dereferencing the *next* pointer of some *node* of the linked list (unless it is NULL, which means this is the last *node* of the list), one gets another *node* called the 'next node'.
- Thus, beginning with the *head* as the current pointer, if one continues with the process of dereferencing the current pointer (unless it is NULL) and reassigning it with the *next* field of the dereferenced *node*, one can visit all the nodes in the linked list in a *definite sequence*. The above fact puts the linked list into the *linear* category of FDSs.
- It is not possible to randomly reference any *node* of a linked list using only the *head*. One must go through the linear traversal described above to locate a particular *node*. It is also not easy to reference the 'previous' *node* of a given *node*.

- Of course, if one holds the *next* field of some *node* in a temporary handle, one can resume traversal from a particular node. In other words, the *next* field of any *node* of a linked list may be viewed as the handle of another linked list that begins at the 'next' item of the current list. However, under no circumstances is fully random access possible.

Diagrammatically, a linked list is represented as shown in Fig. 4.1.

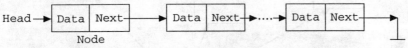

Fig. 4.1 Diagrammatic representation of a linked list.

Note that the *data* field of a linked list *node* may be of any type. It can easily be made the *head* of another (embedded) linked list. In such a case, the entire FDS may be visualized as one that is a linked list of linked lists, diagrammatically represented as in Fig. 4.1. Such an FDS is usually known as the *Doubly Linked List*. The concept can be carried further down indefinitely to multi-linked list.

Linked lists permitting forward and reverse traversal

Imagine a linked list with every *node* having another pointer field called *previous,* and structured in such a way that the *reverse* field of any *node* except the first (the one immediately pointed at by the *head*) points to the *node* whose *next* field points to it. With such a structure, usually called a *Two-way Linked List,* it is easily possible to traverse either forward or backward, starting from any internal node. Additionally, if another auxiliary handle called *last* that points to the last node is maintained, the entire linked list may be traversed in either direction. This technique of structuring a linked list is often used by programmers, where traversal either way is quite frequent. Note that even for such a linked list, total random access is not possible.

Another small improvement may be to make the *next* field of the last item to point to the first item, and the *previous* field of the first item point to the last item. In such a case, notionally, the linked list is 'endless', i.e. the concept of 'first' item and 'last' item cease to exist. The *head* may be made to point to any node at any point of time and even then, the entire list may be traversed, forwards or backwards, whenever desired. Such a structure is often called a *Circularly Linked List.*

Linked list of pointers—Universal list

As we have seen earlier with Universal Vectors, it is possible to conceive of a linked list of pointers to data items, rather than data items themselves. As with Universal Vectors, the *data* field of a *node* of such a list is actually a *pointer* to the required data types. We shall call such a list as a *Universal Linked List* which, as in the case of the universal vector, is a very powerful FDS for container implementation in OOP. Diagrammatically, a universal linked list is represented as in Fig. 4.2. For a C++ declarations of universal linked-list node, see the section on List container.

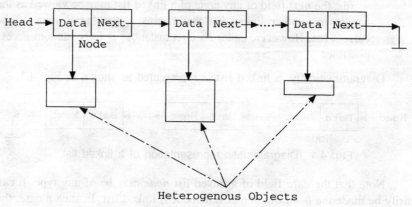

Fig. 4.2 Diagrammatic representation of a universal linked list.

Linked Binary Trees

In this section we shall consider the final FDS—the linked binary tree. Unlike the linked list, which is a linear FDS, the binary tree is non-linear. We must mention here that like the confusion between the linked list FDS and the list ADT (container), there is also a confusion regarding the nomenclature of the linked binary tree and a class of associated containers called 'binary trees' (with suitable adjectives). The term 'linked' binary tree is therefore non-standard. We have used this prefix to distinguish the linked binary tree FDS from associated containers.

The linked binary tree is basically a special type of doubly linked list. The key item here is also generally called a *node*. However, to maintain distinction from a linked list, we shall call it a *bnode*. A *bnode* has a *bdata* (the 'b' prefix used for distinction) data field and *two* pointer fields called *left* and *right* whose pointed item is a *bnode*. The 'handle' of a linked binary tree, called the *root*, points to a *bnode*. Diagrammatically, a linked binary tree may be represented as in Fig. 4.3. Observe the planar view, rather than a linear view of the linked

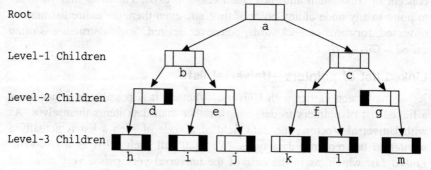

Fig. 4.3 Diagrammatic representation of a linked binary tree.

binary tree in the above figure. It is common practice to use the term 'a linked binary tree is *rooted* at *root*'.

Just as in a linked list, each of the pointers *right* and *left* may be viewed as the *root* (i.e. handle) of two smaller linked binary trees. The linked binary tree rooted at the *left* (resp. *right*) pointer of a *bnode* is called the 'left' (resp. 'right') sub-tree of the node. Clearly, the above description of the linked binary tree is recursive. A more complete recursive definition of a linked binary tree will be given later.

Linked binary tree traversal

We use the term traversal of an FDS to mean visiting every elementary data point of the FDS once and only once in some canonical manner. For linear FDSs (like vector, linked list, etc.), there are only two canonical ways for traversal—front to end or end to front. However, for a non-linear data structure like the linked binary tree, one can talk of three canonical traversal methods, usually known as *pre-order, in-order* and *post-order* traversals.

Consider a linked binary tree B rooted at some root. We can conceive of a canonical traversal of B in which first the *left* sub-tree is traversed, followed by the visiting of the *data* item of the *root,* and, finally, the *right* sub-tree is traversed. Noting that either or both of the left and sub-trees, could be linked binary trees themselves, the concept of the traversal is recursively carried down to each child sub-tree, unless the child in question is actually a *leaf.* This 'Left-Root-Right' or LDR (D for root) traversal scheme is known as *in-order* traversal. If the linked binary tree of Fig. 4.3 is traversed in-order, the *bnodes* visited in order are: h,d,b,i,e,j,a,k,f,l,c,g,m. Similarly, one can describe DLR or pre-order and LRD or post-order traversal of a linked binary tree.

IMPLEMENTATION OF SOME BASIC CONTAINERS

In this section, we shall talk about the basic principles behind implementation of containers.

There are a few different schemes for implementation of containers. For earlier C++ based environments (C++ version below 2.0) not having the `templates` feature, the *Object Based Container Implementation Scheme* is mostly used. The essence of this scheme is to propose a common abstract super-class (called by names like `Object`, `CObject`, etc.) and insist that all items that are to be stored in any of the containers be instances of classes derived from this common class (which we shall refer to as `Object`). The advantage of this scheme is that any of the 'universal' FDSs discussed above may be used to implement the containers. All our following discussions are based on this scheme only.

The `Object` and `SortableObject` Classes

The `Object` class contains no data items—only certain abstract functionalities through virtual functions, some of which are 'pure'.

One important virtual function defined by the `Object` class is `isSortable`. Through this member function, it can be inquired whether the object is sortable, i.e. whether a pair of instances of the class can be checked for orderliness. The `Object` class itself is not sortable and therefore returns a zero value for the above function.

An immediate descendant abstract class of `Object`, called `SortableObject`, heads the hierarchy of all ordered objects. The `SortableObject` class returns a non-zero value for the `isSortable` member function. Additionally, the `SortableObject` defines pure virtual functions `lessThan`, `equalTo` and `greaterThan` to check orderliness of a pair of instances of the object.

Thus, every 'real' class declared by a programmer wanting to use the containers described here must be ultimately derived from the `Object` class— through the `SortableObject` class (along with an implementation of `lessThan` and `equalTo`) if the object is an ordered one. Many functionalities that are common to *all* objects, for example, run-time class determination and mechanism for generating persistence of objects are also declared through the `Object` class. The `Object` and `SortableObject` classes may be declared as:

```
class Archiver; // Pre-declaration of the archiver class. See later.
class Object {

 public:
  Object() {}
  Object( Object& ) {} // Copy constructor.
  virtual ~ Object () {}
  virtual char *nameOf();
  virtual int hashValue() = 0; // Enforces giving a hash value,
                               // required for hash-tables.

  virtual int     isEqual( Object * ) = 0;
     // Even non-sortable objects may be checked for equality.

  virtual int     isSortable() { return 0; }

  virtual int     isAssociation() { return 0; }

// The functions below are required to have persistence storage.
// For explanation, see section on object persistence.

  virtual int  theCode(); // Returns the code vis-a-vis Meta-class.

  virtual void  archiveGet(Archiver *a) = 0; // Read despatcher.
  virtual void  archiveRead(Archiver *a) {} // Actual Read.

  virtual void  archivePut(Archiver *a) = 0; // Write despatcher.
  virtual void  archiveWrite(Archiver *a) {} // Actual Write.
};
```

```
class SortableObject:  public Object {

  public:

            SortableObject() {}
    virtual ~SortableObject() {}

  virtual int lessThan( Object *o) = 0; // 1 if this is less than 'o'.
  virtual int greaterThan( Object *o)
                { return lessThan(o) || isEqual(o) ?
                       0 : 1; } // So greaterThan can
                // be abstracted from lessThan and isEqual.

  virtual int    isSortable() { return 1; }

};
```

Note: To avoid confusion, we shall not declare and implement the following virtual functions in all derived classes of `Object`. However, in a real implementation, they must be included appropriately.

```
virtual char    *nameOf();
virtual int     hashValue();
virtual int     isEqual( Object * );
```

An Early Example of a Container

Let us take up a standard container, *stack*, as an example. We shall declare the `Stack` container class and implement it using a universal vector. Before that, let us make a quick review of the stack container.

· The `Stack` is a sequential LIFO access container of finite size. Three primary operations, namely, `push`, `pop` and `top` are defined. We may also add two more functionalities `isEmpty` and `isFull`, to check whether the stack is empty or full, respectively. Any instance of any class derived from `Object` may be stored in an instance of `Stack`. However, we shall demand that pointers to the class instances, rather than actual instances be used. Also, the actual instances whose references would be held in the stack should be either created in the global data segment or on the heap, and *not* on the stack frame (as automatic instances). The user may create an instance of `Stack` by specifying its maximum size that would be stored as a member variable.

Suppose that the user specifies the size to be *n*. Since we have decided to implement the stack on a universal vector, we may use a dynamic universal vector of size *n,* i.e. a dynamic vector of pointer to `Object` of size *n*, to act as container storage place. The dynamic vector may be held by member variable of type 'pointer to `Object*`' (i.e. `Object **`). Finally, one integer pointer is required to act as the 'stack pointer'. We can therefore make the following declaration of the `Stack` class.

```
class Stack : public Object {

  protected:

  int          stackSize; // The size of the stack.
  int          stackPointer;// Points to topmost empty entry.
  Object     **stackVector;

  public:

  Stack(int size = DEFAULT_STACK_SIZE) // Constructor.
    {stackSize=size; stackPointer=0; stackVector = new Object* [size];}
  ~Stack() // Destructor.
    { delete [] stackVector;}

// Stack operations below.

  int stackEmpty() { return (!stackPointer); } // Empty if stackPointer
                                               // is zero.

  int stackFull() { return (stackPointer==stackSize); }
                 // Full if stackPointer has reached stackSize.

  int push(Object *toPush) // returns 0 if stack full, else 1.
    { return stackFull() ? 0 : stackVector[stackPointer++] = toPush , 1;}

  Object * pop() // Returns NULL if empty, else top entry destructively.
    { return stackEmpty ? NULL : stackVector[-stackPointer]; }

  Object * top(); // Returns NULL if empty; else top entry non-destructively.
    { return stackEmpty ? NULL : stackVector[stackPointer-1]; }
}
```

The above declaration and implementation of the Stack container is more or less self-explanatory. It is a non-abstract container class, meaning thereby, that an instance of stack may be declared and used freely in the program as shown below:

```
#include "stack.h" // Assumes that the declaration of the stack class
                   // is in the file STACK.H
.
.
Stack myStack(10); // Declares a stack of 10 items.
.
.
AClassInheritedFromObject o, *po;
.
.
  myStack.push(&o); // Pushing 'o' onto stack. No checking done.
.
.
  if ( (po=myStack.pop()) ) {
  /*Valid pop from stack.*/ ...
  }
  else {
  /*Stack was empty.*/ ...
  }
```

The `queue` and `dequeue` containers

The Queue or Dequeue (double ended queue, in which entry and exit can be from either end of the queue) container may be implemented along similar lines as the Stack container. Usually, for these containers, the universal vector is handled in a circular manner. The last vector entry is logically considered to be one preceding the first vector entry and, similarly, the first vector entry is logically considered to be one succeeding the last vector entry. Thus, effectively, the vector is 'endless'. The situation can be easily achieved through the use of 'modulo' arithmetic on the vector index.

Serial access containers vs. enumerable containers

Containers like Stack, Queue, and Dequeue are, for obvious reasons, called *sequential* or *serial* access containers. They have very little in common with each other. The concept of enumeration or iteration over these containers is a little obscure.

The non-sequential access containers generally have a meaningful iteration operation and are therefore called *enumerable* (note that in the implementation described below, even the sequential access containers may be enumerated). Unlike sequential containers, enumerable containers may be quite neatly classified in an inheritance hierarchy. One such classification (incomplete) is shown in Fig. 4.4, where the entire container class hierarchy is headed by an abstract class Container. This class does not provide container features (like 'add

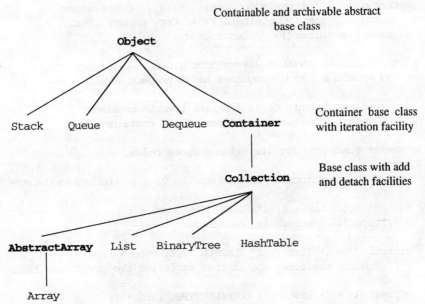

Fig. 4.4 One (enumerable) container class hierarchy (incomplete).

content', 'search for content', etc.), but only sets up the iteration functionality. There is an immediate descendant abstract class of Container called Collection, which actually acts as the head class for enumerable containers.

Container and Collection

At the top of the enumerable container class hierarchy is the class `Container`. This *abstract* class is meant for grouping some other objects together—i.e. it is a skeletal container with no containment specialities defined. It does not provide a method for adding and removing objects from the container, leaving them to be provided by derived classes. Let us first have a look at the declaration of the `Container` class, as well as its iterator class—`ContainerIterator`, declared as a `friend` class of `Container` for convenience.

```
typedef void (ITERFUNCTYPE *)(Object *, void *);
typedef  int (CONDFUNCTYPE *)(Object *, void *);

class Container:  public Object {

  protected:

  countType      itemsInContainer;

  private:

  friend  class ContainerIterator;

public:

    Container() { itemsInContainer = 0; } // Constructor.
    Container( const Container& ); // Copy Constructor.
  virtual ~Container(); // Destructor.

  int  isEmpty() { return (itemsInContainer == 0); }
    // Returns a 1 if the container has no members; else 0.

  int  getItemsInContainer() { return itemsInContainer; }
    // Returns the number of items in the container.

// Member Functions for iteration purpose below.

  virtual ContainerIterator* initIterator() = 0; // Initializes an iterator.

  virtual void forEach( ITERFUNCTYPE, void * );
    //Iteration over whole container.

  virtual Object* firstThat( CONDFUNCTYPE, void * );
    // Returns the first object that satisfies the given condition.

  virtual Object* lastThat( CONDFUNCTYPE, void * );
    // Returns last object satisfying given condition.

};

class ContainerIterator {
```

```
public:

virtual ~ContainerIterator(); // Destructor.

virtual Object      *current() = 0;
virtual Object      *next() = 0;
virtual void        restart() = 0;
virtual int         endReached() = 0;
};
```

Thus, other than establishing certain iteration functionalities through virtual functions, the abstract `Container` class performs only the rudimentary task of keeping track of the number of items in the container.

Let us have a look at the iterating functions. It shall clearly demonstrate that while `Container` is an abstract class, the concept of iteration can be captured even at this level.

```
void Container::forEach(ITERFUNCTYPE iterFunc, void * generic)
{
  ContainerIterator* iterator = initIterator();
          // Automatically re-started.

  while( !iterator->endReached() ) { // Continue iterating.
    Object* theObject = iterator->current(); // Get current item.
    (*iterFunc)(theObject,generic); // Despatch to iterating function.
    iterator->next(); // Move forward.
  } // end while.

  delete iterator; // Must delete, since it was allocated on heap.
}
Object* Container::firstThat(CONDFUNCTYPE condFunc, void *
generic)
{
  ContainerIterator* iterator = initIterator();
          // Automatically re-started.

  while( !iterator->endReached() ) { // Continue iterating.
    Object* theObject = iterator->current(); // Get current item.
    if ( (*condFunc)(theObject,generic) ) {// Check condition.
      delete iterator;
      return theObject;
    }
    iterator->next(); // Move forward.
  } // end while.

  delete iterator; // Must delete, since it was allocated on heap.
  return NULL; // No content satisfies condition.
}

Object* Container::lastThat(CONDFUNCTYPE condFunc, void *
generic)
{
```

```
ContainerIterator* iterator = initIterator();
    // Automatically re-started.

while( !iterator->endReached() ) { // Continue iterating.
  Object* theObject = iterator->current(); // Get current item.
  if ( (*condFunc)(theObject,generic) ) {// Check condition.
   // First satisfying content found.
   iterator->next(); // So, move one step forward.
   while( !iterator->endReached() ) { // Continue iterating.
    Object *oldObject = theObject; // Save the last found.
    theObject = iterator->current();
    if ( !(*condFunc)(theObject,generic) ) {
        // Check for condition failing.
        // Found the first failure.
    delete iterator;
    return oldObject; // Return the last found.
    }
   } // end inner while.
  } // end if.
  iterator->next();
   // Move forward since first satisfying content not found.
} // end while.
delete iterator; // Must delete, since it was allocated on heap.
return NULL; // Not a single content satisfies condition.
}
```

Some more advanced features of enumerable containers are abstracted through the descendant class of Container called Collection. The Collection abstract class is declared below:

```
class Collection: public Container {

public:

virtual ~Collection();

virtual void  add( Object *o) = 0; // For adding an item.

virtual void  detach( Object *o, int toDelete = 0 ) = 0;
    // For removing the object 'o' from container;
    // destroy it too if toDelete is non-zero.

virtual int   hasMember(Object *o) { return findMember(o); }
    // Returns 1 if 'o' is a member, 0 otherwise.

virtual Object*   findMember( Object *o );
    // Returns 'o' if found in container, NULL otherwise.

 void           destroy( Object *o ) { detach( o, 1 ); }
};
```

Observe that the Collection class permits addition and deletion of objects in an abstract manner, as signified by the respective pure virtual functions. In addition, `Collection` supports a membership test. It would be interesting to have a look at the implementation of the membership test function. It will be clearly demonstrated, how, with the use of the concept of iteration, such a functionality can be captured even at this abstract level.

```
Object* Collection::findMember( Object *o )
{
  ContainerIterator* iterator = initIterator();
        // Automatically re-started.

// The idea is to iterate through each object, doing a comparison of objects.
// The iteration is a shallow one, that is, if our collection is made up of
// container objects those containers are not checked internally.

  while( !iterator->endReached() ) { // Continue iterating.

      Object* listObject = iterator->current(); // Get current item.

      iterator->next(); // Move forward.

      if ( listObject == o ) { // FOUND.
       delete iterator;
       return listObject;
    }
  } // end while.

  // Iteration complete without success.

  delete iterator; // Must delete the container iterator, since it
                   // was allocated on heap.
  return NULL;     // item NOT FOUND.
}
```

AbstractArray, *Array* and *SortedArray*

The `AbstractArray` class is the base class for random access and sorted arrays. At construction time, the nominal size of the array is fixed through a constructor parameter. A second constructor parameter is used to determine if the array would increase its size when necessary, and by how much (`delta`). The implementation is based upon the universal vector FDS. Initially, a universal vector of the nominal array size is allocated. If the size must increase on demand, a *reallocation* takes place, from which a new universal vector of size `delta` more than the present nominal size is allocated, the original array is 'copied' onto the newly allocated one, the original universal vector is deallocated and nominal size is increased by amount `delta`. The entire process of reallocation is invisible to the user.

The `AbstractArray` container does not know how and where to add the next item. Thus, it still keeps the `add` functionality abstract.

```
class AbstractArray:  public Collection {

  protected:

    int      delta; // The amount by which array size may increase if required.
    int      arraySize; // Nominal and presently fixed array size.
    int      whereToAdd;
    Object   **theArray; // The universal vector.

    friend  class ArrayIterator;

    Object*  objectAt( int i ) { return *theArray[i]; }
    void     reallocate(int newSize);

  public:

    AbstractArray( int asize, int aDelta = 0 ); // Constructor. Parameter
             // asize determines nominal array size during construction.
             // aDelta, positive, determines size increment amount.
    virtual ~AbstractArray();

    int              size() { return arraySize; }

    virtual ContainerIterator* initIterator()
    { return (ContainerIterator *) new ArrayIterator( this ) ; }

    virtual void add( Object *o ) = 0; // Kept as pure virtual.
          void detach( int at, int toDelete = 0 ); // An
       // additional item removal function. First parameter
       // indicates item position.

    virtual  void        detach( Object *o, int toDelete= 0 );

};
```

Let us have a look at how some of the member functions of `AbstractArray` may be implemented.

```
void AbstractArray::reallocate(int newSize)
// Reallocates array's universal vector to new size = old size + delta.
{
  if ( !delta ) { // Error: Attempting to expand a fixed size array.
    exit(__EEXPAND);// Generate run-time error.
  }
  if ( newSize <= arraySize ) return;

  int i; // Loop counter for moving the pointers.

  int adjustedSize = newSize + ( delta - ( newSize % delta ) );
          // To make adjustedSize to next multiple of delta.

  Object **newArray = new Object *[ adjustedSize ];
```

```
  if ( !newArray ) {  // Error:  Out of Memory.
    exit(__ENOMEM);// Generate run-time error.
  }

  for ( i = 0; i < arraySize; i++ ) {
    newArray[i] = theArray[i]; // Copy old vector to new,
  }
  for (; i < adjustedSize; i++ )
  {
    newArray[i] = NULL; // and make the extra entries NULL.
  }

  delete [ arraySize ] theArray; // Throw away the old vector.
  theArray = newArray; // Set vector to new.
  arraySize = adjustedSize;
}

AbstractArray::AbstractArray( int asize, int aDelta)
{
// The Constructor. Allocates a universal vector of size = asize.

  whereToAdd = 0;
  arraySize = asize;
  delta = aDelta;

  theArray = new Object *[ arraySize ]; // Allocate universal vector,
  for( int i = 0; i < arraySize; i++ ) theArray[ i ] = NULL;
    // and initialize each entry to NULL.
}

AbstractArray::~AbstractArray()
// The Destructor. Must deallocate universal vector.
{
  for( int i = 0; i < arraySize; i++ ) theArray[ i ] = NULL;
  delete [ arraySize ] theArray;
}

void AbstractArray::detach( Object *o, int toDelete )
{
  if ( !toDetach ) return;

  for ( int i = 0; i < arraySize; i++ ) {
   if ( theArray[ i ] == toDetach ) { // Found object asked to detach.
      if ( toDelete ) delete theArray[ i ];
      theArray[ i ] = NULL;
      itemsInContainer--;
      return; // DONE.
    }
  } // end for //
}
```

```
void AbstractArray::detach( int at,  int toDdelete )
{
  if ( theArray[ at] ) { // Some relevant item at requested index.
     if ( toDelete ) delete theArray[ at ];
     theArray[ at ] = NULL;
     itemsInContainer--;
  }
}
```

Now observe the `ArrayIterator` class.

```
class ArrayIterator:  public ContainerIterator {

  private:

  int    currentIndex; // Maintains position info for this iterator.
  AbstractArray *beingIterated; // Maintains a pointer to
                               // the array being iterated.

  public:

    ArrayIterator( AbstractArray *a )
    { beingIterated = a; currentIndex = 0; }

    virtual ~ArrayIterator();
    Object      *current();
                   { return
                    currentIndex   < beingIterated->arraySize ?
                              // Index within range.
                     beingIterated->objectAt( currentIndex ) :
                     NULL; } // Index out of range.

    Object      *next();
    void         restart(); { currentIndex = 0; }
    int          endReached()
                   { return currentIndex >= beingIterated->arraySize;}
};
```

```
// Implementation of Member Function next().

Object* ArrayIterator::next()
// Increments the array iterator and returns the next object.
{
  if ( currentIndex < beingIterated->arraySize - 1 ) {
       // Index within range.
    currentIndex++;
    return ( beingIterated->objectAt( currentIndex ) );
  }
  else { // No more elements in the array.
    return NULL;
  }
}
```

Array

The `Array` is a random access container derived from the `AbstractArray`.
Keeping other functionalities same, it simply overrides the `add` member function
to insert an item at an appropriate empty location. If there are no empty locations
left in the universal vector through which the `Array` is implemented, and if
`delta` (i.e. the amount by which the vector size may be incremented on
demand) is non-zero, a new vector of appropriate size is created, the original
vector is copied to the new one and subsequently discarded, and the new vector
is made to hold the original contents plus the ones that are newly added. In
addition, a new function for randomly inserting a new item to a specified array
location is also supported by the `Array` class. This function, `addAt` deletes
the object, if any, found in the specified location, and inserts the passed object
in that location. A declaration of the `Array` container and implementation of
some of the functions are as follows:

```
class Array:  public AbstractArray {

  public:

     Array( int asize, int aDelta = 0 ) : AbstractArray( asize , aDelta )
{}
     ~Array() {} // Nothing to do here. Destructor for AbstractArray
                  // takes care of destroying the contained objects.

   Object*       operator []( int atIndex) { return objectAt( atIndex
); }

   virtual void      add( Object* );
           void      addAt( Object*, int ); // For adding a given object
                // at a given index, destroying the object (if any)
                // already at that index.
};

void Array::add( Object* o )
{
  // First, we search for the first available space for adding.

  while( theArray[ whereToAdd ] && whereToAdd <= arraySize ) {
    whereToAdd++;
  }

  // Found an appropriate location where to add. May be beyond current size.

  if( whereToAdd > arraySize ) { // Beyond current length. Must reallocate.
    reallocate( whereToAdd + 1 );
  }

  theArray[ whereToAdd++ ] = o;
  itemsInContainer++;
}
```

```
void Array::addAt( Object* o, int atIndex )
{
  if( atIndex > arraySize ) { // Beyond current size. Must reallocate
      reallocate( atIndex + 1 );
  }

  if ( theArray[ atIndex ] ) { // Indicated location full.
      delete theArray[ atIndex ]; // Remove the old entry and delete it !!
      itemsInContainer--;
  }

  theArray[ atIndex ] = o; // Now can add at the indicated location
  itemsInContainer++; // and hence must increment the number of contents.
}
```

SortedArray

The `SortedArray` container is meant to hold only instances of `SortableObject`. It does not permit random insertion. Any object to be added is checked against the existing items of the container and inserted in such a location that all items stored at the lower index of the array are `lessThan` the objects added.

```
class SortedArray:  public AbstractArray {

  private:

    int           lastElementIndex;

  public:
      SortedArray( int asize, int aDelta = 0 ) :
              AbstractArray( asize, aDelta )
              //{lastElementIndex = -1;}
      ~SortedArray() {}

  SortableObject* operator []( int atIndex )
          { return (SortableObject *) objectAt( atIndex );}

  virtual void    add( Object* );
  virtual void    detach( Object*, int = 0 );

};

void    SortedArray::add( Object *o )
{
  if ( !o->isSortable() ) { // Error: object to add is not
                            //        sortable.
    exit(__NOTSORTABLE);
  }
  if ( lastElementIndex == arraySize ) {
    reallocate( arraySize + 1 );
  }

  int i = 0;
```

```
    // Check for appropriate insertion point for 'o'
    while ( i <= lastElementIndex &&
          ( lessThan( (SortableObject *)(theArray[i]),
                        // (SortableObject *)o ) ) {
      i++;
    }


    // Found the appropriate location to insert at i.

    for ( int j = lastElementIndex; j >= i; j-- ) {
      theArray[j+1] = theArray[j]; // Make room for item to be
                                   // inserted.

    }

    theArray[ i ] = o;
    itemsInContainer++;
    lastElementIndex++;


}

void    SortedArray::detach( Object *o, int toDelete )

{
    if ( !o ) return;

    int dPoint, mCount;

    for ( dPoint = 0; dPoint <= arraySize; dPoint++ ) {
      if ( theArray[ dPoint ] == o ) { // Found the one to detach.
        if ( toDelete ) { // Delete the found object, i.e. 'o'.
          delete theArray[ dPoint ];
        }
        for ( mCount = dPoint; mCount < lastElementIndex; mCount++ ) {
            // Now move up the items below the one to detach.
            theArray[ mCount ] = theArray[ mCount + 1 ];
        }

        theArray[ lastElementIndex-- ] = NULL;
        itemsInContainer--;
        return;
      }
    } // end for.
}
```

The List Container

The universal linked list FDS

We have already discussed about the universal linked list and powers of the
same. Let us now declare a universal linked list node.

```
class ListElement {

  private:

  ListElement *next;
  Object      *data;

  friend class List; // The List class and its iterator would
  friend class ListIterator; // use this class extensively.

  public:

    ListElement( Object *o ) { data = o; next = NULL; }
    ~ListElement() { data = NULL; } // Destruction of node does NOT
                                    // destroy data.
};
```

The List class

The list container may be easily implemented using the universal linked list. As container functionalities, these containers permit insertion (always at the head of the universal linked list), a mechanism to peek into the head item and to detach an item randomly from the list. Only the functionality for detaching an item needs discussion. Suppose o is the item to be detached. If o is found at the head node, one need only make the head node a successor of itself, and delete the erstwhile head node after detaching o from it. If o is not found at the head, one must visit the other nodes of the linked list in order and search for o in them. We could have done the search with a list iterator. However, for our purpose, we need to keep track of not only the objects in the list, but also of the list elements, i.e. the pointer nodes. Hence, we may not use the iterator. The declaration of the List class and its iterator are given below, along with the implementations of some of the key functionalities.

```
class List:  public Collection {

  private:

  ListElement  *head;

  friend  class ListIterator;

  public:

    List() { head = 0; }
    virtual ~List();

  Object*       peekHead() { return head? head->data : 0; }
  void          add( Object* );
  void          detach( Object*, int = 0 );
  void          destroy( Object* l ) { detach( l, 1 ); }
```

```
  virtual ContainerIterator* initIterator()
            { return (ContainerIterator *)new ListIterator( this ) ; }
};

  List::~List() // Destructor.
{
  while( head ) { // Still more nodes to delink.
    ListElement *temp = head; // Hold temporary reference to head.
    head = head->next; // Take head forward.
    delete temp; // Delete previous head node. Content NOT destroyed.
  }
}

void List::add( Object* o )
{
  ListElement *newElement = new ListElement( o );
  newElement->next = head;
  head = newElement; // Add at head of linked list.
  itemsInContainer++;
}

void    List::detach( Object* o, int toDelete )
{
  ListElement *cursor = head;

  if ( head->data == o ) { // 'o' is at the head of the list.
    head = head->next; // Remove reference right away.
  }
  else { // The object isn't at the head of the list.
    ListElement *trailer = head;

    while ( cursor )  { // Scan through the list.
      cursor = cursor->next; // 'Cursor' points to node just beyond 'trailer'.
      if ( cursor && cursor->data == o ) { // Found 'o' at trailer.
        trailer->next = cursor->next; // Adjust links.
        break;
      }
      else { // The object isn't the one we want.
        trailer = trailer->next; // Continue moving forward.
      }
    } // end while.
  } // end else.

// Now 'cursor' possibly points to the object that we've found.

  if ( cursor && cursor->data == o ) {
    itemsInContainer--;
    if ( toDelete ) {
      delete cursor->data;
    }
    cursor->data = NULL; // Ensure that we don't delete the data
    delete cursor; // Destroy the node at which 'o' is found.
  }
}
```

```
class ListIterator:  public ContainerIterator {

  private:

  ListElement *currentElement;
  ListElement *startingElement;

  public:

    ListIterator( List* l) { currentElement = startingElement = l->head; }
    virtual ~ListIterator() {}

  Object      *current()
            { return currentElement ? currentElement->data : NULL; }

  Object      *next();
  void        restart() { currentElement = startingElement; }
  virtual int endReached() { return currentElement != NULL; }
};

Object *ListIterator::next()
{
  ListElement *trailer = currentElement;

  if ( currentElement ) { // Still items left to scan.
    currentElement = currentElement->next; // Advance node,
    return trailer->data; // and return data at previous node.
  }
  else {// No more elements in the list.
    return NULL;
  }
}
```

The BinaryTree (Binary Search Tree or AVL Tree) Container

The binary search tree is one of the most fundamental nonlinear containers known to computer scientists. It is most effective in environments where data objects that are being dynamically appended or delinked, leave the container 'sorted' after each such move. The focus is on achieving a speedy reorganization of the container. A binary search tree container is primarily a binary tree—a container where each node holds a data and two other binary trees—called the left and right sub-trees, respectively. This description of a binary tree container is so close to the description of the linked binary tree FDS given below, that issues regarding the two quite often get mixed up.

Note that, in the above description of a binary tree, we have not talked about pointers. Neither have we elaborated how a node of a binary tree contains its children. Indeed, there are schemes whereby binary tree implementation can be mapped on to vectors. Nevertheless, a linked binary tree remains the most plausible choice of FDS for binary tree implementation.

In this section, we shall talk of a special class of binary trees called *height balanced binary search* tree. A binary search tree is a container that is basically a binary tree, but additionally, all data objects that are 'less' (*resp.* 'greater') than the objects held by this tree are to be found in the left (*resp. right*) sub-tree of this tree. This property ensures a search of the container to be properly guided to the appropriate sub-tree till either the item searched for is found, or a tree with no sub-trees (called 'leaf') is reached (when not found).

The height of a binary tree is the maximum sub-tree traversal required to reach a leaf. Clearly, the height of a tree is one more than the maximum of the heights of the two sub-trees. The balance factor of a tree is the difference of the heights of the left and right sub-trees. A height balanced binary search tree is a binary search tree with balance factor of either –1, 0 or +1 for itself as well as for the sub-trees. In literature, a height balanced binary search tree is also referred to as an AVL tree, after the initials of the first investigators of their behaviour.

An AVL tree therefore tends to keep approximately halves of the contained data on the left and right sub-trees respectively. Thus, as a search process is guided into one of the sub-trees, the total search space is halved. This reasoning can be extended to show that with an AVL tree, one requires $O(n)$ time for searching for an item in the worst case, where n is the total number of contained items. Entering a data item into an AVL tree involves first searching for the same. The search process locates a place where the new data should go. However, as a consequence of actually placing the data item in the located position, the balanced condition of the tree may be violated. An AVL tree must have a functionality, which need not be public, to re-organize itself so as to reflect the balanced condition.

We have already provided a rudimentary description of the linked binary tree FDS. Here, we begin by a more comprehensive recursive definition of the same.

The universal linked binary tree

A linked binary tree is a data structure whose primitive item is a node. The node holds a (pointer to a) data object. In addition, a linked binary tree has pointers to two children (one or both may be NULL at a particular juncture), usually called the left and right, which are linked binary trees themselves. A tree that has no child is called a leaf. Usually, therefore, a linked binary tree is one of the children of another tree, which is called the parent. A tree with no parent is called a root.

The FDS associated with a static pointer to a root that in turn develops into a wide hierarchy, is one of the most important non-linear data-structures known to computer scientists. To achieve better manipulation ability, it may be necessary to associate another pointer to the parent tree. With that, we can define and implement the linked binary tree as shown below. Note that both `LinkedBinaryTree` and its embedded object class `BinTreeElement` are private descendant classes of `Object`, with the former being a `friend` of the latter. This helps in easy archiving for the classes, while not providing visibility into details of their implementation to general users of containers.

The declaration of the `LinkedBinaryTree` follows. The linked binary tree is a basic non-linear data structure that may be used by many containers. The functionalities provided are mostly rudimentary ones, mostly for setting and retrieving member data. There is one functionality for deleting the tree, which is non-trivial and recursive. Additionally, two more functionalities— `rotateLeft` and `rotateRight` have been included. Through these functions, a tree may be 'rotated' in the appropriate direction. The concept of rotation is especially important when a linked binary tree is used to implement a height balanced container like the AVL tree. We have incorporated rotation at the level of a general linked binary tree, so as to make the rotation facility available to other users of the data structures. The left rotate operation has been explained through a diagram in Fig. 4.5.

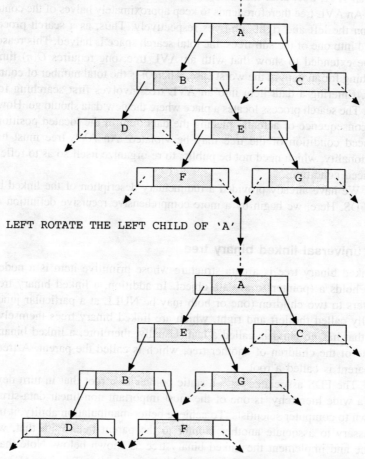

LEFT ROTATE THE LEFT CHILD OF 'A'

Fig. 4.5 'Left' rotation of an AVL tree.

`BalancedLinkedBinaryTree`, which is a descendant data structure class of a `LinkedBinaryTree`, actually introduces the concept of 'height balancing'. For this, it has a member data called the `balanceFactor`, whose value is −1, 0 or +1. Functionalities are provided for rebalancing while inserting or delinking a data item.

```
class LinkedBinaryTree; // Pre-declaration.
class BalancedLinkedBinaryTree; // — ditto —

class BinTreeElement : public Object {

// Definition for the core content of a binary tree. Indeed,
// the LinkedBinaryTree class has a single member which is a
// BinTreeElement. This is required for efficient manipulation.

friend class LinkedBinaryTree; // For obvious reasons.
friend class BalancedLinkedBinaryTree; // For obvious reasons.
protected:

  LinkedBinaryTree *parent, *left, *right ;
  Object        *data;

  void deleteElement(int dataAlso = 0);

     BinTreeElement( Object *o = NULL)
          { data = o; parent = left = right = NULL; }
     ~BinTreeElement() { }
          // Destruction of node does NOT destroy data.
};

void BinTreeElement::deleteElement(int dataAlso)
{
  if (dataAlso) delete data;
  left = right = parent = NULL;
  delete this; // Note this use.
}

class LinkedBinaryTree {
protected:
// The actual linked binary tree class. Observe that tree
// functionalities are all vested to this class.
friend class BinaryTree; // The binary tree container and its iterator
friend class BinaryTreeIterator; // would use this class extensively.

  BinTreeElement *element;


  void deleteTree();

     LinkedBinaryTree() { element = new BinTreeElement; }
     ~LinkedBinaryTree() { deleteTree(); }

  int    isLeaf() { return element->left || element->right ? 0 : 1; }
                // To find whether this is a leaf.

  void   addAt(Object *d) { element->data = d; } // Add a data object.

  void   traverse( ITERFUNCTYPE, void *, int tCode);
```

```
void    setLeft(LinkedBinaryTree *t) { element->left = t; }
void    setRight(LinkedBinaryTree *t) { element->right = t; }
        // To set appropriate child. No deletion done.

void    setParent(LinkedBinaryTree *t) { element->parent = t; }
LinkedBinaryTree *parentTree() { return element->parent; }
LinkedBinaryTree *leftTree() { return element->left; }
LinkedBinaryTree *rightTree() { return element->right; }
        // To get the appropriate child.

Object *rootData() { return element->data; } // Get the data.

int     rotateLeft(); // Left rotate by pointer adjustment.
int     rotateRight(); // Right rotate by pointer adjustment.
};

class BalancedLinkedBinaryTree : public LinkedBinaryTree {
  int   balanceFactor;

friend class BinaryTree; // The binary tree container and its iterator
friend class BinaryTreeIterator; // would use this class extensively.

    BalancedLinkedBinaryTree() : LinkedBinaryTree()
            {balanceFactor = 0; }
    ~BalancedLinkedBinaryTree() { deleteTree(); }
  void insertAndBalance( Object *o, BalancedLinkedBinaryTree *from);
};
```

Let us have a look at the implementations of some key functions of the LinkedBinaryTree class.

```
void LinkedBinaryTree::traverse( ITERFUNCTYPE iterFunc,
                                 void *generic, int tCode)
{
  char order[3]; // Holds the visit sequence.

// Code to create the visit sequence follows.
  switch(tCode) {
    case IN_ORDER:
      order[0] = 'L';order[1] = 'D';order[2] = 'R';break;
    case PRE_ORDER:
      order[0] = 'D';order[1] = 'L';order[2] = 'R';break;
    case POST_ORDER:
      order[0] = 'L';order[1] = 'R';order[2] = 'D';break;
    default: return;
  }

// Now that visit sequence is known, visit accordingly.
  for (int i=0;i<3;i++) {
    if (order[i]=='L') { // Traverse left sub-tree.
      if (element->left) {
        element->left->traverse(iterFunc,generic,tCode);
      }
    }
    else if (order[i]=='R') {// Traverse right sub-tree.
      if (element->right) {
```

```
        element->right->traverse(iterFunc,generic,tCode);
      }
    }
    else {
      (*iterFunc)(element->data,generic); // Despatch this.
    }
  }
}
void LinkedBinaryTree::deleteTree()
{
  // First recursively delete left and right sub-trees
  // if they exist.

  if (element->left) element->left->deleteTree();
  if (element->right) element->right->deleteTree();

  // Now delete this element.

  element->deleteElement();
}


int LinkedBinaryTree::rotateLeft()
{
  if (element) { // This is not a leaf.
    LinkedBinaryTree *temp = element->right,
                     *oldParent = element->parent;
    if (!temp) return ROTATE_FAIL; // No right sub-tree.

    element->right = temp->element->left;

    if (temp->element->left) {
      // Original right sub-tree has left sub-tree.
      temp->element->left->element->parent = this;
    }

    temp->element->left = this;
    element->parent = temp;

    temp->element->parent = oldParent;

    if (oldParent) { // Adjust sibling linkage of old parent
                     // to temp if there exists such a parent.
      if (oldParent->element->left == this)
          oldParent->element->left = temp;
      else oldParent->element->right = temp;
    }
  }
  return ROTATE_SUCCESS;
}

int LinkedBinaryTree::rotateRight()
{
  if (element) {
    LinkedBinaryTree *temp = element->left,
                     *oldParent = element->parent;
```

```
    if (!temp) return ROTATE_FAIL; // No left sub-tree.

    element->left = temp->element->right;

    if (temp->element->right) {
        // Original left sub-tree has right sub-tree.
      temp->element->right->element->parent = this;
    }

    temp->element->right = this;
    element->parent = temp;

    temp->element->parent = oldParent;

    if (oldParent) { // Adjust sibling linkage of old parent
                     // to temp if there exists such a parent.
      if (oldParent->element->right == this)
          oldParent->element->right = temp;
      else oldParent->element->left = temp;
    }
  }
  return ROTATE_SUCCESS;
}
```

It is interesting to observe the implementation of the `insertAndBalance` functionality of `BalancedLinkedBinaryTree`. First, look at the parameter list. One parameter is o, the object to be inserted into this tree, where the tree must be a leaf for the operation to be meaningful. The parameter `1OrR` indicates whether this tree is the left (if non-zero) or right (if zero) child of its parent, which must exist. Finally, the parameter `from` is some ancestral tree to this one, whose balancing has been disrupted as a result of the insertion and must be restored through appropriate rotations.

```
void BalancedLinkedBinaryTree::insertAndBalance
            ( SortableObject *o, BalancedLinkedBinaryTree *from)
{
  if ( !isLeaf() || !element->parent) return;

  addAt(o);

  BalancedLinkedBinaryTree *temp1, *temp2;
  int a;

  if (o->lessThan((SortableObject *), from->rootData()) ) {
    temp1 = temp2 = (BalancedLinkedBinaryTree*) from->leftTree();
    a = -1;
  }
  else {
    temp1 = temp2 = (BalancedLinkedBinaryTree*)from->rightTree();
    a = 1;
  }
  while ( temp1 != this) {
    if (o lessThan (SortableObject *) temp1->rootData()) ) {
       temp1->balanceFactor = -1;
```

```
    temp1 = (BalancedLinkedBinaryTree*)temp1->leftTree();
  }
else if (o->greaterThan((SortableObject*) temp1->rootData()) ){
    temp1->balanceFactor = +1;
    temp1 = (BalancedLinkedBinaryTree*)temp1->rightTree();
  }
  else break;
}

int *fbf = &from->balanceFactor;

if (*fbf == 0) { // Needs no balancing.
  *fbf = a;
  return;
} else if (*fbf == -a) { // Overbalanced.
  *fbf = 0;
  return;
}
else {
  if (temp2->balanceFactor == a) { // Single Rotation.
   if (a==1) from->rotateLeft(); // Left ...
   else from->rotateRight(); // ... or Right as the case may be.
   from->balanceFactor = temp2->balanceFactor = 0;
  }
  else if (temp2->balanceFactor == -a) { // Double Rotation.
    int b = a == 1 ?
  ((BalancedLinkedBinaryTree*) temp2->leftTree())->balanceFactor :
  ((BalancedLinkedBinaryTree*) temp2->rightTree())->balanceFactor;
    if (a==1) {
      temp2->rotateRight(); // First Right,
      from->rotateLeft(); // then Left ...
    }
    else {
      temp2->rotateLeft(); // ... or first Left,
      from->rotateRight(); // then Right, as the case may be.
    }
    from->balanceFactor = b>0 ? -b : 0;
    temp2->balanceFactor = b<0 ? -b : 0;
  }
 }
}
```

AVL tree implementation with linked binary tree

The BalancedLinkedBinaryTree is the most natural FDS for implementation of the AVL tree container represented by BinaryTree, an inherited class of Collection. Note that BinaryTree, being a descendant class of Container is indeed a container. The functionalities are as found with any container.

Observe the implementation of the add functionality. Here, an in-order traversal of the tree rooted at theTree is made to find out: (a) an appropriate leaf to insert the data to be added, and (b) a non-leaf node of the tree rooted at theTree, whose balance condition is likely to be affected as a result of the insertion. The insertAndbalance function for the newly created leaf node (where insertion is to be done) is next invoked after properly connecting the node to the overall tree. The said function then rebalances the tree possibly using none, one, or two rotations.

```
class BinaryTree : public Collection {
// Generalized AVL Tree.
protected:
  BalancedLinkedBinaryTree *theTree;

public:
    BinaryTree() { theTree = new BalancedLinkedBinaryTree; }
   ~BinaryTree() { theTree->deleteTree(); }

  void  add( Object *o); // For adding an item.
  void  iterate(ITERFUNCTYPE iterFunc, void *generic)
        { theTree->traverse(iterFunc, generic, PRE_ORDER); }

  void  detach( Object *o, int toDelete = 0 ) = 0;

};

void BinaryTree::add(Object *p)
{
  BalancedLinkedBinaryTree *tempTree = NULL,
                           *thisTree = NULL,
                           *from     = NULL;
  SortableObject *o = (SortableObject *) p;
  // Thus 'o' is a sortable object.
  if ( theTree->isLeaf() ) { // This is a leaf node.
    theTree->addAt(o);
    return;
  }
  int done = 0;
  from = thisTree = theTree;
  while (!done) {
    if (o->lessThan(thisTree->rootData()) ) {
      // Insert in left sub-tree.
      if ( thisTree->leftTree() ) {
        // A left-subtree exists,
        if (thisTree->balanceFactor) from = thisTree;
        thisTree = (BalancedLinkedBinaryTree *)thisTree->leftTree();
        if (thisTree->balanceFactor) from = thisTree;
      }
      else { // No Left sub-tree, insert here.
        tempTree = new BalancedLinkedBinaryTree;
        thisTree->setLeft(tempTree);
        tempTree->setParent(thisTree);
        tempTree->insertAndBalance(o, from);
        if (from->parentTree() &&
            !( (from->parentTree())->parentTree()) )
          theTree = (BalancedLinkedBinaryTree *)from->parentTree();
        done = 1;
      }
    }
```

```
else if (o->greaterThan(thisTree->rootData()) ) {
   // Insert in right sub-tree.
   if ( thisTree->rightTree() ) {
      // A right-subtree exists.
         if (thisTree->balanceFactor) from = thisTree;
      thisTree = (BalancedLinkedBinaryTree *)thisTree->rightTree();
      if (thisTree->balanceFactor) from = thisTree;
   }
   else { // No right sub-tree, insert here.
      tempTree = new BalancedLinkedBinaryTree;
      thisTree->setRight(tempTree);
      tempTree->setParent(thisTree);
      tempTree->insertAndBalance(o, from);
      if (from->parentTree() &&
          !( (from->parentTree())->parentTree()) )
        theTree = (BalancedLinkedBinaryTree *)from->parentTree();
      done = 1;
   }
}
else { // Same data.
   done = 1;
}
}
}
```

Implementation of the detach function of BinaryTree is left as an exercise.

The Hash Table Container

We have already talked about the hash table in the context of searching a container. In this section, we take up an implementation of a hash table container using an 'embedded' Array container. The *array* is a linear container whose size may be fixed (to *n*, say, *n* being a prime usually). Each content of the Array is another embedded container, this time of variable size—List. All Objects are supposed to return their hash values. A hash table recalculates this value to a remainder modulo *n* to *k*, say. The Object being entered (whose hash value has been re-calculated to *k*) is entered into the list at the *k*-th index of the array.

This embedded storage concept slightly complicates the issue of iteration of a hash table—there must be *two* iterators involved. The implementation given below explains this through appropriate comments.

```
class HashTable:  public Collection {

   private:

   int     size;
   Array   table;
   int     getHashValue(Object *o) { return o->hashValue() % size; }
   // Asking 'o' to hash itself and return that value modulo 'size',

   friend class HashTableIterator;
```

```
   public:

     HashTable( int s = DEFAULT_HASH_TABLE_SIZE )
           {size=s;table(s);} // Initializes the hash table.

     ~HashTable();

     void    add( Object* );
     void    detach( Object*, int = 0 );

     ContainerIterator* initIterator()
       { return (ContainerIterator *)new HashTableIterator(this->table);}

     Object* findMember( Object* );

};

void HashTable::add( Object *o )
{

   int index = getHashValue(o);

   if( !table[index] ) { // NO list at index-th entry of table.
      table->addAt( new List, index ); // Add a new List object at the index.
   }
// Surely a List now exists at the 'index'-th entry.

   ((List *)table[index])->add( o ); // Add 'o' to the list.
}

void HashTable::detach( Object* o, int toDelete )
{
   int index = getHashValue( objectToDetach );

   if(table[index] ) { // A list exists at the hashed index.
      ((List*)table[index])->detach( o, toDelete);
   }
}

Object* HashTable::findMember(Object *o)
{
   int index = getHashValue(o);

   if(!table[index]) { // No list at hashed index. No possibility of a find.
      return NULL;
   }
   // There is a list at the hashed index. Possibility of finding 'o' in list.
   // Must search through the list.

      return ((List*)table[index])->findMember( o );
      // Searches through the list.
}


class HashTableIterator:  public ContainerIterator {
```

```
private:

int           preIterate();
ArrayIterator *indexIterator; // For iterating over the table.
ListIterator  *listIterator; // For iterating over the list at some index.
Array*        beingIterated; // Holds the table of the hash table being
                             // iterated.

public:

HashTableIterator( Array * );

Object        *current()
Object        *next()
void          restart()
int           endReached()

};

HashTableIterator::HashTableIterator( Array *a )
// This iterator requires two internal iterators.
// One for the array, i.e. table, and another over
// the List at the hashed index of the table being iterated.
// The list iterator is initialized to a dummy iterator
// and the array iterator is initialized.
// Function next is used to finish the initialization.
//
{
    listIterator = NULL;
    indexIterator = (ArrayIterator *)beingIterated->initIterator();
    (void)preIterate();
}

Object *HashTableIterator::next()
{
    if ( preIterate() )
        return listIterator->next();
    else
        return NULL;
}

int HashTableIterator::preIterate()
// Prepares a hash table iterator for the next iteration step.
// If our current list iterator is finished, we bump the array
// iterator up. If the element at that index is a valid list,
// we set up an iterator using that list.
{
    while ( !listIterator ) {
        while ( !indexIterator->current() &&
                !indexIterator->endReached() )
            indexIterator->next(); // Move forward along table.
        if ( indexIterator->endReached() ) return 0; // Beyond end.
        else { // Array iteration not over.
            List *l = (List *)indexIterator->next();
            listIterator = (ListIterator *)l->initIterator();
```

```
        do indexIterator->next();
        while ( !indexIterator->current() &&
                !indexIterator->endReached() );
    }
    return 1;
  }
}

int HashTableIterator::endReached()

//      This is used to test for the end of iteration sequence.
{
  return  indexIterator->endReached();
}

Object *HashTableIterator::current()
{
  return  listIterator ?
          listIterator->current() : NULL;
}

void    HashTableIterator::restart()
{
  if (listIterator) delete listIterator;
  listIterator = NULL;
  indexIterator->restart();
}
```

Container of Containers

The reader must have observed that in all our implementations, the containers themselves have been derived classes of `object`. One major motivation for this is to make these containers 'archivable'. The next section describes object persistence in detail. Another motivation behind deriving containers from `Object` is to make all containers 'containable', i.e. one can have a container whose contents are other containers. The concept can be extended further till the limits of the user's imagination. Indeed, in our example, hash tables have been implemented as an `Array` of `Lists`. This way, we could, logically at least, conceive of a `List` of `AVLTree` of `Array` of certain objects. Other than causing a tremendous strain on the mind of the user, such a conception should not pose any implementational difficulties.

OBJECT PERSISTENCE

Quite often, it is required that the data items used in an application be persistently, i.e. in a semi-permanent nature, be stored for later use. The storage medium is usually a secondary storage device. The gravity of the problem must be realized in the context of the existence of many heterogeneous containers holding the data items. Most of the data items as well as most of the containers are created in the primary memory through pointers. Clearly, the intention during archiving is to store a *logical* picture of the dynamically created data, rather than their physical addresses.

A Simple Case

Consider, for example, that a pointer p is pointing to some data item d (say) in the primary memory. For simplicity, let us assume that p is a global variable, and that d contains only non-pointer data. In a particular execution instance, the value of p, i.e. the *l*-value of d is v (say). The value v is of no particular significance to archiving. What is required in this situation is:

- During saving, the command for the same should come through p, the global handle of the data d. Some coded message to that effect must be stored in the archive.

- The (non-pointer) members of d should next be saved in some particular order.

- During retrieval, the file pointer for the archive must, somehow, exactly point to the coded message saved in the first step. Also, the retrieval should have come through the same (global) pointer p.

- Upon reading the message, a new *uninitialized* data d1 (say) must be created in the dynamic memory and p made to point to it.

- Member data of d1 must be retrieved from the archive in the same order as they were saved in the second step.

A Less Simple Case

The problem reveals itself in its full complexity when we dilute the assumption that the data item d above may also contain pointer data. Also that the pointer members of d may point to other instances of data items in the dynamic memory and so forth. The possibility of *cyclic reference* is also not ruled out. As an example, consider the following scenario (diagrammatically shown in Fig. 4.6):

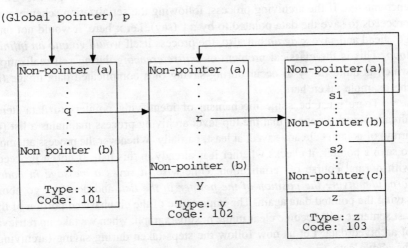

Fig. 4.6 An example set-up to be archived.

- A global pointer p points to a dynamic data instance x.
- Apart from non-pointer members, x has a pointer member q, which is pointing to another dynamic data (not necessarily of the same type) y.
- In a similar manner, y has a pointer member r pointing to another dynamic data z.
- The data z has two pointer members s1 and s2, which are pointing to x and y respectively.
- The request for archiving, as well as, later, for retrieval, comes through p.

Let us assume for the time being that we are not in an object-oriented programming environment, meaning thereby, that the data types are fixed and known before hand.

The Serialization Scheme

While saving p, the contents of x are to be saved. During the process of saving x, the pointer q is encountered. Assuming that there are some more non-pointer data of x to be saved, the question now is whether the archiving process should temporarily suspend saving the remaining members of x and proceed with saving y—the data pointed to by q, or vice versa.

In the *serialization* scheme of archiving, the former option is chosen. Thus, the archiving process first saves a coded message indicating the *type* of the data pointed to by q and begins saving the members of z, the data pointed to by q. At some point of saving y, the pointer r is encountered. Following our scheme, the archiving process should begin saving z, the data pointed to by r.

The process runs smoothly till either the pointer s1 or pointer s2 is encountered. If the archiving process, following the serialization scheme, now proceeds to save the data pointed to by s1 (say), i.e. x here, it would not only go ahead and save x *again* but also, the process itself *would go into an infinite loop*. This is the classical problem of *self-referencing* during self-realization, which is quite likely to occur during saving of a complicated data image (as the example taken here).

There must be some mechanism of identifying pointers to data items already saved. Suppose that the top-level archiving process maintains a list (or array) of pointers already saved, at least, partially. Whenever the process attempts to save a pointer, it checks whether it is already in this list. If not, it proceeds with normal course of serialization. Otherwise, it *saves a message in coded form identifying the position of the pointer in the list,* and does not go about saving the pointed data again. The importance of the emphasized portion of the last sentence will become clear in the next paragraph, when we take up retrieval of archived data. Let us now follow the steps taken during saving (archiving) the above data.

Archiving

Let us make some assumptions:

- The data x, y and z are of types X, Y and Z, respectively. These types are given the codes 101, 102 and 103 (say), respectively.

- There is a top-level archive(void *v, int code) function which assumes that the saving of the data is through the pointer v, which is of a type whose code is code. The appropriate typecasting can thus be done by archive. This is a bit simplified, but would keep issues from getting confused for the time being. The function maintains an internal list of pairs (pointer, code), signifying that an archival of the data pointed to by the pointer and of type 'code', has already been initialized. Upon being invoked, archive() checks whether v is in the list. If not, it first saves i, code in the file (using fprintf() call for example), where i is the position in the internal list of the pair just entered, and invokes the appropriate save?() (see below) function with v as the parameter. However, if v is found in the list, -i-1, code are saved instead, where i is the position in the list where v was found, and the current invocation of archive() returns immediately.

- There are functions saveX(X*), saveY(Y*), saveZ(Z*) that take care of saving data of the mentioned types. These functions are invoked by archive(). A particular function, say saveX, should save the non-pointer data members of the parameter in the usual manner (using a fprintf() call for example). However, if it must save a pointer member, it calls archive() with the pointer and the code for the pointer as parameters.

The following happens when archive(p,101) is invoked, say from main().

1. The archive function saves 0,101 in file, the pair (p,101) in the internal list, and calls saveX(p), since p is a pointer to X.

2. saveX(p) saves some non-pointer data, and invokes archive(q,102) when it decides to save q.

3. archive saves 1,102 in file and (q,102) internally, and invokes saveY(q).

4. saveY(q) saves some non-pointer data, and invokes archive(r,103) when it decides to save r.

5. archive saves 2,103 in file and (r,103) internally, and invokes saveZ(r).

6. saveZ(r) saves some non-pointer data, and invokes archive(&x,101) when it decides to save s1.

7. Since &x, i.e. p, is already in the internal list, archive saves −1,101 in file and returns immediately to saveZ(r).

8. `saveZ(r)` saves some more non-pointer data, and invokes `archive(&y,102)` when it decides to save s2.

9. Since &y, i.e. q, is already in the internal list, `archive` saves −2,102 in file and returns immediately to `saveZ(r)`.

10. `saveZ(r)` saves the remaining non-pointer data, and returns back to the invocation point of `archive(r,103)`. This in turn returns to `saveY(q)`.

11. `saveY(q)` saves the remaining non-pointer data, and returns back to the invocation point of `archive(q,102)`, which in turn returns to `saveX(p)`.

12. `saveX(p)` now saves the remaining non-pointer data, and finally returns to the invocation of `archive(p,101)`. This returns back to original call from `main()`.

See Table 4.1 for a diagrammatic representation of the above process.

Table 4.1 The Example Archiving Process

Invoking Action	FILE	Internal List	Next Action
`main()`	Open empty file	Initialized empty	`archive(p, 101)`
`archive(p, 101)`	0, 101	0: p, 101	`saveX(p)`
`saveX(p)`	0, 101 Non-pointer (a) of x		`archive(q, 102)`
`archive(q, 102)`	0, 101 Non-pointer (a) of x 1, 102	0: p, 101 1: q, 102	`saveY(q)`
`saveY(q)`	0, 101 Non-pointer (a) of x 1, 102 Non-pointer (a) of y		`archive(r, 103)`
`archive(r, 103)`	0, 101 Non-pointer (a) of x 1, 102 Non-pointer (a) of y 2, 103	0: p, 101 1: q, 102 2: r, 103	`saveZ(r)`
`saveZ(r)`	0, 101 Non-pointer (a) of x 1, 102 Non-pointer (a) of y 2, 103 Non-pointer (a) of z		`archive(s1, r)`
`archive(s1, r)`	0, 101 Non-pointer (a) of x 1, 102 Non-pointer (a) of y 2, 103 Non-pointer (a) of z −1, 101		return to `saveZ(r)`

Table 4.1 The Example Archiving Process (cont.)

Invoking Action	FILE	Internal List	Next Action
saveZ(r) resume	0, 101 Non-pointer (a) of x 1, 102 Non-pointer (a) of y 2, 103 Non-pointer (a) of z −1, 101 Non-pointer (b) of z		archive(s2, r)
archive(s2, r)	0, 101 Non-pointer (a) of x 1, 102 Non-pointer (a) of y 2, 103 Non-pointer (a) of z −1, 101 Non-pointer (b) of z −2, 102		return to saveZ(r) resume
saveZ(r) re-resume	0, 101 Non-pointer (a) of x 1, 102 Non-pointer (a) of y 2, 103 Non-pointer (a) of z −1, 101 Non-pointer (b) of z −2, 102 Non-pointer (c) of z		return to archive(r, 103)
archive(r, 103) resume			return to saveY(q)
saveY(q) resume	0, 101 Non-pointer (a) of x 1, 102 Non-pointer (a) of y 2, 103 Non-pointer (a) of z −1, 101 Non-pointer (b) of z −2, 102 Non-pointer (c) of z Non-pointer (b) of y		return to archive(q, 102)
archive(q, 102) resume			return to saveX(p)
saveX(p) resume	0, 101 Non-pointer (a) of x 1, 102 Non-pointer (a) of y 2, 103 Non-pointer (a) of z −1, 101		return archive(p, 101)

Table 4.1 The Example Archiving Process (cont.)

Invoking Action	FILE	Internal List	Next Action
	Non-pointer (b) of z		
	−2, 102		
	Non-pointer (c) of z		
	Non-pointer (b) of y		
	Non-pointer (b) of x		
archive(p, 101)			return to main()
main()	Close FILE		Continue

Retrieving

The retrieval process is the inverse of the archiving process. There is no problem with retrieving non-pointer data if the file pointer is properly synchronized on one hand, and the retrieving process knows exactly which data (most possibly some non-pointer member of some data item) to read. This is particularly suited to the object-oriented scenario, where saving and retrieving the member data of an object is the responsibility of the object, and the respective methods have to maintain the same order of saving and retrieving.

The problem comes when a pointer data is to be retrieved. The retrieving method of the data (object) has no idea (in our scheme) whether the pointed data item has already been retrieved or not. This depends upon whether the archiving method saved the pointed data before or after the data in question. In the latter case, the retrieving process for the pointed object must be immediately invoked. However, before that, *an empty space for the new pointed object must be created in the dynamic memory.*

This is achieved by first reading the coded message which must immediately follow in the archive. Upon reading the coded message, the *type* of the next data is known and hence an empty instance of the type can be easily created! The significance of the exclamation mark at the end of the previous sentence would be explained later. If, on the other hand, the coded message indicates that the pointed data has already been read, the pointer must be stored in some list of the top-level archive retrieval process, and is simply recovered from the list. Let us, for the time being, review the retrieval process of the data items saved above. We shall follow the process in steps.

First, the assumptions, over and above the ones made earlier:

- There is a top-level void *retrieve() function which assumes that the retrieving of the data is through the pointer returned by the function. This function also maintains an internal list of pairs (pointer, code), signifying that the retrieval of the data pointed to by 'pointer' and of type 'code', has already been initialized. Upon being invoked, retrieve() first reads a position number n and a code c from the file. If n is negative, i.e. the data item has been (at least partially) retrieved, retrieve() immediately returns the 'pointer' of the pair whose position is -n-1. If n is positive, it first *creates* an (uninitialized) instance of a data of appropriate type (X if c is 101, and so forth) in the dynamic memory through a pointer temp (say), saves the pair (temp, c) in the internal list—which should be exactly in position n if everything goes well—and invokes the appropriate get?(temp) and returns temp.

- There are functions getX(X*), getY(Y*), getZ(Z*) that take care of retrieving data of the mentioned types. These functions are invoked by retrieve(). A particular function, say getX, retrieves the non-pointer data members of the parameter in the usual manner (using a fscanf() call for example). However, if it must retrieve a pointer member, it calls retrieve() and assigns the return value to the pointer.

The following happens when retrieve(p,101) is invoked, say from main().

1. The retrieve function reads 0,101 from the file, allocates memory to temp1 assuming temp1 to be of type X (exactly what temp1 = new X would do), saves the pair (temp1,101) in the 0-th internal list position and calls getX(temp1), since temp1 is a pointer to X.

2. getX(temp1) reads some non-pointer data, and invokes retrieve(q, 102) when it decides to read q.

3. The retrieve function reads 1,102 from the file, allocates memory to temp2, assuming temp2 to be of type Y, saves the pair (temp2,102) in the 1-st internal list position and calls getY(temp2).

4. getY(temp2) reads some non-pointer data, and invokes retrieve(r, 103) when it decides to read r.

5. The retrieve function reads 2,103 from the file, allocates memory to temp3, assuming temp3 to be of type Z, saves the pair (temp3,103) in the 2-nd internal list position and calls getZ(temp3).

6. getZ(temp3) reads some non-pointer data, and invokes retrieve(s1, 101) when it decides to read s1.

7. Here, retrieve reads –1,101. Since n=–1 is negative, it means that retrieval of the data is already in progress and that the pointer to the retrieved data is in the (–(–1)–1)=0-th position of the internal list. This pointer is returned to getZ.

8. getZ(temp3) first assigns the returned pointer to s1, reads some more non-pointer data, and invokes retrieve(s2, 102) when it decides to read s2.

9. Here, retrieve reads –2,102. Since n=–2 is negative, it means that retrieval of the data is already in progress and that the pointer to the retrieved data is in the (–(–2)–1)=1-st position of the internal list. This pointer is returned to getZ.

10. `getZ()` assigns the returned pointer to `s2`, reads the remaining non-pointer data and returns to the invocation of `retrieve()` in step 5, which returns to `getY()` with the value of the pointer in the 2-nd entry.

11. `getY()` assigns the returned pointer to `r`, reads the remaining non-pointer data and returns to the invocation of `retrieve()` in step 3, which returns to `getX()` with the value of the pointer in the 1-st entry.

12. `getX()` assigns the returned pointer to `q`, reads the remaining non-pointer data and returns to the invocation of `retrieve()` in step 1, which returns to the outermost invocation (from main) with value of the pointer in the 0-th entry. This pointer is presumably assigned to `p` by `main()`.

See Table 4.2 for a diagrammatic representation of the above process.

Table 4.2 The Example Retrieval Process

FILE Contents
0, 101
Non-pointer (a) of x
1, 102
Non-pointer (a) of y
2, 103
Non-pointer (a) of z
–1, 101
Non-pointer (b) of z
–2, 102
Non-pointer (c) of z
Non-pointer (b) of y
Non-pointer (b) of x

Invoking Action	Top of FILE	Retrieve Action	Internal List	Next Action
`main()`	File opened	None	Initialized empty	`p=retrieve()`
`p=retrieve()`	0, 101	temp1 = new X	0: temp1, 101	`getX(temp1)`
`getX(p, 101)`	Non-pointer (a) of X	read from FILE to temp1->Non-pointer(a)		`temp1->q =retrieve()`
`temp1->q= retrieve(q, 102)`	1, 102	temp2 = new Y	0: temp1, 101 1: temp2, 102	`getY(temp2)`
`getY(temp2)`	Non-pointer (a) of Y	read from FILE to temp2->Non-pointer(a)		`temp2->r= retrieve()`
`temp2->r= retrieve()`	2, 103	temp3 = new Z	0: temp1, 101 1: temp2, 102 2: temp3, 103	`getZ(temp3)`
`getZ(temp3)`	Non-pointer (a) of Z	read from FILE to temp3->Non-pointer(a)		`temp3->s1 =retrieve()`

Table 4.2 The Example Retrieval Process (cont.)

temp3->s1= retrieve()	-1,101	None	return temp1. So, temp 3->s1 =temp1 return to getZ (temp3)
getZ (temp3) resume	non-pointer (b) of Z	read from FILE to temp3-> Non-pointer (b)	temp3->s2 = retrieve()
temp 3->s2= retrieve()	-2,101	None	return temp2. So, temp3 ->s2 =temp2 return to getZ (temp3)
getZ (temp3) re-resume	Non-pointer (c) of Z	read from FILE to temp3->Non-pointer(c)	return to temp2->r =retrieve()
temp2->r = retrieve() resume	Non-pointer (b) of Y	None	return temp3. So, temp2->r =temp3 return to getY (temp2)
getY (temp2) resume	Non-pointer (b) of Y	read from FILE to temp2->Non-pointer(b)	return to temp1->q = retrieve()
temp1->q= retrieve() resume	Non-pointer (b) of X	None	return temp2. So, temp1->q= temp2 return to getX (temp1)
getX (temp1) resume	Non-pointer (b) of X	read from FILE to temp1->Non-pointer (b)	return to p= retrieve()
p=retrieve()	End-of-FILE	None	return temp1. So, p=temp1 in main()
main() resume			continue.

Persistence in the OOP Environment

The problem of persistence is further complicated in the OOP environment. Let us investigate why:

- The programmer who coded the top-level archive and retrieve functions had no idea regarding the actual objects to be used in the operating environment, since a later user can add any object class of his choice. Of course, a reasonable assumption that all archivable and retrievable object classes belong to the same hierarchy, can be made.

- A consequence to the above fact is that the above programmer can offer no pre-determined code scheme relating *all* possible classes used in a given environment.

- A necessary step in retrieval is creation of an uninitialized object instance. This can only be done through the constructor of the respective class. However, dynamic construction is possible in C++ *only* through the operator new, for which the class name must be *statically* bound. C++, and most other OOPLs do not support an indirect constructor call.

The 'metaclass' concept—How to achieve it in C++

In more 'proper' object-oriented languages like Smalltalk, the solution is available through the concept of a *metaclass*. A metaclass is a class whose instances are different classes. Generally speaking, a *class* (NOT an instance of a class) can be created through constructor of a metaclass. This created class is dynamic. An invocation of the constructor to the dynamically created class can be dynamic, and solves the problem to quite an extent. Alas, C++ does not have this concept and one must derive a way around the problem.

A painless way around is as follows. The serialization programmer decides upon a top-level (generally abstract) class from which serialization would be supported. The class `Object` in our case could be a viable candidate. The serialization programmer, though insists that first, *all* classes derived from the specified base class, i.e., the ones that may be serialized, have a callable *null* constructor. Next, he insists that corresponding to *all* such classes, say for example class `Class_X`, a function of the following type be included (assuming `Object` to be the specified base class):

```
Object *Class_X_FTAG() { return new Class_X; }
```

The suffix `_FTAG` is an artificial discipline that must be followed. Now, an invocation `Class_X_FTAG()` immediately and indirectly constructs an instance of `Class_X` and returns a pointer to it. The advantage is that *the declaration prototype for all such functions are exactly identical,* and may be expressed as:

```
typedef Object * (* ICP)();
```

We shall call the above function pointer the 'indirect constructor despatcher'. Since the pointers to the above function for every class are distinct, this can not only take the place of 'code' in our above discussion, but can also be used for object construction during retrieval.

Metaclass simulation fundamentals

There are a few more points to be considered.

First, there must be some class to simulate the metaclass, which maintains a list of indirect constructor despatchers of all serializable classes. The actual 'code' that will be saved/retrieved would be a numeric position reference of a despatcher in the saved list, rather than the actual pointer. This is because in different program runs, the actual pointer values of the despatchers would presumably, be different, and hence care must be taken that data saved in one run be retrievable in another.

Through a virtual function, every class must be able to return its code and the metaclass must be able to associate a code with a despatcher and vice versa, *whenever* required during execution of the program. The last condition requires that *all* the code-despatcher associations are established even before the `main()` function begins execution.

The best way to carry out some requisite manipulation before `main()` takes over is to do so at `startup`. An easy way is through construction of global variables, since their constructors are called at startup in that case.

Finally, all these extra things to be done by the actual user of the serializable classes should be conceptually simple. Ideally, the user should not be made to do anything beyond some clearly defined declarations and macro calls using, may be, the name of his/her newly declared class and its parent.

A note is in order here. The above discussions are valid only if the serializable classes are in a 'single-inheritance' hierarchy. Multiple inheritance ruins all our assumptions and have not been considered here.

Serialization specific virtual functions in 'Object'

We begin by including certain virtual functions, pure or otherwise, from the root serializable base class—Object in our case. The extra work of archiving and retrieval will be carried out by the Archiver class, aided in the process by a MetaClass that simulates a metaclass. The extra functions relevant for serialization in Object are:

```
int theCode(); // Returns the code vis-a-vis metaclass.

virtual void   archiveGet(Archiver *a) = 0; // Read despatcher.
virtual void   archiveRead(Archiver *a) {} // Actual Read.

virtual void   archivePut(Archiver *a) = 0; // Write despatcher.
virtual void   archiveWrite(Archiver *a) {} // Actual Write.
```

The user is responsible for implementing the functions archiveRead and archiveWrite. Here, (s)he must read/write only the newly declared identifiers for the class, and *not* the ones declared in any parent.

The non-pointer members are read/written using the member functions readXXX and writeXXX of the Archiver class, where XXX stand for the basic scalar data types like, int, float, char, etc. Actually, the Archiver class implementor may save considerable trouble for the user by overloading operators << and >> for the purpose.

If, however, a newly declared member is a pointer px to a class Class_X, say, then the function should use the statement px=a->getFromArchive() for reading and a->putToArchive(px) for writing data for the embedded object. Here, a is the parameter Archiver object.

MetaClass implementation

The next important concept is the implementation of MetaClass. We use the static declaration feature of C++ here to our advantage. The MetaClass class maintains a linked list of indirect constructor despatchers (using MetaClassItem). However, there is only one linked list for all instances of MetaClass. The constructor of MetaClass takes a despatcher of a class as argument, and attaches it to the linked list. The position of the despatcher in the list is its code and member functions are provided to get the despatcher given its code and vice versa. The declaration and implementation is:

```
typedef Object * (* ICP)(); // The indirect constructor despatcher.
class MetaClass;

class MetaClassItem : public Object {

    ICP              indirectConstructor;
    MetaClassItem *next;

public:

    MetaClassItem() {}

    friend class MetaClass;
};

class MetaClass {

    static MetaClassItem *handle;

    static int              codeTag;

public:

    MetaClass(ICP function);

    static ICP  theICP(int code);
    static int  theCode(ICP f);
};

static MetaClassItem *MetaClass::handle = NULL;

    MetaClass::MetaClass(ICP function)
{
    MetaClassItem *mci = new MetaClassItem;
    mci->indirectConstructor = function;
    mci->next = handle;
    handle = mci;
}

static ICP MetaClass::theICP(int code)
// This program searches the link list of stored function pointers
// and returns the code-th one.
{
    int n=0;
    MetaClassItem *mci = handle;
    while( mci && n<code) {
        n++;
        mci = mci->next;
    }
    return mci ? mci->indirectConstructor : NULL;
}

static ICP MetaClass::theCode(ICP f)
// This program searches the link list of stored function pointers
// and returns the position number of the one that matches f
{
```

```
    int n=0;
    MetaClassItem *mci = handle;
    while( mci && mci->indirectConstructor != f) {
        n++;
        mci = mci->next;
    }
    return mci ? /* i.e. found */ n : -1;
}
```

The `Archiver` class

Next, we come to the `Archiver` class. This class encapsulates the functionalities of both `archive` and `retrieve` discussed earlier. Recall that during both archiving and retrieving, a list of pairs (pointer, code) needs to be maintained. In reality, the code need not be maintained, since a call to the `theCode` virtual function of `Object` is implemented in a way to do this. How this is actually done is described later.

As discussed, the archiver class has functions to read/write all the scalar data items. Additionally, it has two member functions `putToArchive()` for storing objects through pointers and `getFromArchive()` for retrieving objects after creating them and returning the pointers to the created objects.

The `Archiver` class takes care of the finer aspects of serialization described earlier. It appropriately calls the read despatcher `archiveGet` during reading and `archivePut` during writing, the functions being member functions of the class whose pointer is being read/written. The above two functions have typical structures as discussed later.

```
#define ARCHIVER_BASE_SIZE 1024
#define ARCHIVER_INCREMENT 1024

class Archiver {

    FILE    *file;
    Array   *tagTable;

public:

    Archiver(char *fName, int toRead=1)
        { file = fopen(fName, toRead ? "rt" : "wt");
        tagTable = new Array(ARCHIVER_BASE_SIZE, ARCHIVER_INCREMENT);}

    ~Archiver();

    int     readInt(); // Reads an integer from file.
    void    writeInt(int i); Writes an integer to file
    float   readFloat(); // Reads a float from file.
    void    writeFloat(float f); Writes a float to file

        .    // For all scalar data types.
        .

    void    putToArchive(Object *o); // For storing objects.
    Object  *getFromArchive(); // For retrieving objects.
};
```

```
Archiver::~Archiver()
{
  delete tagTable;
  if (file) fclose(file);
  file = 0;
}

void Archiver::putToArchive(Object *o)
{
  for (int i=0; i<tagTable->size();i++) {
    if (tagTable[i] == o) { // Object 'o' already saved.
     fprintf(file,"%d\n",-i-1); // Save only negated tagged position and,
     fprintf(file,"%d\n",o->theCode()); // the code of class of 'o'.
     return;
     }
   }
// Saving 'o' for the first time.
  tagTable->add(o); // Tag the object.
  fprintf(file,"%d\n",tagTable->size()-1); // Save new tagged position and
  fprintf(file,"%d\n",o->theCode()); // the code of class of 'o'.
  o->archivePut(this); // Actually write the data.
}

Object *Archiver::getFromArchive()
{
  int tag, code;
  char buff[81];
  fgets(f,80,buff); sscanf(buff,"%d",tag);
  fgets(f,80,buff); sscanf(buff,"%d",code);
  if (tag<0) // Indicates that object already read.
    return tagTable[-tag-1];
// To initiate reading.
  Object *o = NULL;
  ICP iConstructor = MetaClass::theICP(code);
  o = (*ICP)(); // Construct indirectly.
  o->archiveGet(this); // Actually read the data.
  return o;
}
```

Class specific facilities for serialization

Finally, we come to the additional implementations that must be carried out for every serializable class (for example, Class_X here, whose parent class is Parent_of_X) . We have already seen the nature of the constructor despatcher function. There must be an associated global construction of a MetaClass instance with Class_X as the parameter. This construction must be necessarily global so as to invoke the MetaClass constructor and hence register this class at start-up.

We can implement the theCode virtual member function of Class_X as shown below. The read and write despatcher functions call the corresponding despatcher functions of the parent class before invoking the actual read/write functions of Class_X. This saves the user from the botheration of knowing the individual data members of all the parents right upto Object. Observe that the implementation below is typical and ambiguous only in the names of the class in question and its parent class. A single macro (say registerClass) therefore suffices for the entire implementation. The only additional responsibility of the user is, therefore, to call this macro just after the class declaration and just before either implementation of any of its members, or before its use if there is no implementation. The best suggested location of the macro call is at the top of the .CPP file for a class, just after the inclusion directives. A call in the .h file itself may cause duplicate definition errors.

```
// Macro Definitions for macro.
// registerClass(Class_X, Parent_of_X)
// The definition is not entirely correct syntactically.
// Rather, it shows the expanded form.

Object *Class_X_FTAG() { return new Class_X; }

MetaClass Class_X_MCLASS(Class_X_FTAG); // Pre-start-up constructor call.

int    Class_X::theCode()
{
   return MetaClass::theCode(Class_X_FTAG);
}

void  Class_X::archiveGet(Archiver *a)
{
   Parent_of_X::archiveGet(a);
   archiveRead(a);
}

void class_X::archivePut(Archiver *a)
{
   Parent_of_X::archivePut(a);
   archiveWrite(a);
}

// Macro End
```

Some example classes and their archiving functions

Let us take some examples of actual classes and show the implementations for their archiving functions.

First, we consider the Triangle hierarchy taken up in Chapter 2. However, now the Triangle class is considered to be inherited from Object, i.e. class Triangle : public Object {... }. Similarly, the Point class is also inherited from Object.

```
void Point::archiveWrite( Archiver *a )
{
   a->writeFloat(xCoord);
   a->writeFloat(yCoord);
}
```

```
void Point::archiveRead(Archiver *a )
{
  xCoord = a->readFloat();
  yCoord = a->readFloat();
}

void Triangle::archiveWrite( Archiver *a )
{
  for (int i=0;i<3;i++) vertices[i].archiveWrite(a);
    // Save only the three points.
}

void Triangle::archiveRead(Archiver *a )
{
  for (int i=0;i<3;i++) vertices[i].archiveRead(a);
    // Retrieve the three points.
}

void TriangularLamina::archiveWrite( Archiver *a )
{
  a->writeInt(materialCode);
    // Save only materialCode.
}

void TriangularLamina::archiveRead(Archiver *a )
{
  materialCode = a->readInt();
    // Retrieve only materialCode.
}

void TriangularFrame::archiveWrite( Archiver *a )
{
  // Do nothing !!!
}

void TriangularLamina::archiveRead(Archiver *a )
{
 // Do nothing !!!
}

void HoledTriangularLamina::archiveWrite( Archiver *a )
{
  holePosition.archiveWrite(a);
  a->writeFloat(holeDiameter);
    // Save only hole data.
}

void HoledTriangularLamina::archiveRead(Archiver *a )
{
  holePosition.archiveRead(a);
  holeDiameter = a->readFloat();
    // Retrieve only hole data.
}
```

The List container class and its archiving functions

We choose the List container for the next example. List, being a derived class of Object, can be archived all the same.

```
void List::archiveWrite( Archiver *a )
{
  ListElement *l = head;
  while (l) {
    a->putToArchiveWrite(l->data); // Save data of current node,
    l = l->next; // and proceed forward.
  }
}

void List::archiveRead(Archiver *a )
{
  ListElement *l, *prevL;
  int toRead = itemsInContainer;

  // itemsInContainer already read all the way up at
  // Container::archiveRead.

  head = NULL; // Assume empty list at the outset.

  if (!toRead) return; // Nothing to read.

// Since ListElement is not derived from object, it must be created
// and attached directly.
  l = new ListElement;
  l->next = NULL;
  l->data = a->getFromArchive();
  head = l; // Reading the first node.
  --toRead;
  prevL = l;

  while (toRead) { // Till the end of the list.
    l = new ListElement;
    l->next = NULL;
    l->data = a->getFromArchive();
    prevL->next = l; // Reading the next node.
    --toRead;
    prevL = l;
  }
}
```

A final note

A final note on the `Archiver` class implementation may be in order. One may observe that every time `putToArchive` is invoked, it first searches `table` to find whether the object to be archived is already there. In the above example of implementation, we have chosen `table` to be an `Array`. This compels us to perform a linear search of the table. In a practical environment, where there may be thousands of objects to be saved, this fact can lead to perceptible performance degradation. A better alternative is to make `table` a `HashTable`.

PROBLEMS

A. Container Implementation

1. Implement the Stack container using the universal linked list FDS.

2. Similarly, implement the Queue container using a universal linked list. Do you think the same method for entering (pushing) and removing (popping) as with the implementation of Stack in the above problem can be applied here?

3. A Matrix is a two-dimensional linear container where the maximum sizes in either dimensions must be mentioned at construction time. The container has an addAt functionality, but takes two, rather than one integral parameters indicating the position in the matrix of the data to add. The usual add container function appends the data at the end of the last added item, considering the contents of the matrix in a 'row-major' fashion. Implement Matrix using universal two-dimensional vectors.

4. Try to implement a Matrix container using universal multiply linked list.

5. Introduce 'addition' and 'multiplication' functionalities of matrices in the Matrix class implemented above. Finally, introduce the functionality of 'inversion' of a matrix.

6. Try to implement the delinking functionalities of the balanced binary tree FDS and the BinaryTree container.

7. Implement the BinaryTree container using universal vectors.

    Hint: A clean way of mapping a binary tree on to a vector is as follows. Assume that the root is at level 1, and all children of all nodes at level k are at level $k+1$. Thus, there are 2^{k-1} nodes at the k-th level. Let the vector index begin from 0. Then, the 2^{k-1} nodes at the level k occupy *fixed* indices 2^{k-1}, $2^{k-1}+1$, ..., 2^k-1. Thus, the root is at index 1, the level 2 nodes at indices 2 and 3, level 3 nodes at indices 4 through 7, etc. Index 0 is unoccupied.

8. A PriorityQueue is a sequence container class with functionalities identical to that of a Queue but with different behaviour. First, the objects entered into a priority queue must be sortable. Secondly, during entering, the new entrant gets 'priority', i.e. it is positioned 'ahead' of all other objects in the queue that are lessThan it. Thus, for the data object that comes out of the queue first, there is no other object in the queue which is greaterThan it. Clearly, a reorganization of the queue is necessary for every entry and exit. Implement a PriorityQueue using a universal vector as the FDS.

10. Next, implement the `PriorityQueue` using the linked binary tree. Incidentally, if you are able to properly solve this problem, you would have implemented a new FDS called the *heap*, which is a special type of linked binary tree.

B. Container Usage

1. Consider the `Triangle` objects taken up in an earlier chapter. Use a `List` container to store `Triangles`. You must ensure that the objects entered into your container are indeed `Triangles`.

2. Try to store `Triangle` in a `BinaryTree`, where the area of the triangle acts as the sorting criterion. Make all necessary changes in the declaration and implementations of the `Triangle` class for this purpose.

3. Consider the class `SortablePoint`, a derived class of the `SortableObject` class. It has a member `thePoint` of the `Point` class described in an earlier chapter. There is an additional member data `sortCriterion` in the `SortablePoint` class which, when 0, sets the sorting criterion to the *y*-coordinate and when non-zero, to the *x*-coordinate. Instances of this class are to be stored in a container that is a `BinaryTree` whose 'contents' are again `BinaryTrees`. The latter trees contain `SortablePoints` of equal *x*-coordinates and are themselves sorted on *y*-coordinates. The outer tree considers the *x*-coordinates of the points stored in the embedded trees as the sorting criterion.

4. Construct the enumerator for the above container in line with `HashTableIterator`.

5. Declare the `Polygon` class as a `List` container of `Points`. Store `Polygons` in a `SortedArray`, where the sorting criterion is the area of the polygons.

6. A class `PolyItem` has an `unsigned int` member degree and a `float` member multiplier, representing the term multiplier * x ** degree (where ** indicates raising to power) in a polynomial of one variable. Choose an appropriate container for storing polynomials. Your container must be augmented to `makeComplete` the polynomial, i.e., insert missing terms with zero multipliers, upto some highestDegree.

7. Declare global functions for adding and multiplying polynomials.

5

Object-Oriented Graphical Users' Interface Programming

With the rapid proliferation of GUI platforms, an increasing number of applications are being ported to GUI environments and almost every new application is being developed under GUIs. Historically, most GUIs that are currently well-known, were developed before C++ gained its present popularity. As a result, application development interfaces for these GUIs were provided through a non-OOPL, usually, C.

Nevertheless, the design principles of most currently available GUIs are very much object-oriented. Even the application development interfaces display a strong object-oriented spirit. Microsoft Windows (MS-Windows, or simply Windows[1]) happens to be one of the most popular GUIs in the personal system range. The traditional Windows application development system, the Software Development Kit (SDK), provides a C language based Application Programming Interface (API).

As more and more C++ compilers, including one from Microsoft, became popular and 'Windows capable', the compiler vendors themselves, and sometimes third party suppliers, came up with different object-based Windows libraries. For example, Microsoft supplies the Microsoft Foundation Classes (MFC), a major part of which is an object-based Windows library, as an integral part of their Visual C++ package. Similarly, Borland supplies OWL (Object Windows Library) with the Borland C++ package. The authors have also worked with two third party libraries—CNS++ Views and Zapp.

Along with the libraries, mostly those supplied by the compiler vendors, come several 'visual' tools for automating different stages of application development. With these tools, Windows application development has, apparently, become quite 'easy'. However, while interacting with new and less experienced programmers willing to graduate into Windows programming, we have discovered a communication gap between the programmers' insight (read object-orientedness) and the tools' capabilities. This gap is a result of lack of understanding of the principles upon which the tools themselves have been designed. As a result,

---

[1] Currently (1997), Windows-95 and Windows-NT are the most popular GUIs from Microsoft. However, in this text, discussions are based on Windows 3.1.

somewhere down the line, the programmer fails to identify proper tools, and use the available tools to their full potential.

This chapter is intended to give a broad insight into the whys and hows of an object-based Windows library. We reiterate that the chapter is *not* intended to either speak of a particular commercially available library or development of yet another library. The codes given as examples must be treated exactly as that—examples. They are not meant to be compiled into the readers' own library. Indeed, we warn that such an attempt would most probably fail.

This chapter should also *not* be the first one to be read by a programmer wishing to graduate in Windows programming from (let us say) DOS programming. We suggest a prior reading of some of the following literature— *Windows SDK programmer's reference,*[2] excellently written books on SDK programming, Windows 3.x help files, on-line or off-line (printed) books on development platforms like MS-Visual C++, and Borland C++. While reading this chapter, the spirit should be to understand the basic principles of Windows library design from an object-oriented standpoint with the idea of getting to know a commercial library in a better and fruitful manner.

A GENERAL INTRODUCTION TO GUIs

In the last few years, there has been a marked change in the concept of user interface of application programs, especially those running on personal computers. As computers became more equipped with graphics capabilities, an increasing number of software applications started providing users with visually descriptive interfaces that are standardized upto an extent. The standardization aspect is directed towards making application interfaces more or less similar in look and feel, at least for those applications running on a particular type of platform. This way, users switching to a new application (or a newer version of an older one) need not be retrained with its interface. Graphical Users' Interfaces (GUIs) are operating environments that make this possible with less effort on part of the application programmer.

Currently, GUIs of different types are available for varied hardware platforms. Some of them, for example MS-Windows-95, and Macintosh OS, are full-fledged operating systems, complete with file management capabilities. Some others like MS-Windows 3.x, and the X window system, are application shells that provide GUI capabilities while running under a host OS. Almost all of them provide multi-tasking capabilities that may or may not be pre-emptive (as against co-operative), but only a few of them, like the X window system, offer true multi-user capabilities. In spite of the dissimilarities, most GUIs have some common characteristics.

Some Features Common to Most GUIs

The most important commonality among GUIs is that almost all of them are

---

[2] *SDK Programmer's Reference, Microsoft Windows 3.1*, Vol. 1–4, Microsoft Corp. (Also available with Books Online of Microsoft Visual C++ Ver-1.5.2).

event-driven. The essence of the event-driven nature is that unlike the conventional *command-driven* environments, an application is relieved of the burden of tracking primary user interaction devices like the keyboard and the mouse. The GUI environment takes the tracking duty upon itself through a background process running endlessly. An intercepted user interaction is despatched as a *message* to an appropriate foreground application. This means that an application running under a GUI must have one or more entry points that the operating environment *calls back,* and the code at these entry points receives appropriate messages passed as parameters. Application development platforms permit declaration of these entry points as functions whose reference must be made known to the operating environment at appropriate points.

Another important commonality among GUIs lies in the manner in which they handle the (primary) display. Most GUIs have the concept of a *window*— a well demarcated rectangular region of the screen through which an application presents its output, or part thereof, to the user. The power of GUIs comes from the fact that they are capable of managing several such windows (some of which may even be hidden) from several applications that are *open* at a time. An application may have a number of open windows. Each time a new window needs to be opened by an application, it sends an appropriate window opening command to the GUI kernel indicating, nominally, the window's size, position, *style*, etc. The kernel on its part, does the necessary housekeeping for adding the new window to its list of opened windows, and sends a recognizing reference to the window, called a *handle,* back to the application as a return value of the window opening command. Any further communication between the application owning the window and the GUI kernel refers to the handle of the window as its identifier.

As mentioned above, at any point of time, a number of windows from several applications may be open, and most of them are expected to be visible on the display, wholly, partially or eclipsed behind other windows. Of all visible windows on the screen, at most one window can have *focus*. The kernel despatches all (normal) user interactions to the application owning the window with focus, and sends the handle of the window as one of the call back parameters. A window in a GUI environment plays the dual role of a zone for displaying (partial) output and a user event handler. In fact, the latter role is logically extended such that *all* messages dispatched by the GUI kernel are targeted at *some* window of some application, and individual applications or even different portions of the same application can communicate with each other through user defined messages targeted at appropriate windows. The above described method is the prescribed style for interprocess and intraprocess communication, and a good GUI programmer is expected to have a clear understanding of the mechanism.

Most GUIs also provide further capabilities in the form of specially designed windows dedicated to performing certain special tasks. Over the years, some of these special user interface objects have become virtually standardized in the sense that the look and feel of such objects are similar across most GUIs. Examples of such objects are scroll bars, menus of different types (pop-up, pull-down, etc.), list boxes, message boxes, edit boxes, various combinations of the last three and dialog boxes. In addition, most GUIs provide device-independent facilities for drawing different types of geometric entities and regions as well as texts of different fonts.

With such facilities provided by most GUIs, the application development platforms provided with most of them can easily be viewed as a reasonably complex object-oriented system. A study of such a system under the OOP paradigm would provide the reader with a realistic case-study of object-oriented programming. In this chapter, we discuss an object-oriented formulation of the MS-Windows 3.1 (or above) application development system. It is assumed that the reader has a general understanding of application development using the MS-Windows Software Development Kit (SDK), which offers a C language based, and hence, not a significantly object-oriented development platform.

A General Introduction to MS-Windows

The MS-Windows 3.x GUI is not a full-fledged OS, but works as a shell over the well-known DOS operating systems whose file management system it relies upon completely. Working in a personal computing environment, MS-Windows is a console-based, single-user GUI that supports *co-operative multi-tasking*. The meaning of the latter term is that the kernel of MS-Windows (henceforth to be called Windows—note the 'W' in capital and the pluralizing 's') does not pre-empt a running task. This means that a well-behaved Windows program must periodically relinquish control to the kernel so that the latter can do its housekeeping, particularly, keep track of user interactions.

The Windows SDK provides the function `GetMessage` for this purpose. When an application issues a call to `GetMessage`, CPU control is relinquished to the Windows kernel at a point where it maintains a log of all incoming messages. Some of the messages result out of direct user interaction, for example, the user depressing a mouse button. Some others may have been *posted* by running applications. A significant number of messages are generated by Windows itself. One important Windows generated message is `WM_PAINT` and is directed at a window. This message acts as an indication to the application maintaining the window that Windows has reasons to believe that some visible portions of the window no longer displays valid data.

When Windows detects a despatchable message in its log (called message queue), it picks the most appropriate one and returns from the `GetMessage` call of the application which owns the window for which the message is directed. The application receiving control need not be the one that issued the latest `GetMessage` call.

The `GetMessage` function

The `GetMessage` function is associated with four pointer type parameters, the first of which points to a local `MSG` (for messages) data structure that the Windows kernel fills up before returning from the call. The return value of the function is zero if there is no message, but instead, the application must terminate its execution.

Entry points of a typical windows program

A typical Windows program has at least two entry points. The first and the essential entry point is the function WinMain. This is the one that assigned control by the run-time loader. Apart from performing some initial housekeeping duties that includes setting up of the main window of the application, the WinMain function is expected to notify to Windows, among other things, a second entry point which contains the main message handling functionalities and is usually (but not mandatorily) called WndProc.

There are two associated functions, namely, TranslateMessage and DispatchMessage, to GetMessage. Both take a pointer to an MSG structure as the only parameter. The former translates the message received from GetMessage into a uniform representation. The latter, i.e. DispatchMessage Windows function requests Windows to invoke the message handling entry point (WndProc) of the application with appropriate parameters.

The Window Procedure

The message handling entry point, also known as the window procedure (WndProc in our case), of a program running under Windows, is a call back function with four parameters. The first parameter is the handle of the window for which the message is directed. The second parameter identifies the message. The remaining two parameters represent message specific data.

A typical non-object-oriented implementation of the message handler consists of a switch statement taking care of the relevant messages in individual case blocks. Each such block returns from the function with a zero value, thereby indicating to Windows that the message has been handled. Unhandled messages are delegated back to Windows by calling the API function DefWindowProc.

The window procedure of a sufficiently complex program is, therefore, expected to handle a large number of messages. Many disciplined programmers incorporate an amount of procedural abstraction in this aspect. The essence of this abstraction is to provide handlers for individual (or, sometimes, a small set of) messages handled as separate functions. An additional data structure containing a handled message and a pointer to the handler of the message per entry, is also maintained. The actual window procedure searches for the received message in the above data structure that is usually known as the 'message map'. If found, the corresponding handler function is invoked. A simplistic example of the above scheme is given below:

```
typedef LONG (* MESSAGE_HANDLER)(HWND, UINT, WPARAM, LPARAM);
/* The prototype function handler pointer. The second function
   parameter is the handled message. It is passed just in case
   the handler needs to know the actual message, for example,
   where a single handler handles multiple messages.
*/

typedef struct {
    UINT              message;
    MESSAGE_HANDLER   handler;
} MAPITEM;
```

```
/* Prototypes of some actual handlers below */
LONG paintHandler(HWND, UINT, WPARAM, LPARAM);
LONG destroyHandler(HWND, UINT, WPARAM, LPARAM);
LONG createHandler(HWND, UINT, WPARAM, LPARAM);
LONG mouseMoveHandler(HWND, UINT, WPARAM, LPARAM);

/* The Message Map declared below as a global vector */
MAPITEM         messageMap[] = {
 { WM_PAINT,       paintHandler },
 { WM_DESTROY,     destroyHandler },
 { WM_CREATE,      createHandler },
 { WM_MOUSEMOVE,   mouseMoveHandler }
};

LONG FAR PASCAL WndProc(HWND hWnd, UINT mess,
                        WPARAM wParam, LPARAM lParam)
{
  int i;

  for (i=0; i< sizeof(messageMap) / sizeof(MAPITEM); i++)
    if (mess == messageMap[i].message) /* Message searched */
      /* and dispatched to handler */
      return (*messageMap[i].handler)(hWnd, mess, wParam, lParam);
  /* Message not handled */
  return DefWindowProc(hWnd, mess, wParam, lParam);
}
```

Latent object-orientation in the message mapping concept

Although the above code fragment is not object-oriented in the strict sense, it does incorporate some OOP principles.

The window procedure body is reusable across application in the source code form. Adding (and/or removing) a general purpose handler of some message can be incorporated in a disciplined manner—the message handler must be a function whose prototype matches MESSAGE_HANDLER, and a new entry in the messageMap vector must link the handled message with the function.

One obvious reason why the above code fragment is not strictly object-oriented, is that any change in the declaration of messageMap must be followed by a recompilation of the WndProc function. Nevertheless, the concept has its merits and has been used with suitable extensions in some popular object-oriented Windows libraries, as we shall see later.

There is one more lacuna in the above scheme—it makes an implicit assumption that either there is only one type of window handled by the window procedure, or that alternate behaviours for different windows of an application for the same message are routed to different parts of the code in the message handler. One must remember that most practical Windows applications use multiple windows, which differ considerably from each other in the manner in which they handle certain messages. Such applications must therefore direct control in a message handler to relevant portions of the code. There are traditional ways of solving the problem, but they are quite inelegant and do not offer as much code sharing as the object-oriented approach described below.

WINDOW CLASS LIBRARY BASED ON MESSAGE MAPS

The basis of the object-orientedness of the approach discussed in the last section is to associate the scalar window handle with a class. This class—let us call it the `BaseWindow` class—heads a hierarchy of what we shall refer to as the window object class. We shall take up the other members of the `BaseWindow` class later on in this chapter. For now, we assume that the `BaseWindow` class has a single data member `handle` (say) of type `HWND`. There must be a global 'typecasting' function to convert a `HWND` data to a (pointer to a) `BaseWindow` class instance.

An observant reader may have guessed the solution which is as follows:

1. Each window class, starting from the topmost BaseWindow class, maintains a static message map structure for the class.

2. This structure need be maintained for a particular window class only if it is designed to handle one or more new messages and/or provide new behaviour(s) for handler(s) for one or more messages handled by the parent window class.

3. The message map is a static member because it is a property of the class as a whole and not of individual instances of the class. In other words, all instances of a particular window class share a common message map structure.

4. A virtual member function (say, `handleMessage()`) is maintained by all the window classes from BaseWindow downwards to particularly direct those messages meant for the window to relevant message-handling member functions.

5. Two primitive member functions of `BaseWindow` class (called `createWindow()` and `destroyWindow()`) maintain getting and ungetting of the handle for the particular window instance. These two functions ensure that the handle for the instance is properly associated with (a pointer to) the instance in a *global* association List (called `GLOBAL_WindowTable`, say).

6. The global window procedure (called `GLOBAL_WindowProc()`, say) checks the handle of the window to which the message is directed against handles stored in `GLOBAL_WindowTable` and invokes the `handleMessage()` function of the window instance associated with the handle.

An Early Declaration of the BaseWindow Class

Let us try to understand the above scheme through a few actual declarations and (partial) implementations. We begin by declaring the `BaseWindow` class.

For the sake of simplicity, we assume that this class handles only one message—WM_XXXX.

```
// Pre-declaration of some global functions follow.

void GLOBAL_ConstructWindow(BaseWindow *w);
void GLOBAL_DestructWindow(BaseWindow *w);
LONG PASCAL GLOBAL_WindowProc(HWND, UINT, WPARAM, LPARAM);

// Declaration of class BaseWindow.

class  BaseWindow : public Object { // To be containable.
protected:

    HWND                    handle;
    BaseWindow              *parent;
    WNDCLASS                *wClass;
    char                    title[81];
    .
    .
    // Other relevant data declared above.

public:

    void showWindow();
    void updateWindow();

    BaseWindow() { // A NULL protected constructor used by dialog boxes.
        parent = NULL; wClass = NULL; title[0] = 0;

    virtual void createWindow() {
        if ( (handle = ::CreateWindow(wClass->lpszClassName,
                                      title, ....)) {
            GLOBAL_ConstructWindow(this);
            showWindow();
            updateWindow();
        }

    virtual void destroyWindow() {
        GLOBAL_destructWindow(this);
        ::DestroyWindow(handle);
    }

    void setInstance(HANDLE h) { wClass->hInstance = h; }

friend class Application; // See later.

public:

    BaseWindow *windowHandle() { return handle; }
    BaseWindow *windowParent() { return parent; }

    BaseWindow( BaseWindow *pWindow,
                LPCSTR *name = NULL,
                WNDCLASS *class = NULL) {
        parent = pWindow;
```

```
        if (name) strcpy(title, name); else strcpy(title, "No Name");
        // Other housekeeping jobs above.
        wClass = class ? class : &GLOBAL_BaseWindowClass;
        // Additional housekeeping jobs below.
    }

    LONG onlyMessageHandler(UINT, WPARAM, LPARAM);
        // Consider only one message handler for the BaseWindow class,
        // handling only message WM_XXXX (say).
```

```
// THE DECLARATION AND CODE FROM HERE TILL THE COMMENT LINE WITH
// *s ONLY
// CAN BE EASILY GENERATED BY MACROs. THE PREFIX "Base" HAS BEEN
// APPENDED TO THE LEFT OR TO THE RIGHT OF CLASS SPECIFIC DECLARATIONS.
```

```
// Declarations upto function handleMessage can be expanded by a MACRO,
// say, DECLARE_MESSAGE.
```

```
// Declarations required to describe the message handler for
// BaseWindow.
```

```
typedef LONG (BaseWindow::*Base_WINDOW_MESSAGE_HANDLER)
            (UINT, WPARAM, LPARAM);
```

```
// Declarations for the window message map entry for
// BaseWindow.
```

```
typedef struct {
    UINT                       message;
    Base_WINDOW_MESSAGE_HANDLER   handler;
} Base_WINDOWMAPITEM;
```

```
// The message map, initialized later for
// BaseWindow.
```

```
    static Base_WINDOWMAPITEM   handlerFunctions_Base[];
```

```
// Dispatcher of messages for this window only, for
// BaseWindow.
```

```
    virtual LONG handleMessage(UINT, WPARAM, LPARAM);
```

```
// Declaration upto this is expanded by MACRO DECLARE_MESSAGE, indicating
// willingness to handle at least one new message or handle at least one
// message differently from the parent window class.
```

```
// So, the closing brace is NOT expanded by any MACRO.
;
```

```
// One MACRO, say, DEFINE_MESSAGE, can expand to initialization of message.
// Map entries upto the opening brace.
```

```
// Initialization of message map entries for
// BaseWindow.
```

```
static Base_WINDOWMAPITEM    handlerFunctions_Base[] = {

// One line each can be added by a MACRO, say, ADD_MESSAGE, for every message
// to be handled.

  { WM_XXXX, onlyMessageHandler }

// The closing brace of the message map initialization and the message
// despatcher following it can be expanded by another MACRO, say, END_MESSAGE
};

// Implementation of message dispatcher for
// BaseWindow.

LONG BaseWindow::handleMessage(UINT m, WPARAM w, LPARAM l)
{
  for ( int i=0;
         i<sizeof(handlerFunctions_Base)/sizeof(Base_WINDOWMAPITEM); i++)
    if (handlerFunctions_Base[i].message ==m)
      return (handlerFunctions_Base[i].*handler)(m, w, l);
  return 0;
}
```

Definition of Global Data Structures and Functions

For the sake of completeness, we give below the definitions of the relevant
global data structures and functions used above.

```
// The declaration and code below is to maintain a Global Association
// of created windows. Function GLOBAL_WindowProc() Directs Message to
// relevant window.

struct GLOBAL_WindowListItem : public Object { // To make it associable
  HWND             handle;
  BaseWindow       *thisWindow;

    GLOBAL_WindowListItem(HWND h, BaseWindow *w)
      {handle = h; thisWindow = w; }
;

List             GLOBAL_WindowTable;

void GLOBAL_ConstructWindow(BaseWindow *w)
{
  GLOBAL_WindowTable.add(
            new GLOBAL_WindowListItem( w->windowHandle(), w));
}

void GLOBAL_DestructWindow(BaseWindow *w)
{
  ListIterator l(GLOBAL_WindowTable);

  while (!l.endReached()) {
    if ( ((GLOBAL_WindowListItem *)l.current()).thisWindow == w)
{
```

```
            GLOBAL_WindowTable.destroy((GLOBAL_WindowListItem*)l.current());
            return;
        }

    }

LONG PASCAL
    GLOBAL_WindowProc( HWND hWnd, UINT mess,
                        WPARAM wParam, LPARAM lParam)
{
    ListIterator l(GLOBAL_WindowTable);

    while (!l.endReached()) {
      if ( ((GLOBAL_WindowListItem *)l.current()).handle == hWnd) {
      // A window object for this handle has been found.
          return ((GLOBAL_WindowListItem*)l.current()).
                    thisWindow->handleMessage(mess,wParam,lParam);
      }
      return DefWindowProc(hWnd, mess, wParam, lParam);
}
```

A short discussion about the above two code fragments may be in order.

As has been commented in the first of these, a major part of the same would be repeated, with well-defined parametric variations depending only on the position of the window class in the class hierarchy, for window classes derived (ultimately) from BaseWindow. Indeed, this observation highlights partial object-orientedness of the approach. However, as would become more evident when compared with a purer object-oriented scheme, code-sharing in this scheme is not seamless.

An obvious non-object-oriented aspect is from the observation that a window class derived from BaseWindow cannot meaningfully inherit its message map (handlerFunctions_Base). The biggest advantage of the scheme is that at any level of the hierarchy of the window class, the class designer need only declare and implement handlers precisely and only for messages that have special significance to the class. It is for this reason, that two of the most popular C++ based Windows libraries (Borland's OWL and Microsoft's MFC) use the message map approach.

Declaration of Child Window Classes

To get a clearer idea of the approach, let us try to declare and partially implement a child window class to BaseWindow. This class handles two additional messages — WM_YYY1 and WM_YYY2 and is called DerivedWindowWithHandler. First, we provide the expanded code.

```
// The declarations and code below is for a window class derived from
// BaseWindow that handles two new messages.
```

```
class DerivedWindowWithHandler : public BaseWindow {
protected:
//   .
//   .
// Other member data/functions.
//

public:
//   .
//   .
// Other member data/functions including constructor.
//

   LONG newMessageHandler1(UINT, WPARAM, LPARAM);
   LONG newMessageHandler2(UINT, WPARAM, LPARAM);
// Consider two message handlers for the DerivedWindowWithHandler class,
// handling only message WM_YYY1 and WM_YYY2 (say).

// THE DECLARATION AND CODE FROM HERE TILL THE COMMENT LINE WITH *s ONLY
// HAS BEEN GENERATED BY MACROs.
// THE PREFIX "DWH" (for DerivedWithHandler) HAS BEEN APPENDED TO
// THE LEFT OR TO THE RIGHT OF CLASS SPECIFIC DECLARATIONS.

// DECLARE_MESSAGE expansion begins.

// Declarations required to describe the message handler for
// DerivedWindowWithHandler.

typedef
   LONG (DerivedWindowWithHandler::*DWH_WINDOW_MESSAGE_HANDLER)
       (UINT, WPARAM, LPARAM);

// Declarations for the window message map entry for
// DerivedWindowWithHandler.

typedef struct {
   UINT                       message;
   DWH_WINDOW_MESSAGE_HANDLER   handler;
} DWH_WINDOWMAPITEM;

// The message map, initialized later for
// DerivedWindowWithHandler.

   static DWH_WINDOWMAPITEM   handlerFunctions_DWH[];

// Dispatcher of messages for this window only, for
// DerivedWindowWithHandler.

   virtual LONG handleMessage(UINT, WPARAM, LPARAM);

// DECLARE_MESSAGE expansion ends.
;


// DEFINE_MESSAGE expansion begins.
```

```
// Initialization of message map entries for
// DerivedWindowWithHandler.

static DWH_WINDOWMAPITEM   handlerFunctions_DWH[] = {
//DEFINE_MESSAGE expansion ends.

// Each following line (except the final comma) expanded by
// ADD_MESSAGE.

  { WM_YYY1, newMessageHandler1 },
  { WM_YYY2, newMessageHandler2 }

// END_MESSAGE expansion begins.
};

// Implementation of message dispatcher for
// DerivedWindowWithHandler.

LONG DerivedWindowWithHandler::handleMessage(UINT m, WPARAM w, LPARAM l)
{
  for (int i=0;
     i<sizeof(handlerFunctions_DWH)/sizeof(DWH_WINDOWMAPITEM); i++)
    if (handlerFunctions_DWH[i].message ==m)
      return (handlerFunctions_DWH[i].*handler)(m, w, l);

// The message is not handled by this window. Perhaps the parent window
// **class** (NOTE: **NOT** parent window pointed by member "parent")
// handles it.

  return BaseWindow::handleMessage(m, w, l);
  // Since BaseWindow is the parent class of this window.
}

// END_MESSAGE expansion ends.

class DerivedWindowWithoutHandler : public BaseWindow {
protected:
//   .
//   .
// Other member data/functions.
//

public:

//   .
//   .
// Other member data/functions including constructor.
//

    // NO message handler for this class.
    // Handlers of parent window class assumed.
    // So, no declaration for the handleMessage function.
};
```

At the later part of the above code fragment, we have given the declaration for the class `DerivedWindowWithoutHandler`. This class does not introduce any new message handler or modify the handler of any message handled in the parent window class.

Macro Encoding of Code for `DerivedWindowWithHandler`

The code for `DerivedWindowWithHandler` can be much shortened using macros. The macro-encoded code is given below.

```
// The declarations and code below is for a window class derived from
// BaseWindow that handles two new messages.

class DerivedWindowWithHandler : public BaseWindow {
protected:
// /  .
//       .
// Other member data/functions.
//

public:

//       .
//       .
// Other member data/functions including constructor.
//

    LONG newMessageHandler1(UINT, WPARAM, LPARAM);
    LONG newMessageHandler2(UINT, WPARAM, LPARAM);
    // Consider two message handlers for the
    // DerivedWindowWithHandler class,
    // handling only message WM_YYY1 and WM_YYY2 (say).

    DECLARE_MESSAGE(DerivedWindowWithHandler)
};

DEFINE_MESSAGE(DerivedWindowWithHandler, BaseWindow)
    ADD_MESSAGE(WM_YYY1, newMessageHandler1),
// Note the comma at the end,
    ADD_MESSAGE(WM_YYY2, newMessageHandler2)
// and the absence of comma after the last one.
END_MESSAGE(DerivedWindowWithHandler)
```

We are sure that the reader would not fail to appreciate the finesse evident in the above code.

WINDOW CLASS LIBRARY BASED ON VIRTUAL FUNCTIONS

Could there be a 'purer' object-oriented approach for designing a window class library? It is not difficult for one with a reasonable grasp of the discussions in the earlier chapters to guess the answer: Declare a common super class to all possible window object classes and declare an appropriate number of `virtual` message handling functions in this class.

The Two Extremes of the Approach

At one extreme, there may be only one such polymorphic message handling function. The scheme is naive because if an inherited window class is required to modify the behaviour of the parent class only for a small subset of messages, the message handler for the inherited class must take care to filter out other messages and invoke the parent's message handler explicitly. Additionally, if the derived window class behaviour for a particular message requires only some extensions over the parent's behaviour for the message, it must re-implement the portion of the parent's code for the message. This clearly violates our principle of code sharing.

The scheme on the other extreme is to provide individual virtual functions for *all* messages envisaged to be handled by any descendant window class. While this approach is perhaps the purest from an object-oriented point of view, it is naive in a different way. A pragmatic scheme is to provide virtual functions for handling an appropriate subset of messages only, the choice of the subset being based on a judicious balance between the two extremes discussed above, and with an idea of the nature of applications envisaged to be created with the designed class library. As a matter of fact, most practical commercially available libraries choose an approach which is a mixture of the two approaches.

Some Common Messages Handled Better through Virtual Functions

We now enumerate some common messages that (in our opinion) are better handled through virtual functions:

- Mouse and virtual key notification messages—`WM_LBUTTONDOWN`, `WM_RBUTTONDOWN`, `WM_LBUTTONDBLCLK`, `WM_KEYDOWN`, etc.
- The `WM_PAINT` message.
- Resizing, hiding, etc., message.

To justify this position, let us consider the `WM_LBUTTONDOWN` message as an example.

The `WM_LBUTTONDOWN` message is sent by Windows to the window procedure of a window when the user has pressed the left mouse button somewhere within the client area of the window. The `wParam` parameter encodes the status of all the three buttons of the mouse as well as the special keys `SHIFT` and `CONTROL`. The parameter `lParam` encodes the position, i.e. the *x* and *y* co-ordinates of the mouse, at the time when the button press was detected.

Handling of mouse events like this one is such a fundamental aspect of windows programming, that it may be freely assumed that most window classes would provide their distinctive handler for the event and that any such handler would almost certainly need to decode out the co-ordinates and the key status of the mouse. One can therefore propose a handler for the WM_LBUTTONDOWN right at the BaseWindow level, and let this handler decode out the co-ordinates and the key status and finally call a virtual member function (say) leftMoseDown(int x, int y, unsigned int status). This ensures that the designer of a window class need not perform the repetitive task of decoding, but simply be concerned with overloading and re-implementing the leftMouseDown() function.

Another example could be the message WM_PAINT. Here again, most user designed window classes are expected to incorporate their own handlers for the message. Moreover, most of these handlers are expected to perform some 'device-independent graphics' within the handler. The key to device independence lies in the use of a Windows internal data structure called the 'device context'. A properly invoked BeginPaint() function returns a handle to a Windows internal device context. Care must be taken by the handler to release the device context by calling the ReleaseDC() function with the window and device handles as parameters. Again, the above two tasks are fairly routine and may be directly carried out within a handler. A virtual member function (say) paint() is invoked in between calls to BeginPaint() and ReleaseDC(). The device context handle, or better still, a device class built around the handle, is used as a parameter to the paint() function.

Virtual Message Handler Implementation Example

The handlers for the messages listed above may be implemented as a separate function or may be embedded in a switch statement within the main message handling function as shown below:

```
class DeviceContext {

protected:
    HDC          hDC;
    PAINTSTRUCT *ps;
    HWND         hWnd;
public:

    DeviceContext(HWND h)
    {
        hWnd = h;
        ps = new PAINTSTRUCT;
        hDC = BeginPaint(hWnd, ps);
    }

    ~DeviceContext() { EndPaint(hWnd, ps); delete ps; }

    friend class BaseWindow;
};
```

```
LONG BaseWindow::handleMessage(UINT m, WPARAM w, LPARAM l)
{
    .
    .
    .
    PaintDeviceContext *dc = 0;
    int r;
    .
    .
    .
    switch (m) {
        case WM_LBUTTONDOWN: return leftMouseDown(LOWORD(lParam),
                                        HIWORD(lParam), wParam);
        .
        .
        .
        // Other similar cases.

        case WM_PAINT:
            dc = new PaintDeviceContext(hWnd);
            r  = paint(dc);
            delete dc;
            return r;
        .
        .
        .
        // Other cases.
        .
        .
        .
    }
    for  (int i=0;
        i<sizeof(handlerFunctions_Base)/sizeof(Base_WINDOWMAPITEM); i++)
        if (handlerFunctions_Base[i].message ==m)
            return (handlerFunctions_Base[i].*handler)(m, w, l);
    return 0;
}
```

THE APPLICATION CLASS

As discussed earlier, every Windows application has a primary entry point
WinMain(). Most Windows applications perform some routine housekeeping
duties within this function before going into a 'message loop' headed by a
GetMessage() function call that yields control back to the Windows kernel.
In the code fragment below, we give the implementation of the WinMain()
function of a typical Windows application reproduced with small changes from
the manual *Guide to Programming* of the Software Development Kit (SDK)
for MS-Windows.

```
HANDLE     GLOBAL_hInst;

BOOL GLOBAL_InitApplication(HANDLE hInstance,
                      char *wClassName, char *menuName)
                                  /* current instance .      */
{
  WNDCLASS        wc;
/* Fill in window class structure with parametres that
   describe the main window.       */

  wc.style = NULL;                    /* Class style(s). */
  wc.lpfnWndProc = GLOBAL_WndProc    /* Function to retrieve messages
                                         for windows of this class. */
  wc.cbClsExtra = 0;                 /* No per-class extra data. */
  wc.cbWndExtra = 0;                 /* No per-window extra data. */

  wc.hInstance = hInstance;    /* Application that owns the class. */
  wc.hIcon = LoadIcon(NULL, IDI_APPLICATION);
  wc.hCursor = LoadCursor (NULL, IDC_ARROW);
  wc.hbrBackground = GetStockObject(WHITE_BRUSH);
  wc.lpszMenuName = menuName;    /* Name of menu resource in .RC file. */
  wc.lpszClassName = wClassName;/* Name used in call to CreateWindow. */

/* Register the window class and return success/failure code. */

  return (RegisterClass(&wc));
}


BOOL GLOBAL_InitInstance (HANDLE hInstance, int nCmdShow,
                       char *wClassName, char *title)

{
  HWND              hwnd;            /* Main window handle.   */

/* Save the instance handle in a global variable, to be used in  */
/* many subsequent calls from this application to windows.    */

  GLOBAL_hInst = hInstance;

/* Create a main window for this application instance.   */

  hWnd = CreateWindow(
        wClassName,               /* See RegisterClass () call.  */
        title,                    /* Text for window title bar.  */
        WS_OVERLAPPEDINDOW,       /* Window style.   */
        CW_USEDEFAULT,            /* Default horizontal position. */
        CW_USEDEFAULT,            /* Default vertical position.  */
        CW_USEDEFAULT,            /* Default width.   */
        CW_USEDEFAULT,            /* Default height.  */
        NULL,                     /* Overlapped windows have no parent. */
        NULL,                     /* Use the window class menu.   */
        hInstance,                /* This instance owns this window.  */
        NULL                      /* Pointer not needed.   */
    );
```

```
/* If window could not be created, return "failure".    */

    if (!hWnd) return (FALSE);
/* Make window visible, update its client area and return "success". */

    ShowWindow(hWnd, nCmdShow); /* Show the window.          */
    UpdateWindow(hWnd);          /* Sends WM_PAINT message. */
}

int PASCAL WinMain( HANDLE hInstance,        /* Current instance. */
                    HANDLE hPrevInstance,    /* Previous instance. */
                    LPSTR lpCmdLine,         /* Command line. */
                    int nCmdShow) /* show-window type (open/icon) */
{
    MSG msg;                    /* Message. */
    if (!hPrevInstance)        /* Other instances of application running? */
        if (!GLOBAL_InitApplication(hInstance))
/* initialize shared things */
            return FALSE;              /* Exits if unable to initialize. */

/* Perform initializations that apply to a specific instance. */

    if (!GLOBAL_InitInstance(hInstance, nCmdShow)) return FALSE;

/* Acquire and dispatch messages until a WM_QUIT message is received. */

    while (GetMessage(  &msg /* Message structure. */
                      NULL, /* Handle of window receiving the message. */
                      NULL,      /* Lowest message to examine. */
                      NULL)) {   /* Highest message to examine. */
        TranslateMessage(&msg);     /* Translates virtual key codes. */
        DispatchMessage(&msg);      /* Dispatches message to window. */
    }
    return (msg.wParam); /* Returns the value from PostQuitMessage. */
}
```

The above code fragment has been adequately commented upon and should be self-explanatory. What is quite clear is that almost the whole of the above code is same for every application, and therefore, easily encapsulated. The decision that remains to be taken is what should be the class that would carry the encapsulated code. Different object-based libraries for Windows treat this aspect differently. We shall discuss the most popular approach among them.

Looking at the code for the `WinMain()` function, one finds that there are three distinct parts—creation of the application, creation of the instance and the by now familiar, *message loop*. Out of these, the second part, i.e. the one involving a call to the function `GLOBAL_InitInstance()`, also creates the main window of the application. As the code stands, this window is a typical 'frame window' type registered in the `GLOBAL_InitApplication()` function.

A `FrameWindow` class is a derived class of `BaseWindow` except that its window class is `GLOBAL_FrameWindowClass`. Additionally, it ensures the availability of a main menu object (see later) which can, however, be empty. Most libraries, on the other hand, encapsulate the frame window with a vertical and a horizontal scroll bar and associate each of them to a `ScrollBar` control object. Similarly, many other functionalities associated with frame windows provided by most libraries have not been included in our class. Hence, the declaration of the `FrameWindow` class given below is by no means complete.

The `FrameWindow` Class—The Main Window of an Application

```
WNDCLASS GLOBAL_FrameWindowClass = {


};

class Menu; // Pre-declaration of a menu class. See later.

class FrameWindow: public BaseWindow {
protected:
  char *mainMenuName;

  void createWindow() {
    if ( (handle = ::CreateWindow(wClass->lpszClassName,
                          title, ....)) {
      GLOBAL_addWindow(handle, this);

      if (mainMenuName) { // Main menu to be loaded from resource
        windowMenu = new Menu(this, mainMenuName, GLOBAL_hInstance);
      }
      else { // Initialize an empty main menu.
        windowMenu = new Menu(this);
      }
      showWindow();
      updateWindow();
    }
  }

public:

  FrameWindow( BaseWindow *pWindow, LPCSTR *name = NULL,
               char *menuName = NULL)
      : BaseWindow(pWindow, name, GLOBAL_FrameWindowClass)
  {
    mainMenuName = NULL;
    if (menuName) { // Menu resource name mentioned.
      mainMenuName = new char [strlen(menuName) + 1; ];
      strcpy(mainMenuName, menuName);
    }

  };
```

Application Class Encapsulation

Most modern libraries introduce an `Application` class to encapsulate the common behaviour of most applications. The base `Application` class does precisely what the first two parts of the code for `WinMain` does, i.e. it initializes the application and the instance, respectively. The window class name, the menu resource name and the title can be member variables.

Some libraries offer a host of window classes implemented within the library or user extended versions of them, as possible candidate for the first of these variables, with a standard one selected by default. To provide the library user with the flexibility to add code after creation of the instance and before the message loop is begun, the constructor does not invoke the message loop directly. A special member function `runApplication()` must be invoked for this purpose.

Declaration and implementation of the `Application` class

Let us have a look at the declaration and partial implementation of the Application class.

```
int        GLOBAL_RunFlag = 0;
HANDLE     GLOBAL_hInstance, GLOBAL_hPrevInstance;
int        GLOBAL_nCmdShow;

int PASCAL WinMain( HANDLE hInstance,        /* Current instance. */
                    HANDLE hPrevInstance, /* Previous instance. */
                    LPSTR lpCmdLine,         /* Command line. */
                    int nCmdShow)    /* Show-window type (open/icon). */
{
    GLOBAL_hInstance = hInstance;            // Save the necessary
    GLOBAL_hPrevInstance = hPrevInstance;  // parameters in
    GLOBAL_nCmdShow = nCmdShow;              // global variables.

    // Invoke the user written entry point.
    return userWinMain(hInstance, hPrevInstance, lpCmdline, nCmdShow);
    // The user entry point function should create an instance of
    // Application class that would trigger initialization of the
    // application and instance. Invoking the runApplication() member of
    // the Application object would initiate the message loop.
}

int PASCAL GLOBAL_MessageLoop()
{
    MSG msg;

    while (GetMessage( &msg    /* Message structure. */
              NULL,    /* Handle of window receiving the message. */
              NULL,    /* Lowest message to examine. */
              NULL)) {       /* Highest message to examine. */
        TranslateMessage(&msg);  /* Translates virtual key codes. */
        DispatchMessage(&msg);   /* Dispatches message to window. */
    }
```

```
    return (msg.wParam);   /* Returns the value from PostQuitMessage. */
}

class Application {
protected:

  char         *className, *menuName, *appTitle;
  FrameWindow  *frame;

public:

    Application(FrameWindow *w = 0, char *mName = 0, char *title = 0);
    ~Application();

  virtual    void runApplication();

  FrameWindow *getMainWindow() { return frame; }

  void       setTitle(char *title);
  char       *getTitle() { return appTitle; }
  void       setMenu(char *mName);
  char       *getMenu() { return menuName; }

};

  Application::Application(FrameWindow *w, char *mName, char *title)
{
  frame = w ? w : new FrameWindow(this);
  frame->setTitle(appTitle);
  frame->setInstance(GLOBAL_hInstance);

  if (mName) {
    menuName = new char [strlen(mName) + 1];
    strcpy(menuName, mName);
  }
  else menuName = NULL;
  if (title) {
    appTitle = new char [strlen(title) + 1];
    strcpy(appTitle, title);
  }
  else {
    appTitle = new char [13];
    strcpy(appTitle, "Default Name");
  }

  // Initialization of application
  if (!GLOBAL_hPrevInstance) ::RegisterClass(frame->getClass());

  // Initialization of instance.
  frame->createWindow();
}

int Application::runApplication()
{
  return GLOBAL_MessageLoop();
}
```

The simplest user written program is therefore:

```
int     userWinMain( HANDLE hInstance,        /* current instance */
                     HANDLE hPrevInstance,    /* previous instance */
                     LPSTR lpCmdLine,         /* command line */
                     int nCmdShow)            /* show-window type
(open/icon) */
{
  Application a(new FrameWindow, NULL, "My Small Program");

  return a.runApplication();
}
```

which is appreciably more compact and precise than what needs to be written without the benefit of the library.

Associating Data with Application and Window

The simplest program listed above obviously does not do much in term of data storage and display. A more realistic program would have data stored internally, display it on windows and, possibly, interact with the user to augment the stored data and/or alter its values.

The next question to be answered, therefore, is where the data must be stored. There are several options for the same, the simplest being storing the data in global variables. To illustrate how this may be done, let us consider a small problem that we would code as a Windows program.

A small problem

The problem is to maintain a set of `Triangle` objects which have been read from a file (say 'triangle.dat') and list out their co-ordinates, one triangle per line, on the client area of the main window of the application. To do this, we may perform the following tasks:

1. Maintain a global container of triangles.
2. At start-up, load the triangle container from the archive triangle.dat.
3. Capture the WM_PAINT message targeted at the main window of our application to actually print the data.

Note that we have assumed that the object-based Windows library that we are using is based totally on event capturing through message maps.

Towards a solution

With knowledge gathered from Chapter 3, we may declare a global `List` container of triangles as:

```
List GLOBAL_TriangleList;
```

Of course, we need an archiver object to read the triangles.

```
Archiver GLOBAL_TriangleArchiver("TRIANGLE.DAT");
```

The next step, i.e. reading triangle data from the archive can be done by the following line of code in the `userWinMain()` before running the application:

```
GLOBAL_TriangleList.archiveGet(&GLOBAL_TriangleArchiver);
```

The Windows message `WM_PAINT` is sent to a window whenever some portion or whole of the windows client area has been 'invalidated'. This can happen when Windows detects that the invalidated portion of the window that was hitherto hidden behind other windows (or was iconized) has now become visible. The situation can also be simulated by program code to forcefully invalidate the whole or portion of a window. The accompanying `wParam` parameter with the `WM_PAINT` message encodes the invalidated portion. However, in our problem, we shall assume that every time the message is delivered, the whole window has been invalidated.

In our previous ('simplest') program, we chose a `FrameWindow` as the main window of our application. However, this window type is not designed to handle the `WM_PAINT` message as we would like it to be. We must, therefore, declare a new window class derived from `FrameWindow` and insert declarations and definitions in this class to achieve the desired behaviour.

```
class TriangleFrame : public FrameWindow {

public:

    TriangleFrame(BaseWindow *p = NULL) : FrameWindow(p) {}

  LONG myPaintHandler(UINT, WPARAM, LPARAM);

    DECLARE_MESSAGE(TriangleFrame);
};

DEFINE_MESSAGE(TriangleFrame, FrameWindow)
  ADD_MESSAGE(WM_PAINT, myPaintHandler)
END_MESSAGE(DerivedWindowWithHandler)

LONG TriangleFrame::myPaintHandler(UINT, WPARAM, LPARAM)
{
  ListIterator l(GLOBAL_TriangleList);

  while (!l.endReached()) {
    Triangle *t = (Triangle *)l.current();

    char line[81];
    sprintf(line, "(%6.2f,%6.2f), (%6.2f,%6.2f), (%6.2f,%6.2f)",
            t->vertex(0)->x(), t->vertex(0)->y(),
            t->vertex(1)->x(), t->vertex(1)->y(),
            t->vertex(2)->x(), t->vertex(2)->y());
    ..
  Code to output the next triangle's co-ordinates stored in 'line'
    ..
    ..
    l.next();
  }
}
```

Note that we have not put the actual code for writing text in the window here. We would like to defer this aspect of Windows programming till a later stage.

To complete the picture, the following is the code for the `userMain()` function, preceded by declarations of the global variables:

```
List     GLOBAL_TriangleList;
Archiver  GLOBAL_TriangleArchiver("TRIANGLE.DAT");

int      userWinMain( HANDLE hInstance,     /* Current instance. */
                      HANDLE hPrevInstance, /* Previous instance. */
                      LPSTR lpCmdLine,      /* Command line. */
                      int nCmdShow)         /* Show-window type.
(open/icon) */
{
  GLOBAL_TriangleList.archiveGet(&GLOBAL_TriangleArchiver);

  Application a(new TriangleFrame, NULL,
              "Small Program with Global Data");

  return a.runApplication();
}
```

Storing application data as `Application` class members

A better object-oriented approach for storing application data in global variables is to store them as member data of the application object itself. For this, one needs to derive a new application class from `Application` as follows:

```
class TriangleApp : public Application {

protected:

  List     triangleList;

friend class TriangleFrame;

public:

    TriangleApp(TriangleFrame *w, char *mName, char *title) :
      Application(w, mName, title)
    { triangleList.archiveGet(&GLOBAL_TriangleArchiver); }

};
```

The only change in the `TriangleFrame::myPaintHandler()` function would be in the first line, which must now be:

```
ListIterator l(((TriangleApp *)myApp)->triangleList);
```

Observe the typecast of `myApp` from `Application *` to `TriangleApp *` so as to access the data member `triangleList`.

The `userMain` program can be simplified even more to a single line:

```
return
   TriangleApp((myApp=new TriangleFrame),
              NULL,
              "Program with Member Data").runApplication();
```

We shall take up a still better object-oriented approach while discussing the 'document-view' program architecture.

Had we begun with the assumption that our library captures some essential messages like `WM_PAINT` and directs them to virtual functions/function `paint()` for the `WM_PAINT` message, we could do away with the declaration of the message map and the `myPaintHandler()` function and, instead, redeclare the virtual function `paint()` within the scope of the `TriangleFrame` window class and incorporate the code now included in `myPaintHandler()` in `TriangleFrame::paint()`.

MENUS, MENU RESOURCES AND MENU OBJECTS

Perhaps one of the most interesting aspects of programming with GUIs like MS-Windows is the ease with which menu-based user interfaces can be designed. Most GUIs support menus of different types—*Pull-down, Pop-up, Drop-down*, etc. There may be different levels of nesting among them.

Menus are considered so fundamental an aspect of GUI programming that most GUI development platforms (even the so called non-object oriented ones) provide mechanisms whereby menus can be declared outside the scope of the main code, to be compiled and bound to the run-time module as separate entities called *resources*.

Menus are just one form of a resource. Usually, GUI platforms permit declaration and use of many different types of resources. An inherent object-oriented concept is associated with resources in the sense that the programmer using a resource is almost totally relieved from the burden of understanding in detail how the particular resource works. In this section, we shall discuss how an object-based library shell around a typical GUI like Windows can further ease the programmer's job of using menus. Similar concepts for other resources shall be discussed later.

Resource Creation and Binding in a Windows Program

The use of externally declared resources and eventually binding them to a Windows application is done as follows:

- The resources are declared in text form in a simple but formal format is a *resource script* file—a text file usually with a .RC extension.

- The Windows development platform comes with a utility, RC.EXE, called the *resource compiler*. This utility can compile a resource script file to a resource file (with extension .RES) in a more efficient internal format of Windows.

- As a final step of application generation, the linked run-time module (a .EXE file) is further linked with a resource file by the same resource compiler. The resulting .EXE file is complete for running under Windows.

The Main Menu of an Application

Let us take the example of creating the 'main' menu of the main frame window of the application. The items of this menu are listed side by side on one (usually; sometimes more than one line may be required) line between the title bar and the client area of the window. Clicking the mouse on a menu item (or alternately, pressing the 'hot-key' combination Alt-K, where K is the underlined letter in a menu item) can lead to one of the following:

- Some aspect of the program related to the menu item would be executed. For example, it is a standard practice of most Windows programs to have a main menu item called About, clicking of which pops up a small window (called a Message Box) providing a brief information about the application.

- A rectangular box containing further menu items pops up just below the main menu item selected. The user may now select an item in the popped-up menu by clicking upon the line containing the item (or alternately, pressing the underlined 'hot-key' letter of the item), which might lead to either some program action or pop-up a further menu. Menu items may therefore be nested to a number of levels.

Declaration of a Menu Resource

The language for declaring a menu in the resource script file is quite simple. Let us introduce the language with an example.

The example application provides the user with a choice of software facilities. The main menu contains only two items—'Software' and 'Help'. Selecting the latter invokes a help screen, while selecting the 'Software' item pops up another menu that offers a choice of three types of software—word processors, spreadsheets and language compilers. Compilers are again provided for the languages C/C++, Basic and Pascal. As a number of compilers for C/C++ are available, selecting this item pops up a further menu naming the compilers. Actually, the C/C++ compilers come from two different manufacturers, a fact which is highlighted by separating them into two parts, with a delimiting horizontal line across the menu box. A resource script declaration for the menu is given below:

```
MyMainMenu BEGIN

   POPUP "&Software" BEGIN
    POPUP   "&Word Processing" BEGIN
      MENUITEM "MS-Word &2.0", IDM_WORD_2
      MENUITEN "MS-Word &6.0", IDM_WORD_6
    END
```

```
   POPUP "&Spreadsheets" BEGIN
     MENUITEM "MS-&Excel", IDM_EXCEL
     MENUITEM "Lotus &123", IDM_123
     MENUITEM "&Quattro", IDM_QUATTRO
   END

   POPUP "&Language" BEGIN
     POPUP "&C/C++" BEGIN
       MENUITEM "MS-C &7.0", IDM_MSC_7
       MENUITEM "&Visual C++", IDM_VCPP
       MENUITEM "&Quick C", IDM_QUICKC
       MENUITEM SEPARATOR
       MENUITEM "&Borland C++", IDM_BORLANDCPP
     END
     MENUITEM "&Basic", IDM_BASIC
     MENUITEM "&Pascal", IDM_PASCAL
   END
 END

 MENUITEM "&Help" ID_HELP
END
```

Several aspects of the language defining a menu are clear from the above example. The general form of declaring a menu is:

```
<Menu name> MENU BEGIN
   <Menu Items>
END
```

<Menu Name> is a name identifying the menu. A <Menu Item> can either be a leaf level item or another pop-up menu.

A pop-up menu has a similar format of declaration, except that it does not have any name, and the identifying keyword is Popup. A leaf level item is indicated by the keyword Menuitem, and can take upto four parameters—the first two of which are mandatory and important.

The first parameter of a menu item is the text to be displayed for the item. An ampersand in this text is displayed as an underline below the character following the ampersand which acts as the 'hot-key' for the item. The second parameter, a positive integral constant (or, as here, a previously #define-d symbol), is known as the menu-id. Every menu item in a menu generally has unique identifiers, which are sent as the wParam parameter of a WM_COMMAND message invocation of the window procedure of the window owning the menu.

Windows API Functions for Menu Creation

Windows also permits declaring entire menus from within the program, that is, menus may be created independently without declaring them in a resource file. Moreover, Windows permits adding items to or removing items from an existing menu created programmatically or through a menu resource. The Windows API functions relevant for creation, altering and use of menus are listed below:

- The `CreateWindow()` function takes a string parameter for the menu name. Windows binds the menu resource by that name to the created window. If this parameter is NULL during call, the menu resource of name entered in the field lpszMenuName of the window class structure parameter is loaded instead.

- The function `GetMenu(HWND)` returns the menu handle of the window whose handle is the only function parameter. Conversely, the function `SetMenu(HWND, HMENU)` sets the menu associated with the window indicated in the first parameter to the one whose handle is the second parameter.

- A menu can be loaded from the application's resources with the `LoadMenu()` function, providing the application's instance handle and the menu name as the parameters.

- Function `CreateMenu()` has no parameter and returns the handle to a newly created but empty menu.

- Functions `AppendMenu()`, `InsertMenu()`, `ModifyMenu()` and `DeleteMenu()` may be used to make changes in an existing menu.

Encapsulation of Menus

To provide an object-oriented shell for ease of menu usage, we propose the following:

- Declare a class `MenuItem` for a menu item that roughly corresponds to an item declared in the resource script by the `MENUITEM` keyword. This class encapsulates the menu identifier, a pointer to a function corresponding to the menu item, a status flag, etc.

- Declare a class `Menu` that encapsulates a menu handle and contains a variable-sized array of MenuItems. All Windows API menu functions are also encapsulated within this class.

- Within the `BaseWindow` class, introduce a Menu object for the menu associated with the window.

- The window procedure of the `BaseWindow` class would select the WM_COMMAND message and perform a newly introduced `scanMenu()` action.

- The `scanMenu()` function would match the menu identifier encoded in the wParam parameter of the window procedure, one by one against all menu items of the menu associated with the window. In case of a match, the function associated with this menu item is invoked. If no matching item is found in any of the menus, the newly introduced virtual function, viz. `defaultWMCommand()` function, is invoked.

- The Menu class maintains an Array of MenuItems called menuItemArray, that maintains all leaf level menu items of the menu. The

`BaseWindow::scanMenu()` function performs its matching operation on `menuItemArray` and invokes the menu function pointed to by the `menuFunction` member of the item. To dissociate the matching operation even further from the `BaseWindow` class, the matching operation is actually carried out by a member function `runMenuCommand()` of the class `Menu`.

- The Menu class may be constructed either from a resource or through a program. In the latter case, an empty menu is created at the beginning. In either case, further member functions are provided to add and/or alter menu items of the menu. If the menu is constructed from a resource, the relevant construction process ensures proper building up of menuItemArray through judicious use of Windows API functions `GetMenuItemCount()`, `GetMenuItemID()` and `GetSubMenu()`.

```
typedef LONG (BaseWindow::*MENUFUNCTION)(); // Type declaration for
menu function.

class Menu;

class MenuItem : public Object { // To allow a menu container.
protected:
    WORD          menuId;
    WORD          menuStatus;
    MENUFUNCTION menuFunction;
    Menu          *ownerMenu;

public:

    MenuItem( WORD id, BOOL enable, BOOL check,
              MENUFUNCTION function = 0, Menu *owner = 0)
    {
        menuId = id;
        menuStatus = (enable ? 1 : 0) | (check ? 2 : 0);
        menuFunction = function;
        setOwner(owner);
    }

    Menu *theOwner() { return ownerMenu; }
    void setFunction(MENUFUNCTION function) { menuFunction = function; }
    void adjustMenu() // To actually change the owner menu.
    {
        if (ownerMenu) {
            ownerMenu->enableItem(this, isEnabled() ? TRUE : FALSE);
            ownerMenu->checkItem(this, isChecked() ? TRUE : FALSE);
        }
    }

    void setOwner(Menu *owner)
    {
        if (ownerMenu = owner) ownerMenu->addMenuItem(this);
        adjustMenu();
    }
```

```
  BOOL isEnabled() { return menuStatus & 1; }
  BOOL isChecked() { return (menuStatus >> 1) &1; }
  void enableMenuItem(BOOL enable)
  {
    menuStatus &= 0xFFFE;
    menuStatus |= enable;
    adjustMenu();
  }

  void checkMenuItem(BOOL check)
  {
    menuStatus &= 0xFFFD;
    menuStatus |= check;
    adjustMenu();
  }

  void toggleCheck() { checkMenu Item( isChecked() ? FALSE : TRUE); }

friend class Menu;

};

class Menu {
protected:

  BaseWindow    *ownerWin;
  HMENU         menuHandle;
  Array         *menuItemArray;

  void init()
  {
    menuItemArray = new Array(5, 1);
   // Assuming initial size of 5 with increment 1.
  }

  int findItemPosition(MenuItem *m)
  {
    ArrayIterator a(menuItemArray);
    int i = 0;
    while (!a.endReached()) {
      if ( (MenuItem *)a.current() == m ) return i;
      i++; a.next();
    }
    return -1; //  Not found;
  }

  MenuItem *findItemById(WORD id)
  {
    ArrayIterator a(menuItemArray);
    while (!a.endReached()) {
      MenuItem *m = (MenuItem *)a.current();
      if ( m->menuId == id ) return m;
      a.next();
    }
    return NULL; //  Not found;
  }
```

```
    void loadMenu(HANDLE, char *);
    void adjustMenuArray(HMENU);

public:

    Menu(BaseWindow *w)
    { ownerWin = w; menuHandle = CreateMenu(); init();   }
// To create an empty menu.

    Menu( BaseWindow *w, char *menuName, HANDLE hInstance =
          GLOBAL_hInstance)
    // To create menu from a resource.
    {
        ownerWin = w;
        init();
        loadMenu(hInstance, menuName);
    }

    ~Menu() { if (menuItemArray) delete menuItemArray; }

  LONG runMenuCommand(WORD wParam)
  {
    MenuItem *m = findItemById(wParam);
    if (m) return  (ownerWin->*(m->menuFunction))();
    return FALSE;
  }
};

void Menu::loadMenu(HANDLE hInstance, char *menuName)
{
  menuHandle = LoadMenu(hInstance, menuName);
  if (menuHandle) adjustMenuArray(menuHandle);
  else menuHandle = CreateMenu();
}

void Menu::adjustMenuArray(HMENU hMenu)
{
  for (int i = 0; i < GetMenuItemCount(hMenu); i++) {
    switch ((UINT id = GetMenuItemID(hMenu, i))) {
    case -1: if (hMenu) adjustMenuArray(GetSubMenu(hMenu, i)): break;
                         // Pop-up, so make a call recursively.
      case  0: break; // Separator.
      default: menuItemArray->add(new MenuItem(id,
              GetMenuState(hMenu, id, MF_BYCOMMAND) & MF_ENABLED,
                                                   // Enabled?
              GetMenuState(hMenu, id, MF_BYCOMMAND) & MF_CHECKED,
                                                   // Checked?
              0, // No function set.
              ownerWin));
    }
  }
}
```

```
class BaseWindow {
    .
    .
    .

protected:
    Menu          *windowMenu;
    .
    .
    .
protected:
    virtual LONG scanMenu(WORD wParam)
      { return windowMenu ? windowMenu->runMenuCommand(wParam): FALSE; }

    virtual LONG defaultWMCommand(WORD, LONG) {}

    virtual LONG handleWMCommand(WORD wParam, LONG lParam)
    {
        if (scanMenu(wParam)) return TRUE;
        .
        .
        // Other WM_COMMAND actions.
        .
        .
        return defaultWMCommand(wParam, lParam);
    }
};

LONG BaseWindow::handleMessage(UINT m, WPARAM w, LPARAM l)
{
    .
    .
    .

    switch (m) {
    case WM_COMMAND: return handleWMCommand(LOWORD(wParam, lParam);
    .
    .
    }
    .
    .
}
```

CONTROL WINDOWS AND CONTROL CLASSES

Apart from menus, most GUIs provide with special purpose window-like entities that facilitate getting input from the user. In GUI parlance, these entities are usually referred to by a common term called *control*.

Some typical controls are buttons of various types (like push buttons, radio buttons, check boxes, etc.), edit boxes, list boxes, combo-boxes (a combination of the previous two), scroll bars, etc. Almost every user of any of the common GUIs are so familiar with the above entities that we assume that they need no further introduction.

In some aspects, a control entity (or control object) is similar to a menu in the sense that both generate reasonably pin-pointed user interaction messages for the underlying application. However, unlike menus, control objects are actually window objects in their own right and are therefore associated with all of the duties of a typical window. What makes them special as window objects is that most of their duties (for example, 'painting') are performed by the GUI kernel itself.

The reason why controls are so powerful for use as user interface objects is that one aspect of their duty as performed by the GUI kernel is to send directed messages to the underlying application. To understand this and other aspects of control objects, let us review the controls as provided with Windows.

Definition of a Control

A *control*, as defined in the Windows SDK manual, is a pre-defined child window that carries out a specific kind of input or output. The main point to be noted here is that a control is itself a window, i.e. it has an associated window class and a valid window handle. Additionally, a control is a child window of some other window, i.e. one must always specify a valid parent window while creating a control.

The built-in control classes provided in Windows are BUTTON, EDIT, LISTBOX, COMBOBOX, SCROLLBAR and STATIC.

Like normal windows, controls are created using the Windows API CreateWindow() function with the control class name supplied as the window class parameter of the function. Each control must be assigned a unique identifier—an unsigned integer that is supplied as the menu handle parameter to the creating function.

Unlike normal windows but more like menus, a control sends a notification message to the parent window, rather than to itself. A control notification by a control having identifier ID comes in the form of a WM_COMMAND message directed at the parent window where the wParam parameter has the value ID while the lParam parameter supplies further control-specific information.

A control may also be created within a *Dialog Box,* which is again a special type of window for user interaction, and is discussed in detail in a later section. Controls within a dialog box may be created even outside the program through appropriate resource scripts.

Encapsulation of an Abstract Control Class

To provide a class representation for controls, one can conceive of a common BaseControl class derived from class BaseWindow (because, as discussed, a control is also a window) and encapsulate the following behaviour:

- The control identifier, passed as one of the constructor parameters, is passed as the hMenu parameter in the call to the CreateWindow() function. Controls within a dialog box are, however, created automatically when the dialog box containing them are created. Hence, there must be a separate constructor for control objects that correspond to dialog box control items. Depending upon which constructor is used, a flag is maintained to indicate the type of the associated control object—a directly created control object or a dialog box item.

- A pointer to a member function of the parent window object that actually initiates program response corresponding to the control is also obtained as a parameter both the control's constructor. This parameter may be also be kept NULL, indicating that the intended handler is a member function of the control object itself rather than one of the parent windows.

As mentioned above, the parent window of a control which receives the control's notification through a WM_COMMAND message. The window class of the parent window must be able to re-direct the same to either its own handler member function responsible for the Control class or to the handler function within the control class itself as the case may be. An easy way to achieve this is to maintain a List (say) of Control objects in the parent window object and filter every WM_COMMAND message through this list. Since BaseWindow is the common base class for all window classes, the most appropriate place to incorporate the above behaviour is in BaseWindow. Let us consider some extensions and modifications in the BaseWindow class as a result of this.

Extensions in the BaseWindow class

```
typedef LONG (BaseWindow::*CONTROLFUNCTION)(WORD, LONG);
         // Type declaration for menu function.

class BaseDialogBox; // See later.

class Control;
class BaseWindow {
   .
   .
   .
protected:
  List          controlList;
   .
   .
   .
protected:
   .
   .
   .
  void    addControl(Control *c)
     { controlList.add(c);

  virtual LONG scanControls(WORD id, LONG lParam)
     {
```

```
// BaseWindow::scanControls is declared friend of Control. See later.

    ListIterator l(controlList);
    while (!l.endReached()) {
      Control *c = (Control *)l.current();
      if ( c->controlId == id ) {
          if (c->handler) return (*(c->handler))(id, lParam);
          else { // No handler specified,
                  // dispatch for default action of control.
              return c->theControl->defaultAction(id, lParam);
      }
      l.next();
    }
    return FALSE; //  Targetted control not found.
  }

  virtual LONG handleWMCommand(WORD wParam, LONG lParam)
  {
    if (scanMenu(wParam)) return TRUE
    .
    .

    // Other WM_COMMAND actions.
    if (scanControls(wParam, lParam)) return TRUE; // Control Handling.
    .
    .
    .

  }

class Control : public BaseWindow {}

friend LONG BaseWindow::scanControls(WORD, LONG);

protected:

  LPCSTR                controlClass, controlStyle;
  WORD                  controlId;
  CONTROLFUNCTION       controlFunction;
  int                   posX, posY, width, height;
  int                   fromDialog; // Created through dialog box or not.

  virtual LONG defaultAction(WORD, LONG) { return TRUE; }// Do nothing
  virtual LONG validate() { return TRUE;}

  Control(BaseWindow *pWindow,
          LPCSTR class, UINT style,
          int x, int y, int w, int h,
        WORD id, CONTROLFUNCTION cfn = NULL, LPCSTR caption = NULL)
// The constructor is protected to avoid creation of a bare "Control"
// object.
    : BaseWindow(pWindow, caption)
    {
      fromDialog = 0;
      controlClass = class; controlId = id;
       controlStyle = style; controlFunction = cfn;
      posX = x; posY = y; width = w; height = h;
    }
```

```
Control(BaseDialogBox *pWindow, WORD resId, CONTROLFUNCTION cfn);
// See later.
  .
        .
        .
LONG scanControls(WORD id, LONG lParam) { return FALSE;} // Overloaded
void createWindow()
// Overloaded to take care of the window class parameter.
{
    if (parent)
    if ( !fromDialog) {
      if (handle = CreateWindow( controlClass,
                                 title,
                                 controlStyle,
                                 posX, posY, width, height,
                                 parent->handle(),
                                 controlId,
                                 GLOBAL_hInstance, NULL))
    {
      parent->addControl(this);
      showWindow();
      updateWindow();
    }
  }
    else { // From a dialog box.
      handle = GetDlgItem(parent->windowHandle(), controlId);
// The control is added to the parent window by the dialog box
// compatible constructor
    }
  }
};
```

'Button' Control Objects

It is clear from the above code that the `Control` class behaves like an abstract base class (as no instances of it can be easily created because the constructor is protected), although it is not an abstract class in the C++ sense. Real control object classes are derived directly from the `Control` class or from derived classes of `Control` which also have abstract class-like properties. For example, consider the declaration of the class `Button`, which is somewhat abstract, and the various derived 'real' button classes.

```
class Button : public Control {
protected:

  int  state;

  LONG defaultAction(WORD, LONG)
  {
    state = handle ? SendMessage(handle, BM_GETCHECK, 0, 0L) : -1;
    return TRUE;
  }

  void createWindow() // Overloaded to take care of state.
  {
```

```
    Control::createWindow(); // Create the control window and then
    state = handle ? SendMessage(handle, BM_GETCHECK, 0, 0L) : -1;
            // Get state.
}


    Button(BaseWindow *pWindow,
            int x, int y, int w, int h,
        WORD id, CONTROLFUNCTION cfn = NULL, LPCSTR caption = NULL)
// The constructor is still protected to avoid
// creation of a bare "Button" object.
    : Control(pWindow, "Button", WS_CHILD | WS_VISIBLE,
            x, y, w, h, id, cfn, caption) { state = 0; }

  Button(BaseDialogBox *pWindow, WORD resId, CONTROLFUNCTION cfn = NULL) :
    Control(pWindow, resId, cfn) { state = 0; }

public:
  int   getState() { return( state = handle ?
                        SendMessage(handle, BM_GETCHECK, 0, 0L): -1 ); }

  void  setState(int newState) { if (handle)
          SendMessage(handle, BM_SETCHECK, (state = newState), 0L); }

};

// Note that for the derived button classes declared below, the
//constructors are public.

class PushButton : public Button {
protected:

public:

  PushButton(BaseWindow *pWindow,
              int x, int y, int w, int h,
          WORD id, CONTROLFUNCTION cfn = NULL, LPCSTR caption = NULL)
    : Button(pWindow, x, y, w, h, id, cfn, caption)
    {
        controlStyle |= BS_PUSHBUTTON;
    }
  PushButton(BaseDialogBox *pWindow, WORD resId,
              CONTROLFUNCTION cfn = NULL) :
    Button(pWindow, resId, cfn) {}
};

class DefPushButton : public Button {
public:

  DefPushButton(BaseWindow *pWindow,
                int x, int y, int w, int h, WORD id,
                CONTROLFUNCTION cfn = NULL, LPCSTR caption = NULL)
    : Button(pWindow, x, y, w, h, id, cfn, caption)
    {
        controlStyle |= BS_DEFPUSHBUTTON;
    }
```

```
    DefPushButton(BaseDialogBox *pWindow,
                  WORD resId, CONTROLFUNCTION cfn = NULL) :
       Button(pWindow, resId, cfn) {}
};

class RadioButton : public Button {

public:

    RadioButton(BaseWindow *pWindow,
                int x, int y, int w, int h, WORD id,
                  CONTROLFUNCTION cfn = NULL, LPCSTR caption = NULL,
                  int initState = 0)
       : Button(pWindow, x, y, w, h, id, cfn, caption)
       {
           controlStyle |= BS_RADIOBUTTON;
       }
    RadioButton(BaseDialogBox *pWindow, WORD resId,
                CONTROLFUNCTION = NULL,
                int initState = 0) :
       Button(pWindow, resId, cfn) { state = initState; }

};

class CheckBox : public Button {

public:

    CheckBox(BaseWindow *pWindow,
          int x, int y, int w, int h,
          WORD id, CONTROLFUNCTION cfn = NULL, LPCSTR caption = NULL,
          int initState = 0, int auto = 1)
       : Button(pWindow, x, y, w, h, id, cfn, caption)
       {
           controlStyle |= auto ? BS_AUTOCHECKBOX : BS_CHECKBOX;
       }

    CheckBox(BaseDialogBox *pWindow, WORD resId, CONTROLFUNCTION = NULL,
                int initState = 0) :
       Button(pWindow, resId, cfn) { state = initState; }

};

// Similarly, other button classes (derived from class Button) and
// other control classes derived from class Control.
```

The 'ListBox' Control Class

The list box control is very useful where the underlying application offers a number of choices, of which the user selects some (usually one). The Windows API permits list boxes to display certain properties selectively. The programmer chooses the properties by setting appropriate bits of the 'style' parameter during the creation of the list box (for list boxes created programmatically), or by enumerating the properties in the dialog script itself (for list boxes that are contained in a dialog box). Setting one of these style parameters, namely LBS_NOTIFY, ensures that a notification message is sent to the parent window of the list box whenever the user selects an item.

Besides, the Windows API permits adding, inserting and deleting strings to/from a list box. Adding a string appends it at the end of the list box, which may then be sorted if the LBS_SORT parameter was set for the list box. Insertion may be done anywhere and bypasses sorting. We shall not discuss other aspects of list box like multiple selection and keyboard interfaces, here, and the reader is encouraged to refer to the Windows SDK manual (or help files) for further reference.

Communication between a list box and application

The underlying application, usually the window procedure (or dialog procedure) of the window (or dialog) owing the list box, communicates with the list box through message passing. We have already talked about addition, insertion and deletion of text items to/from a dialog box. These are achieved by sending messages (LB_ADDSTRING, LB_INSERTSTRING and LB_DELETESTRING, respectively) to the list box in question. For the first two cases, the string is supplied through the lParam parameter of the SendMessage Windows API function. For the last two cases, a zero based index position of the string is sent through the wParam (lParam is NULL if LB_DELETESTRING is the message).

The index of the currently selected string in the list box may be obtained by sending a LB_GETCURSEL message. Similarly, the current selection can be programmatically altered through a LB_SETCURSEL message. The number of strings in the list box can be recovered through a LB_GETCOUNT message. Specific strings can be retrieved with the LB_GETTEXT message by specifying the index number of the string in wParam, and a far pointer to the buffer to be filled up by the string text in lParam. The length of the currently selected string is obtained with the LB_GETTEXTLEN message.

List boxes with the LBS_NOTIFY style set send WM_COMMAND messages to the parent window of the list box. These messages contain the list box control identifier in the wParam parameter, and the list box's window handle in the lower word of lParam. The high word of lParam could be one of the following: LBN_SELCHANGE, LBN_SELCANCEL or LBN_DBLCLK, indicating change of selection, cancellation of selection or double-click on a list box item, respectively.

```
class ListBox : public Control {
protected:
    int     currentItem;

    virtual LONG SelectionChange(UINT item)
        { currentItem = (int) item; return TRUE; }
    virtual LONG SelectionCancel(UINT item)
        { currentItem = -1; return TRUE; }
    virtual LONG SelectionDblClick(UINT item)
        { currentItem = (int) item; return TRUE; }
```

```
LONG defaultAction(WORD, LONG lParam) // Overloaded from Control.
{
    int n = SendMessage(handle, LB_GETCURSEL, NULL, NULL);
    switch ( HIWORD(lParam)) {
    case LBN_SELCHANGE: return SelectionChange(n);
    case LBN_SELCANCEL: return SelectionCancel(n);
    case LBN_DBLCLK:    return SelectionDblClick(n);
    }
    return TRUE;
}

public:

ListBox(BaseWindow *pWindow, UINT lStyle,
        int x, int y, int w, int h,
        WORD id, CONTROLFUNCTION cfn = NULL, LPCSTR caption = NULL)
    : Control(pWindow, "Listbox", lStyle ? lStyle : LBS_STANDARD,
        x, y, w, h, id, cfn, caption) { currentItem = -1; }

ListBox(BaseDialogBox *pWindow, WORD resId,
        CONTROLFUNCTION cfn = NULL) :
    Control(pWindow, resId, cfn) { currentItem = -1; }

int addString(LPCSTR str)
    { return SendMessage(handle, LB_ADDSTRING, NULL, (LONG) str); }
int insertString(LPCSTR str, UINT at)
    { return SendMessage(handle, LB_INSERTSTRING, at, (LONG) str); }
int deleteString(UINT at)
    { return SendMessage(handle, LB_DELETESTRING, at, NULL); }
int getCurrentSelect()
    { return
        (currentItem = SendMessage(handle, LB_GETCURSEL, NULL, NULL));
    }
int setCurrentSelect(UINT at)
    { return
        (currentItem = SendMessage(handle, LB_SETCURSEL, at, NULL));
    }
int getCurrentTextLength()
    { return SendMessage(handle, LB_GETTEXTLENGTH, at, NULL); }
int getCurrentText(LPCSTR str, UINT at)
    { return SendMessage(handle, LB_GETTEXT, at, (LONG) str); }
};
```

The 'EditBox' Control Class

The Windows' 'edit' control is used to obtain text input from the user. An edit control can have a variety of features such as multiple-line editing, and automatic horizontal and vertical scrolling. There may even be edit controls that let the user enter a password or some private text which is not displayed and instead, an arbitrary character (default the asterisk '*') gets displayed for every input character. Advanced text selection, cut-paste-and-copy to clipboard and similar features are also available.

Most of the facilities available with edit controls may be turned on or off by setting or resetting appropriate style parameter bits. For example, the ES_AUTOHSCROLL style makes Windows automatically scroll text to the right by 10 characters when the user types a character at the end of the line. When the user presses the ENTER key, the control scroll all text back to position zero. Similarly, the ES_AUTOVSCROLL style means that Windows automatically scrolls text up one page when the user presses ENTER on the last line. Styles ES_CENTER, ES_LEFT and ES_RIGHT are used to align the text. Style ES_PASSWORD lets all characters to be displayed as the character set through the EM_SETPASSWORDCHAR message (default asterisk). The ES_MULTILINE style designates a multi-line edit control (MLE, the default is single-line edit control, SLE).

A few words on an MLE may be in order. When the multiline edit control is in a dialog box, the default response to pressing the ENTER key is to activate the default button. To use the ENTER key as a carriage return, an application should use the ES_WANTRETURN style.

The different edit control operations can be controlled by sending messages to the appropriate edit control. Windows SDK API specifies 26 different messages for the purpose. Additionally, the WM_GETTEXT and WM_SET_TEXT messages may also be used. Every message requires a different set of message-specific parameters be sent through the wParam and lParam parameters. For example, the EM_GETLINE message retrieves a line from an MLE where the wParam parameter is used to pass the line number and the lParam parameter is used to pass the reference to a character array to where Windows would copy the line. The length of the line may be obtained through a EM_LINELENGTH message.

Another message, EM_LINEINDEX, retrieves the character index of an MLE line, which is the position of the first character of the line from the beginning of the edit buffer.

Messages EM_GETSEL, EM_REPLACESEL and EM_SETSEL may be used to perform select and replace operations, while EM_UNDO may be used to undo the last operation in an edit control. Edit control notification messages are quite a few in number and need not be discussed in detail. As usual, the notifications are sent via a WM_COMMAND message sent to the window owing the edit control where the HIWORD of the lParam parameter encodes the message.

For the sake of completion, we may discuss two notification messages. The message EN_ERRSPACE indicates to the underlying application (through the owner window of the edit control) that the edit control has run out of memory space. The EN_CHANGE message indicates that the contents of the edit control, as well as what is being displayed, has undergone a change due to some user interaction. With these, the EditBox class that encapsulates the behaviour of an edit control item may be declared as follows:

```
class EditBox : public Control {
protected:
  virtual LONG EditChange() { return TRUE; }
  virtual LONG AllocationError() { return TRUE; }
```

```
LONG defaultAction(WORD, LONG lParam) // Overloaded from Control.
{
    switch ( HIWORD(lParam)) {
    case EN_CHANGE: return EditChange();
    case EN_ERRSPACE: return AllocationError();
    }
    return TRUE;
}

public:

EditBox(BaseWindow *pWindow, UINT lStyle,
        int x, int y, int w, int h,
        WORD id, CONTROLFUNCTION cfn, LPCSTR caption = NULL)
    : Control(pWindow, "Editbox",
              lStyle ? lStyle : ES_MULTILINE | ES_LEFT | ES_WANTRETURN |
                               ES_AUTOHSCROLL | ES_AUTOVSCROLL,
              x, y, w, h, id, cfn, caption) {}

EditBox(BaseDialogBox *pWindow, WORD resId, CONTROLFUNCTION cfn) :
    Control(pWindow, resId, cfn) {}

int getLine(LPCSTR str, int len)
    { return SendMessage(handle, EM_GETLINE, len, (LONG) str); }
int noOfLines()
    { return SendMessage(handle, EM_GETLINECOUNT, 0, 0L); }
int getBuffer(LPCSTR buffer, int len)
    { return SendMessage(handle, WM_GETTEXT, len, (LPARAM) buffer); }
int getCurrentSelect()
    { return SendMessage(handle, EM_GETSEL, NULL, NULL); }
int setCurrentSelect(UINT from, UINT to)
    { return (currentItem = SendMessage(handle, EM_SETSEL, at, NULL)); }
int getLineLength()
    { return SendMessage(handle, EM_LINELENGTH, at, 0L); }
int replaceText(LPCSTR str)
    { return SendMessage(handle, EM_REPLACESEL, at, (LONG) str); }
};
```

Special Edit Controls

Many object-based Windows libraries provide with special edit control objects
that help the programmer in obtaining different types of user input—integers,
reals, etc. These edit boxes are usually single line edit boxes. The validate
function is overloaded in these classes to reflect whether the string entered by
the user conforms to the format for which the object is designed. Usually, these
special edit control objects provide a typecasting operator to convert the input
string to the appropriate type. Let us consider, as an example, two special edit
control classes for inputting int and float variables, respectively.

```
class SpecialEditBox : public EditBox {
protected:
  char      formatString[11];

  void init()
  {
    if (format) strcpy(formatString, format);
    char initString[41];
    formatData(initString);
  SendMessage(handle, WM_SETTEXT, 0, (LPARAM) (LPCSTR) initString);
    setCurrentSelect(-1, -1);
  }

  SpecialEditBox( BaseWindow *pWindow, int x, int y, int w, int h,
                  WORD id, char *format = NULL )
    : EditBox( pWindow, ES_LEFT | ES_WANTRETURN,
                x, y, w, h, id, NULL, NULL ) { init(); }

  SpecialEditBox( BaseDialogBox *pWindow, WORD resId,
                  char *format = NULL ) :
    EditBox(pWindow, resId, NULL) { init(); }

// Note that constructors are protected to give a pseudo-abstract nature.

  virtual LONG scanString(char *) { return FALSE; }

  virtual void formatData(char *s) {}

public:

  LONG validate()
  {
    char        input[41], *p = input, *q;

    if (getLine( (LPCSTR) input, 41)) return FALSE;
    q = input + strlen(input) -1; // q points to last character of input
    while (*p == ' ') p++; // Left trim blanks
    while (*q == ' ') q--; *(q+1) = 0; // Right trim and truncate input.

    return scanString(p);
  }
};

class IntegerEditBox : public SpecialEditBox {
public:

  IntegerEditBox( BaseWindow *pWindow,
                  int x, int y, int w, int h, WORD id,
                  char *format = NULL, int initData = 0)
    : SpecialEditBox( pWindow, x, y, w, h, id,
                      format ? format : "%d") { data = initData; }

  IntegerEditBox( BaseDialogBox *pWindow,
                  WORD resId, char *format = NULL, int initData= 0)
    : SpecialEditBox(pWindow, resId, NULL,
                      format ? format : "%d") { data = initData; }
```

```
    void operator int () { return data; }

protected:

  int     data;

  void formatData(char *s) { sprintf(s, formatString, data); }

  LONG scanString(char *p)
  {
    int n;
    if (sscanf(p, formatString, &n)) {
      data = n;
      return TRUE:
    }
    return FALSE;
  }
};

class FloatEditBox : public SpecialEditBox {
public:

  FloatEditBox( BaseWindow *pWindow,
             int x, int y, int w, int h, WORD id,
             char *format = NULL, float initData = 0.0)
    : SpecialEditBox( pWindow, x, y, w, h, id,
                   format ? format : "%f") { data = initData; }

  FloatEditBox( BaseDialogBox *pWindow,
             WORD resId, char *format = NULL, float initData = 0.0)
    : SpecialEditBox( pWindow, resId, NULL,
                   format ? format : "%f") { data = initData; }

  void operator float () { return data; }

protected:

  float     data;

  LONG scanString(char *p)
  {
    float f;
    if (sscanf(p, formatString, &f)) {
      data = f;
      return TRUE:
    }
    return FALSE;
  }
};
```

Other Control Classes

Most GUIs offer a plethora of other controls like 'Scroll Bars', and 'Combo
boxes'. Since it is not our intention to provide the deepest possible insight into

any GUI (Windows or others), we do not give the details of encapsulation of all these controls into classes. The encapsulation of the other classes are left as exercises for the user.

DIALOG BOXES AND DIALOG CLASSES

One distinguishing feature of almost all GUIs is allowing complex user input through a single form like window called a dialog box. Obtaining user input through a dialog box is a big leap in user input methodology from conventional text-based terminals. There are several points of advantages in using dialog boxes over text-based terminals as discussed below.

Advantages of Using Dialog Boxes

In text-based terminals, the basic unit of input is a line of text. Once the user signals the end of one line of input (possibly through pressing the 'Return' key), there is no way of going back unless the underlying application takes special measures for that. In a dialog box on the other hand, several 'units' of input are on display and open for interaction simultaneously. The user therefore gets a global view of the entire input data set, and can also modify one or more particular 'units' simply by transferring the 'focus' (discussed later) to the 'unit.'

Unlike text terminals, a 'unit' of input in a dialog box need not be a single line of text. A 'unit' in a dialog box is actually a control object and can therefore offer all the facilities that the particular control object provides. For example, if it is required that the user specify one out of several possibilities in an input unit, a text terminal can only prompt the user for typing in the possibility (may be in a coded form) and expect that the user has remembered what exactly to type in and has been careful enough in giving an error-free input. If validation is necessary, it must be done by the underlying program. In a GUI environment, the particular unit would be replaced by a list box that is loaded with all the possibilities—the user need simply to browse through the list and select the appropriate entry. The burden of remembering what exactly to type in is removed and validation, to some extent, is automatic. Note also that the underlying application needs no special validation. It simply checks whether the user input belongs to the list of possibilities.

In many applications, the input data validation process could be quite complex—a number of user input units together may determine the validity of a data set. In a text-based terminal, the validation step can therefore be employed only after the last of the input units are obtained from the user, and if the set is found non-valid, every individual input unit will have to be prompted for and obtained from the user.

With a dialog box, on the other hand, it is possible for both the application and the user to have a 'view' of all the individual data units. The (complex) validation process may be either employed when the user indicates the end of input session (usually by pressing a 'button' labeled OK) or, sometimes, when the user has provided one new value to some item (through an appropriate 'control') that renders a set of input values non-valid. Let us take an example.

Let us suppose that the application is one which needs to obtain instances of `Triangle` objects as input. We shall concentrate only on obtaining the co-ordinates of the two base vertices of the triangle, assuming the third vertex to be at the origin. The validation step checks that the area of the triangle given as the input is always greater than k units (say).

With a text-based terminal, the underlying application would presumably prompt for the co-ordinates of the two vertices—a total of two input items if a co-ordinate is input as a single entity, or a total of four units if the abcissae and the ordinates are considered. In either case, the validation step can be triggered only after input of both the vertices is over. If the data is found non-valid, the application must go back and resume the entire input process.

With a dialog box, on the other hand, the coordinates could be obtained through two pairs of edit box controls. An OK button may act as an indicator for end of input. When the user clicks on the OK button, the validation step may be triggered, which reads the control data into actual variables and removes the dialog box if the input is valid. If however, the data on the edit boxes are found non-valid, the user may be given an appropriate error message and the dialog box is not removed.

Creation and Handling of a Dialog Box

What exactly is a dialog box? In most GUIs, including Windows, a dialog box is basically a pop-up window that contains one or more controls with which the user can enter text, choose options, etc. Three entities are associated with a dialog box—a *dialog template* that 'describes' its look and feel (how many controls, of what types, where located, etc), a *dialog function* that is the window procedure for the dialog and a means whereby the dialog box is invoked.

The easiest way to provide a dialog template in Windows is through a resource script. We shall take up this aspect shortly.

The dialog function

The dialog function of a dialog box is very much like the window procedure of a normal window. However, since default processing of dialog boxes are handled internally, the `DefWindowProc` function is not called. Dialog messages are despatched to the dialog function through the `message` parameter. If the function processes the message, it returns a value `TRUE`, else it returns `False`. Although a number of messages are despatched to a dialog function, most dialog functions process only two of them—the `WM_INITDIALOG` and `WM_COMMAND` messages.

Invocation of a modal or modeless dialog box

A dialog box can be invoked by calling either of the functions `DialogBox` and `CreateDialog`. The former creates a *modal* dialog box, while the latter creates a *modeless* one.

A *modal* dialog box temporarily disables the parent window (of the dialog box) and forces the user to complete the requested interaction before returning control to the parent window. As a matter of fact, a modal dialog box starts its own message loop to process messages from the application's message queue maintained by Windows, without returning to the `WinMain` function.

A *modeless* dialog box on the other hand, does not disable the parent window, which means that the user can go on working in the parent window while the dialog box is displayed. Modeless dialog boxes are of interest only in some special cases and shall not be taken up in this book.

Resource script for a dialog box

Let us describe the mechanism of declaring a dialog box as a resource script with an example. Our example application (see later) creates a dialog box to get one triangle object as input.

The dialog box provides a list box of the possible triangle classes presently known (for example, `TriangularLamina`, `TriangularFrame` and `HoledTriangularLamina`). It has two pairs of edit boxes to read in the co-ordinates of two vertices of the triangle object (as before, the first vertex is assumed to be at the origin). A 'combo-box' displays the presently available material codes along with their relevant weight per unit length or area (as the case may be). The user may select an existing code or may add a new one, specifying the code and the data. Two typical buttons, labeled OK and Cancel may be used to indicate end of input or rejection of this input session, respectively.

The Two Faces of a Dialog Box

Considering the definition of a Control in an earlier section, we see that a dialog box fits in as a control object. Like any control object, the main purpose of a dialog box is to obtain user input. However, unlike normal controls described in the section, a dialog box has more window-like properties, in that the window procedure of a dialog box is not an internal aspect of the Windows kernel.

For every dialog box to be created and used in a program, a 'window procedure' must be provided for it and we have already seen that this procedure is commonly known as the 'dialog function' of the dialog box. Structurally, a dialog function is exactly similar to a window procedure, i.e., four parameters, the dialog box handle, a message identifier, a word parameter and a long parameter are passed by Windows to a dialog function in response to user interaction or otherwise.

Another point of difference between a dialog box and a normal control is that a dialog box can contain controls nested into it. In fact, the power of a dialog box in performing user interaction is achieved through the controls nested into it.

Controls within a Dialog Box

The statements between BEGIN and END in the above resource script declares controls of the corresponding type in the dialog box at the indicated positions.

One identifier just after the control type keyword or the item next to it (depending on what control type it is) is a (unique) #defined number which is the control's identifier. Note that some of the controls have a '–1' as the identifier. These are almost invariably STATIC controls. Such controls do not respond to the user's action and hence no message is generated for them. They are mostly used (as here) to annotate other controls.

Whenever the user interacts with any of the (non-Static) controls within a dialog box (to be called dialog 'items' henceforth), Windows despatches a WM_COMMAND message to the dialog function of the dialog box. The wParam and lParam parameters encode appropriate properties associated with the invoked control. For example, if the user presses the button labeled OK, a WM_COMMAND message is despatched to the dialog function with the wParam parameter having the value ID_OK, which is the identifier of the pressed button. As another example, if the user highlights a new item in the triangle list box (whose identifier is IDC_TR_LIST) using the mouse (or the keyboard), a WM_COMMAND message is again despatched to the dialog function with the wParam parameter now having the value IDC_TR_LIST and the high order word of lParam having the value LBN_SELCHANGE (a Windows pre-defined message).

Windows sends the dialog function the predefined message WM_INITDIALOG just after it has created the dialog box, but just before it is displayed. As we shall see a little later, this message should be effectively handled to pass the initialization data to the various controls of the dialog box.

Data Binding with a Dialog Box

As we shall see, shortly, a straightforward object-oriented view of a dialog box may be obtained by associating a dialog class with every distinct dialog box template. Most individual controls defined in the template are associated with a member variable of an appropriate type within the class.

As an example, consider a dialog template that has a list box control lb (say), a radio button group consisting of three radio buttons b0, b1 and b2 and the usual two push-buttons OK and Cancel. One can declare a dialog class with a ListBox and a ButtonGroup member variables with the ButtonGroup member containing three RadioButton members. Push-buttons usually give rise to special behaviour or actions and are therefore mostly associated with member functions of the dialog class, although the possibility of associating them with PushButton members is not ruled out.

Data exchange between the dialog box and the application

In the object-oriented scenario described above, it is desirable that the data displayed in a dialog item always reflect the value stored in the associated control object within the dialog class of the dialog box, and vice versa. This requires certain things to be ensured.

First, the initial data to be displayed on every dialog item must reflect the value in the corresponding class member.

Secondly, any change made in any dialog item by the user must immediately be reflected in the member associated with the item.

To ensure the strict data exchange between a dialog box and its dialog class requires involved programming effort on part of the designer of the base dialog class. However, by doing so, a better object-orientation is achieved in the sense that such code may be more easily transferred to a different GUI environment. Nevertheless, one must be aware of the fact that there are some commercially available object-based Windows libraries that leave the onus of data exchange entirely upon the programmer. The key steps for providing data exchange in a base dialog class are described below:

Base dialog box class derived from `BaseWindow`

The base (presumably abstract) dialog class maintains a container for Control objects nested within the dialog class. This can be done simply by deriving the base dialog box class from the class `BaseWindow`.

Association of dialog items appropriate `Control` objects

The designer of any dialog class derived from the base dialog class must ensure that the relevant dialog items (that is, window handles of resource identifiers thereof) in the dialog box for the class are associated with appropriate `Control` objects within the dialog class.

To be able to do this, there must be constructors of control classes that can create control instances given only a resource identifier and remember during its life-time that it was created that way. Indeed, it is for this reason that, the member data `fromDialog` is used in the declaration of the `Control` class and separate constructors are provided for creating controls directly or through the script of a dialog box.

Unavailability of control handles at dialog box start-up

One complication in the described scenario is that the handles of control identifiers of a dialog box are not available till the dialog box itself is created. If we assume that the constructor of a dialog class creates the dialog box and then proceeds to associate member controls to dialog items, it would give rise to a communication gap.

In most cases, a dialog box is a *modal* one, i.e. once the dialog box is created, all keyboard, mouse and other dialog box specific messages are despatched to the dialog function of the dialog box. A modal dialog box is created by invoking the Windows API function `DialogBox`. This functions returns control to the function invoking it only after the dialog function has terminated the dialog box. One of the earliest messages despatched to a dialog function is `WM_INITDIALOG`, which indicates to the dialog function that the dialog box window has just become valid.

Let us come back to the question of communication referred to above. It is expected that the constructor of the dialog class would invoke the `DialogBox` function (possibly indirectly through another member function).

Thus, for any constructor code executed before the invocation of the

`DialogBox` function, the dialog box has not been created. Similarly, for any constructor code executed after the invocation of the `DialogBox` function, the dialog box has already been terminated. In other words, at no position in the constructor for a dialog class, can the code assume validity of the dialog box.

A number of ways are employed to circumvent the problem. Almost all of them have two commonalties. First, the programmer of the dialog class constructor is advised to call the `DialogBox` function (actually the shadow member function for the same) as the *last* effective code in the constructor body. Secondly, the `WM_INITDIALOG` message is captured and dispatched to a member function that performs control data initialization.

Different object-based Windows libraries differ in whether the above-mentioned message handler member function is virtual or not. If it is not virtual, the designer of a new dialog class derived from an existing class would have to set up the entire code for control data initialization. With virtual `initDialog()` functions, the library might provide a default initialization routine, namely, scanning the `Control` object list and initializing the associated items.

Control message despatched to `Control` object

A proper dynamic data exchange between dialog box control items and the associated `Control` object requires that whenever the user performs any interaction with a control item, the resulting message should be despatched to the associated `Control` object.

Philosophically, there is not much difference between this aspect and the initialization of control items, except that here the message involved is `WM_COMMAND`. The handler for this message must scan the list of `Control` objects and despatch the message parameters to the handler of that `Control` object whose identifier matches with the dialog item identifier received through the `wParam` parameter of the dialog function.

Handling `OK` and `Cancel` buttons

Almost all dialog box sessions are terminated by the user by pressing one of the two buttons labelled `OK` or `Cancel`. Some dialog boxes, however, lack the `Cancel` button. These buttons are so common that Windows provides some pre-defined identifiers (`IDOK`, `IDCANCEL`) to identify them.

A good object-based Windows library is expected to relieve the user from the burden of declaring any `Button` control for these buttons and should take upon itself to provide handlers for them outside the list of `Controls`. These libraries usually call two pre-defined virtual functions one after the other during dialog box termination. The first of these is expected to carry out the final housekeeping job before the dialog box is destroyed. The second actually destroys the dialog box and is quite unlikely to be modified by any descendant dialog classes.

Encapsulation of Dialog Boxes—The `BaseDialogBox` *Class*

The `BaseDialogBox` is the abstract base class for all dialog box classes. It provides functionalities that performs dynamic data exchanges with the user specified list of `Control` objects corresponding to the control items of the dialog box. The member functions `modal()` and `modeless()` encapsulate the API call for opening a modal and modeless dialog box, respectively. As mentioned earlier, every non-abstract dialog box must call either of the above functions as the last effective code in their respective constructors.

We begin with declaration and (partial) implementation of the `BaseDialogBox` class, followed by the implementation of the constructor of the `Control` class. In addition, we have listed the code for a default global modal dialog procedure. This function is almost similar to the global window procedure, except that it always despatches the dialog message to the topmost modal dialog box maintained in a `Stack` of dialog boxes.

```
Stack        global_DialogBoxStack;

LONG PASCAL
    GLOBAL_ModalDialogProc(HWND hWnd, UINT mess,
                           WPARAM wParam, LPARAM lParam);

class BaseDialogBox : public BaseWindow {
protected:

  List          controlList;
  int           modality; // 1 => modal; 0 => modeless.
  int           retVal; // 0 => Cancel, 1 => OK.

  virtual LONG initDialog(HWND hDlg)
  {
    handle = hDlg;

  // Must validate the Control handles here.

    ListIterator l(controlList);
    while (!l.endReached())
    ((Control *)l.current())->createWindow();
    return userInitDialog(hDlg); // Despatch for user's initialization.
  }

  virtual LONG userInitDialog(HWND) { return TRUE; }

  virtual LONG closeDialog() = 0;

  virtual LONG invalidAtClose() { return TRUE; }

  virtual handleDialogCommand(WORD wParam, LONG lParam) { return TRUE; }

  LONG handleWMCommand(WORD wParam, LONG lParam)
// Overloaded from BaseWindow to exclude Menu and other cases.
  {
```

```
    if (scanControls(wParam, lParam)) return TRUE; // Control Handling
      return handleDialogCommand(wParam, lParam);
  }


  virtual void terminate() { if (modality) EndDialog(handle, NULL);
                            else DestroyWindow(handle); }
    BaseDialogBox(BaseWindow *pWindow, char *resName, int mod = 1)
        : BaseWindow()
    {
      parent = pWindow;
      modality = mod;
      strcpy(title, resName);
    }

    ~BaseDialogBox()
    {
      ListIterator l(controlList);
      while (!l.endReached()) l.current()->delete();
      // Delete each dialog item in controlList.
    }
    virtual void modal()
    {
      modality = 1;
      FARPROC dlgFn = MakeProcInstance( (FARPROC) GLOBAL_ModalDialogProc,
                                        GLOBAL_hInstance);
      global_DialogBoxStack.push(this);
      DialogBox(GLOBAL_hInstance, title, parent, dlgFn);
      FreeProcInstance(dlgFn);
      global_DialogBoxStack.pop();
  }

  virtual void modeless(); // Not implemented here.

  virtual LONG dialogFunction(UINT mess, WPARAM wParam, LPARAM lParam)
  {
    LONG l = TRUE;;
    switch (mess) {
      case WM_INITDIALOG: return initDialog(hDlg);
      case WM_COMMAND: switch (wParam) {
                        case IDOK: l = closeDialog();
                                     if (!l &&
                                         !invalidAtClose()) return TRUE;
                        case IDCANCEL: terminate(); return l;
                  default:return  handleWMCommand(wParam,lParam);
                        // Overloaded from BaseWindow to
                        // despatch to the handler for the
                        // control in dialog box or the
                        // default handler of control if
                        // none found.
                        }
                        break;
      default: return FALSE;
    }
  }
```

```
public:

    void addControl(Control *c) { controlList.add(c);   }
};

    Control::Control(BaseDialogBox *pWindow, WORD resId CONTROLFUNCTION cfn)
       : BaseWindow()
{
    parent = pWindow;
    fromDialog = 1;
    controlId = resId;
    controlFunction = cfn;
    parent->addControl(this);
}


LONG PASCAL
    GLOBAL_ModalDialogProc(HWND hDlg, UINT mess,
                           WPARAM wParam, LPARAM lParam)
{
  BaseDialogBox *db = (BaseDialogBox *) globalDialogBoxStack.top();
  if (db) { // A valid dialog box object on top of stack.
     return db->dialogFunction(hDlg, mess, wParam, lParam);
  }
  else return(FALSE); // Something wrong.
}
```

Real Dialog Box Classes

Real dialog box classes are inherited from the abstract BaseDialogBox class described above. It is essential that the closeDialog function be properly overloaded.

The constructor of the real dialog class must take at least two parameters— a pointer to the parent window object of the dialog box, and a resource identifier to locate the dialog box. Various additional parameters may be introduced to establish connection with external data.

Instances of (pointers to) Control objects (except possibly Button objects, see later) should be declared as member data items of the dialog box and constructed within the dialog box constructor, binding them to appropriate dialog items and appending them to the controlList member data or through the addControl member function. The destructor of BaseDialogBox ensures that these control objects get destroyed.

The last executable statement in the constructor should be a call to the member function modal() for a modal dialog box or to the member function modeless() for a modeless dialog box.

The initDialog function of the BaseDialog class establishes the handles of the contained control objects. Control specific data initialization, for example, adding a list of strings to an EditBox, should be carried out in the overloaded userInitDialog function.

Similarly, validation and read-back of control values should be carried out in the overloaded closeDialog function which gets invoked only if the user quits from the dialog box by pressing the OK button. If on the other hand, some action is required during closing down of a dialog box irrespective of whether the OK or the Cancel key was pressed by the user, the action should be put in an overloaded terminate function. However, there must be an explicit call at the end of this function to the terminate function of the parent dialog class (to ensure proper dialog box shutdown).

Button control objects need not be added to the controlList as they are used not to get actual user input but, rather, user notifications. These notifications are best handled in an overloaded handleDialogMessage function. The ideas are explained through an example in the following sub-section.

An Example with a Dialog Box

Let us try to design a dialog box class for getting input data for a host of Triangle type objects. We assume that three types of triangles could be specified, namely, TriangularLamina, TriangularFrame and HoledTriangularLamina.

The choice of the triangle type can be indicated through a list box. This way, further triangle types may be offered for selection without changing the design of the dialog box. As the designer of the present dialog box, we are not aware of what types of triangle objects will our dialog box ultimately cater to. Hence, we assume that because Triangle is an archivable class, all triangle classes have an indirect constructor pointer (of type TCP, say). Furthermore, there is a *global* function (say triangleToTCP(char *)) that takes a triangle class name string (as displayed on the list box), and returns the indirect constructor pointer of the appropriate triangle class. The process that created the dialog box being designed must send a list of pairs of char * and TCP corresponding to the types of triangle objects to be handled.

Two pairs of float-input edit boxes are used to input the co-ordinates of two base points of the triangle, the third point assumed to be at the origin. An additional integer-input edit box is used to input the material code. A checkbox is used to indicate whether the triangle being input would participate in weight calculation. For this purpose, we assume that the Triangle classes of objects maintain a flag that can be set and read by member functions setCalculateWeight and toCalculateWeight, respectively.

As we know that some triangle objects (like HoledTriangularLamina) require further input parameters which the dialog box being designed is not capable of handling, a further PushButton control labelled More Input is used to indicate that a further dialog box should pop up to get additional input(s). Again, we assume that there is a global function (say triangleInputStrategy) that takes a pointer to a triangle object as parameter and decides about the strategy for getting further input, may be, by popping up a further dialog box. We shall discuss later that the functions triangleToTCP(char *) and triangleInputStrategy are candidates for the View and Document modules, respectively, in a 'Document-View' architecture (see Chapter 6).

The resource script for Example Dialog Box

```
/***************** The Resource script for the Dialog Box follows.
***************/
DLG_TRINPUT DIALOG DISCARDABLE  0, 0, 219, 117
STYLE DS_MODALFRAME | WS_POPUP | WS_VISIBLE | WS_CAPTION |
WS_SYSMENU
CAPTION "Triangle"
FONT 8, "MS Sans Serif"
BEGIN
    DEFPUSHBUTTON    "OK",IDOK,8,96,50,14
    DEFPUSHBUTTON    "Cancel",IDCANCEL,88,96,50,14
    PUSHBUTTON       "More Input",ID_TRMORE,168,96,50,14
    LISTBOX          IDC_LIST1,8,20,71,65,LBS_SORT | LBS_NOINTEGRALHEIGHT |
                     WS_VSCROLL | WS_TABSTOP
    LTEXT            "0-th : (",IDC_STATIC,96,28,28,8
    LTEXT            "1-st : (",IDC_STATIC,96,40,28,8
    LTEXT            "2-nd : (",IDC_STATIC,96,52,28,8
    EDITTEXT  ID_TRVERT1X,124,40,16,12,ES_AUTOHSCROLL | NOT WS_BORDER
    EDITTEXT  ID_TRVERT1Y,148,40,16,12,ES_AUTOHSCROLL | NOT WS_BORDER
    EDITTEXT  ID_TRVERT2X,124,52,16,12,ES_AUTOHSCROLL | NOT WS_BORDER
    EDITTEXT  ID_TRVERT2Y,148,52,16,12,ES_AUTOHSCROLL | NOT WS_BORDER
    LTEXT            ")",IDC_STATIC,164,40,8,8
    LTEXT            ")",IDC_STATIC,164,52,8,8
    LTEXT            ")",IDC_STATIC,164,28,8,8
    LTEXT            ",",IDC_STATIC,140,40,8,8
    LTEXT            ",",IDC_STATIC,140,28,8,8
    LTEXT            ",",IDC_STATIC,140,52,8,8
    LTEXT     "Material Code :   ",IDC_STATIC,96,68,52,8
    LTEXT     "Participate in weight calculation ",IDC_STATIC,96,80,
                     107,8
    CONTROL   "Check1",ID_TRWEIGHTPARTICIPATE,"Button",BS_AUTOCHECKBOX |
                     WS_TABSTOP,204,80,8,9
    EDITTEXT         ID_TRMATERIAL,150,65,24,12,ES_AUTOHSCROLL
    LTEXT            "0.0",IDC_STATIC,148,28,12,9
    LTEXT            "0.0",IDC_STATIC,124,28,12,9
    CTEXT     "Vertices",IDC_STATIC,109,12,43,9
    CTEXT     "Triangle Type",IDC_STATIC,16,8,50,10
END
/***************** The Resource script for the Dialog Box above.
***************/
```

See Fig. 5.1 for a picture of a dialog box constructed from the above resource
script.

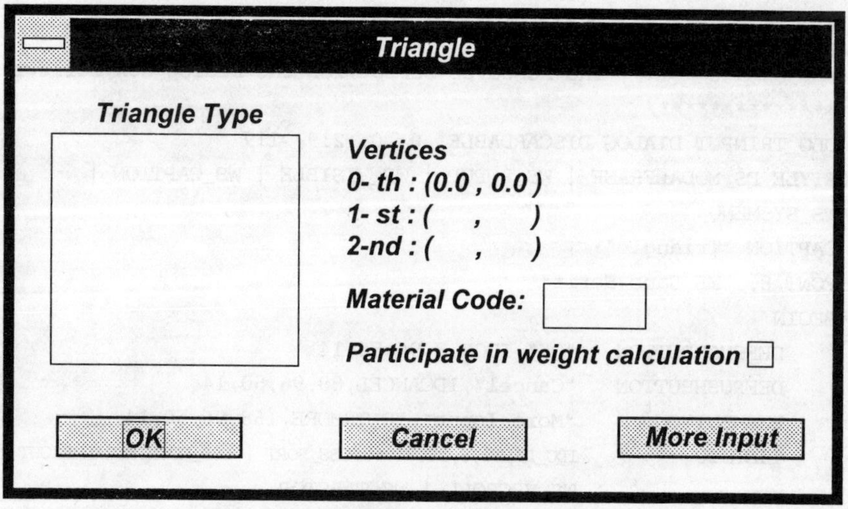

Fig. 5.1 Illustration of Example Dialog Box.

The class structure for Example Dialog Box

```
class TriangleDialogBox : public BaseDialogBox {
protected:

    char        **triangleList; // Storing array of Triangle type names.
    int         listSize; // Number of type names.
    ListBox     *triangleListBox;// The Listbox displaying the names.

    float       vertices[3][3];
// The three vertices of the triangle

    FloatEditBox *verticesEditBox[2][2]; // A FloatEditBox to read
                // two pairs of co-ordinates for two vertices,
                // the third vertex assumed to be at the origin.

    int         material;
    IntegerEditBox *materialEditBox;
// IntegerEditBox to read material code.

    CheckBox    toCalcCheckBox;
// If checked, this triangle participates in weight calculation.

    Triangle    *theTriangle; // The Triangle object being input.

    virtual LONG moreFunction(WORD, LONG)
    // Called if user presses the "More Input" push button.
    {
        makeTriangle(); // Create the Triangle
        return triangleInputStrategy(theTriangle);
        // If required, get more inputs and return the Triangle created.
```

```
LONG userInitDialog(HWND)
{
  addControl( ( triangleListBox =
                  new ListBox(this, ID_TRLIST, NULL) ) );
  triangleListBox->setCurrentItem(0);
  addControl( ( verticesEditBox[0][0] =
                  new FloatEditBox(this, ID_TRVERT1X, NULL,
                                    vertices[1][0])) );
  addControl( ( verticesEditBox[0][1] =
                  new FloatEditBox(this, ID_TRVERT1Y, NULL,
                                    vertices[1][1])) );
  addControl( ( verticesEditBox[1][0] =
                  new FloatEditBox(this, ID_TRVERT2X, NULL,
                                    vertices[2][0])) );
  addControl( ( verticesEditBox[1][1] =
                  new FloatEditBox(this, ID_TRVERT2Y, NULL,
                                    vertices[2][1])) );
  addControl(( materialEditBox =
                  new IntegerEditBox(this, ID_TRMAT , NULL, material)) );
  addControl( ( toCalcCheckBox =
                  new CheckBox(this, ID_TRWEIGHTPARTICIPATE, 1)) );
  addControl( new PushButton(this, ID_TRMORE, moreFunction) );

  return TRUE;
}

LONG closeDialog()
{
  makeTriangle();
  return TRUE;
}

void makeTriangle()
{
  int t;

  if ( ( t = triangleListBox->getCurrentSelect() ) >= 0 ) {
    vertices[1][0] = (float) verticesEditBox[0][0];
    vertices[1][1] = (float) verticesEditBox[0][1];
    vertices[1][0] = (float) verticesEditBox[1][0];
    vertices[2][1] = (float) verticesEditBox[1][1];
    material = (int) materialEditBox;
    if (!theTriangle) theTriangle = triangleToTCP(triangleList[t]);
    if (theTriangle) { // Indirect Construction O.K.
      theTriangle->setVertices( vertices[0][0], vertices[0][1],
                                vertices[1][0], vertices[1][1],
                                vertices[2][0], vertices[2][1]
                              );
      theTriangle->setMaterial(material);
      theTriangle->setCalculateWeight(toCalcCheckBox->getState());
    }
  }
}
```

```
    TriangleDialogBox(BaseWindow *pWindow, char *resName,
                    char **tList, int tSize) :
      BaseDialogBox(pWindow, resName, 1)
  {
    triangleList = tList;
    listSize = tSize;
    theTriangle = NULL;
    triangleListBox = NULL;
    vertices[0][0] = vertices[0][1] = vertices[0][0] =
    vertices[0][1] =vertices[0][0] = vertices[0][1] = 0.0;
    verticesEditBox[0][0] = verticesEditBox[0][1] =
    verticesEditBox[1][0] = verticesEditBox[1][1] = NULL;
    material = DEFAULT_TRIANGLE_MATERIAL;
    materialEditBox = NULL;
    toCalcCheckBox = NULL;
  }

public:

    static Triangle *dialog(BaseWindow *pWindow, char *resName,
                        char **tList, int tSize)
  {
    TriangleDialogBox *tdb =
            new TriangleDialogBox(pWindow, resName, tList, tSize);
    Triangle *t = tdb->theTriangle;
    delete tdb;
    return t;
  }
};
```

An input session with the Example Dialog Box

```
// An example input session.

char      *tList[]; // Global variable containing triangle names,
int        tSize;   // size of above list.

    .
    .
    .

    // From within some window member function, the call
    Triangle *t =
        TriangleDialogBox::dialog(this, DLG_TRINPUT, tList, tSize);
    // would return a new triangle input, if any.
```

Dialog Boxes are not 'Graphics'

From the discussions carried out in this section, we may conclude that the facilities of obtaining user input in GUIs through dialog boxes and/or other controls is not truly 'graphics'. The programmer using dialog boxes and other controls need not necessarily be burdened with graphical aspects like drawing, painting, and resizing. The inputs obtained are also non-graphical, mostly being character strings or indices to sets of other items, again mostly character strings. Whatever facilities are available through dialog boxes might also be simulated on text-based terminals, albeit with limited globality. Nevertheless, the use of controls and dialog boxes have definitely revolutionized user interface technology. In the following section, we initiate discussions on what we mean by 'true' graphics.

Device Independent Graphics

Quite often, we use the term 'graphics' to distinguish it from 'text', thereby implicitly introducing a line of difference between the two. In a GUI environment, the borderline between text and graphics remains quite ill-defined and controversial. However, we explain what we broadly mean by graphics as follows:

When a programmer of an application is actively interested in 'drawing' certain entities, we call that graphics. A drawing entity can be a line or a curve in some colour, a rectangle or some other close shape in some colour and filled with some brush pattern and colour, a text in some font, colour or orientation, bitmaps, etc. Drawing a picture needs at least a few things to be specified. First, there must be a *theme*—the conceptual content of the picture to be drawn. Secondly, there must be a set of *tools* to create the drawing—pens, brushes, colour palettes, etc. Finally, there must be a *medium* on which the drawing is · to be created for view.

In 'graphics', all the above aspects are nearly equally important. The confusion regarding distinguishing graphics from text in a GUI environment stems from the fact that in such environments, text is also drawn. However, there still is a difference. The burden of drawing the text is much more on the GUI kernel than upon the programmer. The theme of the drawing is rarely more complicated than a string of symbols, each symbol having a nearly fixed pictorial representation once the character set is specified. The tools are also limited to a small number of 'fonts' provided with (or added to) the GUI being used.

In computer graphics, the *medium* is one of the various graphical devices connected to the hardware. In non-GUI environments, usually, the underlying operating system has, at best, a limited knowledge of the graphical *capability* of a device to act as a medium for graphics. It therefore becomes the burden of the programmer to possess knowledge about the capability, create (or buy from a third party) the tools necessary for drawing on the medium and only then go about drawing on the medium. As a result, the cost of porting the same drawing to a different medium sometimes becomes quite high, frequently boiling down to creating an entirely separate set of tools as was created for the previous medium.

Essentials of Device Independence—The Device Context

Graphics is GUIs is generally expected to be 'device independent'. The tools for drawing are available as kernel services. The programmer generates pictures using these tools without requiring much knowledge about the medium, i.e.

the device on which the picture is drawn. The GUI kernel has all the necessary knowledge about every such device connected to the hardware. A programmer wishing to provide graphical artifacts in an application, therefore, need not depend much upon any source other than the primary development systems of the GUI environment being used. Porting pictures from one device to another is also considerably simplified.

Windows performs device-independent graphics through a kernel structure that stores, among other things, information regarding certain salient aspects of the driver for the device as might be required for drawing. In Windows terminology, this structure is known as the *device context*.

The device context and the GDI toolbox

To draw graphics on a device, the application program must obtain a device context compatible to the device and created for the same. Once this is done, the actual drawing steps are reasonably device independent. Windows offer a host of functions, called the GDI (Graphics Device Interface) functions, which can be used as a powerful toolbox for drawing graphics.

The main display is treated as just another device by Windows. Thus, even to draw graphics on a window (which we know by now to be a rectangular demarcated zone owned by an application but maintained by Windows), the mechanism is to first obtain a device context for the window. Since the display is an intricate part of Windows, a window device context need not be separately created. Apart from this major difference, drawing on a window is qualitatively the same as drawing on any device.

Compatible DC, bitmaps, the `BitBlt` function and other tools

One can even conceive of creating logical drawing in *memory*, which can later be 'superimposed' on an existing picture on some device. Windows allows this to be done through creation of 'compatible device contexts' to draw in memory. The superimposition can then be done through a very powerful drawing tool called `BitBlt` that copies a *bitmap* from one device context to another compatible device context (which may be the same as the previous one).

A bitmap is a rectangular 'sub-picture' of a picture, essentially a two-dimensional array of pixels. Bitmaps can be monochrome or coloured. During the `BitBlt` process, Windows performs a pixel-by-pixel logical operation between the source bitmap and the destination device. Controlling this logical operation through the GDI function `SetROP2`, one can control the nature of superimposition. `BitBlt` is also the function employed to move/copy sub-pictures of a picture from one zone to another—the two fundamental steps employed in animation.

Apart from the `BitBlt` function mentioned above, Windows GDI provides a host of other functions to draw various geometrical entities—*lines, arcs,* and *rectangles*. The entities are drawn with a Windows defined structure (also called GDI object or simply, *object* in Windows terminology) called a `Pen`. A pen is of a defined thickness and colour.

Similarly, closed zones may be filled up by different types of Brush objects. Printing text on a display device is also considered as a graphical operation, the object used in this case being a Font. A created object must be selected into a device context for it to be effective. To draw text, graphics, and bitmaps, different GDI functions may be used. Most of these functions take a device context as an essential parameter and further functions specific parameters. The drawing is performed on a logical *window coordinate* system, a feature that leads to further device independence as described below.

Painting Windows

We have already discussed in an earlier section how Windows sends the WM_PAINT message to the window procedure of a window that has been partially or totally invalidated. Drawing on a window done as a response to this message is slightly different from drawing done elsewhere. This is because Windows needs to be informed that the message has indeed been processed. The way to do this is to use special functions BeginPaint and EndPaint to obtain and release device contexts, respectively.

The BeginPaint function also does some additional useful duties:

- It erases the background of the invalidated region.

- It fills up a data structure (PAINTSTRUCT) with special information that includes the details of the zone of the window that has actually been invalidated (and hence can be used by the painting process to carry out partial painting at faster speed).

Window and Device Coordinate Systems

Graphics or graphical drawing is always based upon a coordinate system that is essentially digital in nature. In the two dimensional graphics facilities offered by Windows GDI, the coordinate system is integral and Cartesian. However, to provide device independence, Windows deals with two sets of coordinates that are non-ambiguously mapped to each other.

As we know, every (raster) device capable of displaying (printing) graphics provides a discrete two-dimensional dot pattern (pixel pattern) view of its display surface. The distance between consecutive pixels in the horizontal (x-gap) or vertical directions (y-gap) are fixed for such devices, at least once the operating 'mode' of the device (assuming that the device has multiple operating modes) is fixed. In general, the x-gap and y-gap are not equal and the ratio of the y-gap to x-gap is known as the device *aspect ratio*.

Moreover, the directions of increasing abcissae and increasing ordinate and the position of the device *origin* is also from one device to another. In many cases, the origin is at the top left corner of the display surface and ordinates increase downwards, quite contrary to the natural human way of treatment where (usually) the origin is taken at the left bottom corner and ordinates increase upwards.

Given the origin factor and the one of aspect ratio, a graphics programmer needs to be very careful in performing transformations from the 'normal' system in which the pictures are presumably conceived of, to the device system. Also, the transformation needs to be repeated for every new device.

Windows GDI offers a way around it by providing two sets of coordinates. The one on which the GDI function parameters are based is known as the logical or *Window coordinate* system. When Windows kernel translates GDI functional calls to actual interactions with the device, it naturally uses the device or *Viewport coordinate* system. By default, the window and viewport coordinate systems are identical (except for an origin translation).

Mapping modes

However, Windows GDI allows to `SetMapMode` a device context before actual drawing. Of the eight possible mapping modes in Windows (apart from the default `MM_TEXT` mode), six of them provide a 'natural' view of the world, where aspect ratio is unity and ordinates increase upwards. Distances are measured in thousandths of an inch (`MM_HIENGLISH`), hundredths of an inch (`MM_LOENGLISH`), hundreths of a millimeter (`MM_HIMETRIC`), tenths of a millimeter (`MM_LOMETRIC`) or twentieth of a printers point (1/1440 inch, `MM_TWIPS`).

The other two modes, `MM_ANISOTROPIC` and `MM_ISOTROPIC` let the programmer set up a window coordinate system with the aspect ratio not equal to one or equal to one, respectively. In the latter case, setting the mapping mode must be followed by setting the *x*- and *y*-extents of the window and the device through functions `SetWindowExt` and `SetViewportExt`, respectively.

Window and viewport extents and origins

The *x*- and *y*-extents of the window define how much GDI must stretch or compress units in the logical coordinate system to fit units in the device coordinate system. Additionally, the extents define the relative orientation of the *x*- and *y*-axes of both coordinate systems. If the signs of matching window and viewport extents are the same, the axes have the same orientation. If the signs are different, the orientation is reversed.

Apart from setting the extents, the GDI functions `SetWindowOrg` and `SetViewportOrg` set the origins of the window and the viewport, respectively. By changing either of the origins, an application can change the way GDI converts logical coordinates to device coordinates.

Encapsulation of Device Context and Graphics Objects

Although not providing an interface through any OOPL, the Windows API, at least the GDI, is object-oriented to a great extent. This should be obvious from the discussion carried out earlier in this section.

It takes very little effort to build an encapsulated shell around the GDI functions to have a C++ style class structure. Many object-based Windows libraries (for example, MFC of the Visual C++ package) do not go much beyond that, to the extent that even the member functions retain the names of the corresponding API functions they encapsulate.

In many ways, the above approach is quite pragmatic. It neither blocks nor greatly enhances the basic GDI capabilities. However, the users of GDI classes still need to have an appreciable amount of information about the working of the various GDI functions.

Many other libraries have attempted to reduce the burden of information acquisition on the part of the GDI class user. However, quite often, in an attempt to simplify the function call interface, these libraries tend to block some of the facilities available through normal GDI calls. For example, in the CNS++ Views library, the device context class (called `Port`) offers the mapping mode, window and viewport extents as well as their origins to be set by calling, at most, two functions. However, the facility to map simply through the natural mapping modes has been obscured in the process.

A class structure for GDI objects and device context

We offer, on our part, a class structure for GDI objects and the device context in line of what is provided in MFC.

```
class DeviceContext;

class GDIObject : public Object { // Abstract base class for GDI
objects like pen, brush, etc
protected:
    HANDLE          objectHandle, oldHandle;
    DeviceContext   *onDC;

public:

    GDIObject() { objectHandle = oldHandle = 0;
    ~GDIObject() { detach(); onDC = NULL;

    virtual void create() = 0;

    void attach(DeviceContext *dc)
      {
          if (dc) {
            onDC = dc;
            if (!objectHandle) create();
            oldHandle = ::SelectObject(dc->handle(), objectHandle);
            dc->attach(this);
          }
      }

    void detach()
    {
      if (onDC && objectHandle) {
        onDC->detach(this);
        ::SelectObject(dc->handle(), oldHandle);
        objectHandle = 0;
      }
    }
};
```

```
class Pen : public GDIObject { // Real class Pen.
protected:

  WORD      penType, penThickness;
  DWORD     penColour;

public:

    Pen(WORD type, WORD thickness, DWORD colour) : GDIObject()
      { penType = type; penThickness = thickness; penColour = colour; }

    Pen(DeviceContext *dc, WORD type, WORD thickness, DWORD colour) :
GDIObject()
        { penType = type; penThickness = thickness;
          penColour = colour; attach(dc); }

  void create()
     { objectHandle = ::CreatePen(penType, penThickness, penColour); }
};

// Similarly, classes Brush, Font and Bitmap.

class DeviceContext {
protected:

  HDC       deviceHandle;
  List      objectsList;

public:

    DeviceContext() { deviceHandle = 0; }

    DeviceContext(BaseWindow *client)
      { deviceHandle = ::GetDC(client->handle()); }

    // Other constructors for other type of displays.

    ~DeviceContext()
    {
      ListIterator l(&objectsList);
      while (!l.endReached()) l.current()->delete();
// Delete each GDI object list.
    }

    void attach(GDIObject *gdi) { objectsLits.add(gdi); }
    void detach(GDIObject *gdi) { objectsLits.detach(gdi); }

// Different groups of member function for various purposes
// NOT declared or implemented here.

    // Device Context functions, e.g. saveDC();

    // Drawing tool functions e.g.

    void usePen(Pen *p) { if (p) p->attach(this); }
```

```
// Done easily by creating
// Pen while mentioning this device context.

  // Drawing attribute functions, e.g.

  void setRasterOp(WORD rop) { ::SetROP2(deviceHandle, rop); }

  // Mapping Functions,
  // e.g. setViewportExt: map to corresponding GDI functions

  // Line drawing functions, e.g. moveTo, arc, etc.

  // Brush functions, e.g. fillRect

  // Bitmap functions, e.g. bitBlt

  // Text functions, e.g. textOut

  // and so on ...
};
```

```
// Derived classes of DeviceContext cater to special cases. For example,
// PaintDeviceContext encapsulates the BeginPaint and EndPaint functions.
```

```
class PaintDeviceContext : public DeviceContext {
protected:
  PAINTSTRUCT  ps;
  BaseWindow   *window;
public:
  PaintDeviceContext(BaseWindow *w) : DeviceContext()
    { window = w; deviceHandle = ::BeginPaint(w->handle(), &ps); }
  ~PaintDeviceContext() { if (window)
                ::EndPaint(window->handle(), &ps); }
};
```

CONCLUSION

In this chapter we have endeavoured to bridge the gap between a conventional programmer's knowledge and the prudence behind the design of most object-based GUI libraries.

We have covered a few essential aspects of programming in a GUI platform like MS-Windows, in the light of object-orientation with respect to C++. A careful reader must have noticed that because the original Windows API is sufficiently object-oriented, building a class structure around several of its units was not a difficult task.

In Windows, a *window* is on the one hand a demarcated zone on the display surface and a receptor of Windows messages on the other. We have not dealt with the display specific nature of a window to any great depth. However, we have discussed at length how the message handling aspect of a window might be encapsulated in a class structure. In this respect, we have talked about certain extreme approaches and have shown that most object-based Windows libraries choose an intermediate approach. We have given our version of this encapsulation through a base `BaseWindow` class in which we have provided a shell around the message handling system of a window.

Actually, most commercial libraries clearly dissociate the two aspects of a window. In most of these libraries, an abstract `MessageHandler` (or a similarly named) class takes care of message handling. The base `Window` (or some similarly named) class is derived from the `MessageHandler` class and takes care of, mostly, the display specific activities of a window. In the course of our discussion, we have also discussed about the philosophy behind encapsulation of specialized GUI entities like menus, controls and dialog boxes. Finally, we have provided a short discussion on device independent graphics.

In the next chapter, we shall take up some advanced aspects of GUI programming like the 'Document-View' architecture of GUI programs, some abstract GUI actions, and the general principles of design of CAD applications that depend heavily on GUIs for smooth running.

PROBLEMS

1. Assume that in a combined message map and a virtual functions-based library for Windows, the base message handling class BaseWindow declares the handler for the WM_PAINT message as a virtual function. Explain with reasons the outcome of a programmers effort to add a message map entry for WM_PAINT in a class derived from BaseWindow.

2. Expand the macros DECLARE_MESSAGE, DEFINE_MESSAGE, ADD_MESSAGE and END_MESSAGE described in the text using the C++ #define construct.

3. Design a window class that has a status bar and continuously displays the coordinates of the mouse cursor on the status bar. Refer to the relevant messages from the SDK manual or help file.

4. An application does the following. Its display is split vertically into two equal zones. There is a button each at the centre of each of the zones. The label on the button on the left zone is >> while the button on the right zone is labelled <<. When the application is executed for the first time, the background of the left zone is white and the button >> is enabled. However, the background of the right zone is black and the button << is disabled. Every time the user clicks on the only enabled button, the white background of the zone becomes black, the button becomes disabled, the background of the other zone becomes white now and the button within that zone is enabled.

5. Design a dialog box that looks like a simple four function (+, −, * and /) calculator. Bind this dialog box to an appropriate dialog class designed by you. The dialog function of your class should be able to take care of the standard calculator operations.

6

Object-Oriented GUI Programming—Advanced Concepts

In Chapter 5, we have seen how an object-based GUI library lets a programmer dissociate certain routine aspects of GUI programming from the application-specific aspects. We have discussed two major class hierarchies—one that encapsulates the top-level handling of the application (the `Application` class), and another which encapsulates message handling and display aspects of the building blocks (windows, controls and dialog boxes) of a GUI program. A library, along with the tools provided for automatic parametric generation of application specific extensions of the classes provided in the library, forms the foundation of a GUI development platform.

While pointing out the role of a GUI 'window' as a display surface, not much was talked about this specific aspect of a window's behaviour in the last chapter. What was however pointed out, was that a GUI window and hence a window object, can be associated with a 'context' through which a programmer can perform device independent graphics.

'What' is to be drawn on a display window of an application is of course entirely dependent on the application. Various factors, usually related to some user interaction, determine 'when' and 'where' (i.e. on which window), a drawing operation would be carried out. A natural object-oriented thinking would be to delegate the above aspects of drawing to different objects. A reasonable abstraction of the process can therefore be expressed as follows: *An object responsible for receiving user input decides 'when' to draw by invoking another object whose responsibility is to generate 'what' to draw on the object 'where' to draw.* An abstract study in the above lines of GUI programs with a lot of display overhead is known as the *Model-View-Control* (or MVC) paradigm where the *Model, View* and *Control* are sub-abstractions for the 'what,' 'where' and 'when' aspects, respectively.

Historically, in MS-Windows programming, the dual nature of a window as a display as well as a message handler, has led to conceptual unification of the control and the view above. The MVC paradigm is therefore looked at in the same manner, resulting it being commonly known as the *Document-View Architecture*. The document is just another name for the model of the MVC

209

paradigm. The view of the document-view architecture is a combination of the control and view aspects of the MVC paradigm.

In this chapter, we begin with a discussion of the document-view architecture beginning from the next section. Different issues concerning object-oriented programming for interactive presentation graphics is discussed in the next section. Geometric modelling is one of the most efficient and well-used techniques for representing 'what' must be drawn in a typical GUI application. Several aspects of geometric modelling is discussed in the final section.

THE DOCUMENT-VIEW ARCHITECTURE

The document-view architecture is a manifestation of an attempt to further disassociate the various components of an application, usually those meant to be run on GUI platforms. In Chapter 5, we have established the importance of GUI platforms, especially MS-Windows, in design of standardized user interfaces. The user interface is only one necessary aspect of an application whose importance cannot be less stressed. However, the core of the application—the code and data-structural manipulations on a model of the problem being solved, remains quite independent of the user interface. A good object-oriented behaviour could therefore be to formalize this independence, which is the basis of the document-view architecture, also known as the model-view architecture.

The document-view paradigm involves the separation of an application into three distinct abstract layers:

1. The *document* or *model,* which is the principal layer incorporating the application's functionality. Different applications necessarily differ at this level. Application-specific activities like data management, data base, processes, simulation, etc., are done at this level. The activities could be carried out through simple objects or even through complex structures. An application may have a single document or several documents. In Windows programming, a clear distinction is made between the two. Applications with a single document is described to be providing a Single Document Interface (SDI). However, an application could also provide a Multiple Document Interface (MDI).

2. The *view* layer, which deals with how the model is presented to the user. The objects in this layer implement the pictorial elements of the application. The objects extract information from the document layer and display it through a variety of mechanisms like graphs, charts, editors, etc. The objects also provide a capability to perform view transformation. They can request information from the user and provide feedback to user requests. A view (layer) may contain *sub-views* for further division of presentation. However, for a given document, there is usually a well-defined *top-level view*.

3. The *control*, which is more of a dispatching layer that performs user interaction on one end, directly or through view, and interacts with the document on the other.

The key idea of the paradigm is to separate an application into the above interchangeable layers. This way, the notion of *how* a user sees an application can be changed without the need to re-program the application's central structure, the document. The flexibility of changing layers not only provides greater possibilities of porting the same application to different computing environments, but also provides greater flexibility in meeting different use requirements. A major drawback of the software development community, namely, good modellers, are generally not good user-interface designers (and vice versa), can also be removed to quite an extent.

The View Class

The view has a display surface and event handling capabilities. It is therefore a window. It would be quite safe to inherit the class View from class BaseWindow. Member data of View should include a pointer to its Document. There must be a number of member functions to perform interaction with the document. Conversely, there must be other member functions that the document invokes to notify the view of several aspects.

A View class instance (i.e. a view object) is a child of a frame window. More than one view object can share a frame window. A view object can be attached to only one document (an instance of the Document class), but a document can have multiple views attached to it. For example, a word-processing program might provide both a complete text view of a document as well as an outline view that shows only the section headings. The different types of views can be placed in separate frame windows or in separate panes of a single frame window if one uses a splitter window.

A view object is responsible for handling several different types of input— keyboard input, mouse input, commands from menus, toolbars and scroll bars. A view object receives commands forwarded by its frame window. The view is responsible for displaying and modifying the document's data, but not for storing it. The document provides the view with the necessary details about its data. When a view detects changes in its document's data changes, it should typically, call the updateViews functionality of its document, which in turn notifies each of the other views by calling its update member function. The default implementation of the above function invalidates the entire client area of the view.

```
class View : public BaseWindow {
protected:

    Document            *theDocument;
    DWORD               rop;

friend class Document;

public:

    View( BaseWindow *pWindow, char *name = NULL)
      : BaseWindow(pWindow, name, &GLOBAL_ViewClass) { }
```

```
    virtual ~View();

    virtual DWORD drawROP() { return rop; }
    void     setROP(DWORD r) { rop = r; }

    Document* getDocument() { return theDocument; }
    void SetDocument(Document *d) { theDocument = d; }

    virtual LONG initialUpdate() { return update(); }
       // First time update after construction.
       // Could be overloaded in derived views.

    virtual LONG update()
    // Called by document if updation of view required.
    {
       DeviceContext *dc = new DeviceContext(handle);
       long r  = paint(dc);
       delete dc;
       return r;
    }

    LONG paint(DeviceContext *dc)
       { return theDocument ? theDocument->draw(dc) : TRUE; }

};
```

The Document Class

```
class View;

class Document {
protected:
   char  docTitle[81];
   char  *docFilePathName;

   List  docViewList; // List of views associated with this document.
   int   docSticky; // Document changed since last saved.

public:

    Document()
    {
       docTitle[0] = 0;
       docFilePathName = NULL;
       docSticky = 0;
    }

    char    *getTitle()
    {
       char *t = new char [ strlen(docTitle) + 1 ];
       strcpy(t, docTitle);
       return t;
    }
```

```
virtual void setTitle(char* pTitle)
{
  if (pTitle) strcpy(docTitle, pTitle);
}

char    getFilePathName() { return docFilePathName; }

virtual void setFilePathName(char* pFilePathName)
{
  if (pFilePathName) {
    docFilePathName = new char [ strlen(pFilePathName) + 1 ];
    strcpy(docFilePathName, pFilePathName);
  }
}

virtual int  isModified() { return docSticky; }
void setModified(int m = 1) { docSticky = m; }

virtual void addView(View* pView) // Adds a View and puts it on top.
{
  if (pView && pView->theDocument() == this) {
    docViewList.add(pView);
    viewListChanged();
  }
}

virtual void removeView(View* pView, int toDeleteView = 0)
{ docViewList.detach(pView, toDeleteView); viewListChanged(); }

View *getTopView() { return (View *)docViewList.peekHead(); }

void bringViewToTop(View *pView)
{
  removeView(pView, 0); // Remove view from list without destroying it.
  addView(pView); // Add it on top.
  pView->bringToTop();
  viewListChanged();
}

virtual int readFromFile() { return 0; }
virtual int saveToFile() { return 0; }

virtual void viewListChanged() {}

virtual int  newDocument()
{
  if ( isModified() ) return 0;
  strcpy(docTitle, "New Document");
  docFilePathName = NULL;
  docSticky = 0;
  return 1;
}

virtual int  openDocument(char* pFilePathName)
{
```

```
    if ( isModified() ) return 0;
    docFilePathName = pFilePathName;
    if (readFromFile()) {
      docSticky = 0;
      return 1;
    }
    return 0;
  }

  virtual int saveDocument()
  {
    if (saveToFile()) {
      docSticky = 0;
      return 1;
    }
    return 0;
  }

  virtual int saveAsDocument(const char* pFilePathName)
  {
    if (docFilePathName) delete docFilePathName;
    docFilePathName = pFilePathName;
    saveDocument();
  }

  virtual void closeDocument()
  {
    if ( isModified() ) saveDocument();
  }

  virtual ~Document()
  {
    ListIterator l(&docViewList);
    while (!l.endReached()) {
      delete l.current();
      l.next();
    }
    if (docFilePathName) delete docFilePathName;
  }

  virtual int isDrag() { return 0; }
    // Indicates whether drag drop feature is supported.

  virtual void draw(DeviceContext *) {}
  // Called when the entire document must draw itself.
};
```

OBJECT-ORIENTED PROGRAMMING FOR PRESENTATION GRAPHICS

Perhaps the most spectacular industrial applications of computers in the recent times have been in the field of computer-aided design CAD. While the internal aspect of CAD tools are domain specific, most modern versions of marketed

CAD tools have one property in common, namely, rich visual interface. Not only are the results of design displayed graphically, but in many cases, user inputs are also obtained graphically.

In this section, we shall discuss in some detail, about certain aspects of presentation graphics of CAD tools in a GUI environment and within the document view paradigm. A general discussion of CAD tools may be in order.

CAD Tool Software, An Introduction

The term CAD software essentially refers to the vast collection of commercial computer programs which when run on a suitable computer turns the latter into an effective design tool. Clearly, these software must capture the basic concepts of 'design' in the particular field of application it is meant for. There is no formal definition of design. Yet, every industrially produced commodity, must go through what is generally known as the 'design phase'. We therefore try to provide a workable definition of design to act as the starting point of the discussions to follow.

Designing of a commodity means producing the most detailed specifications of the same such that any expert associated with the manufacture and use of the commodity is able to visualize (i.e. create a mental model of) the commodity with relative ease.

The specifications should be viable under the particular technology under use and must conform to the rules and regulations (international, national or local) appropriate for the commodity.

Last but not the least, the commodity produced under the given specifications must be aesthetically pleasing to the general population who would (and might in the future) make use of the commodity.

Let us discuss certain issues arising out of the above discussion in a little more detail.

To experts of the field, laying down of the basic specifications is perhaps the easiest factor to tackle. In most cases, it essentially means formulation of a set of equations and/or formulae and figuring out a set of parameters that satisfy the equations and formulae. The parameters form the pillars around which the final specifications are laid.

The rules and regulations factor, while sometimes considered as a necessary evil by designers, they are actually very much necessary and are usually products of collective wisdom and experiences of leading experts of the field. They serve to minimize the risks of commodities being created that might turn out to be harmful for mankind with immediate or far-reaching effect.

The computer can relieve the designer's burden of checking technical viability by providing with software tools for the same. The tools could be:

Number Crunching Tools like solver for linear and non-linear equations, differential equations (ordinary and partial), matrix manipulations, iterative optimization, etc.

Logic Based Rules, even those incorporating artificial intelligence and expert system features in the design rule checking and validation.

Validation Tools, i.e., standard tools for validating against statutory regulations relevant for the product, provided such regulations are sufficiently objective. Quite often, the statutory regulations are not sufficiently objective or have so many regional variations that incorporation of them in a single CAD software becomes a difficult proposition.

Simulation tools that are useful when the logic of design validation is either less understood or is difficult to model. Simulation allows the designer to verify design efficacy through *logical and dry runs.*

Visual and audio-visual presentation tools.   Aesthetics, and sometimes, design efficacy, are essentially subjective factors. Aesthetic appraisal is carried out by human beings through almost every sensory perception—sight, auditory, touch and, for certain products at least, taste and olfactory. In most cases however, the visual appeal carries the maximum impact. A product that is good to look at, while being technically sound, almost always wins the show. The primary objective of the tools in question is to provide the designer with appropriate (audio-)visual feedback at different stages of design. Evidently, graphical rendering of design models through visual tools remains a key aspect of most CAD software.

CAD Software Presentation Graphics and the Document-View Paradigm

From our discussions above, we find that there could be a clearly-defined demarcation in a CAD software in terms of actual modelling (and/or simulation) and presentation of the model (and/or simulation results). The document-view paradigm is therefore most suitable for description and specification of most CAD software.

The document aspect of the software should formulate a proper model of the commodity being designed, that captures the relevant information needed to carry out various design manipulations. Simultaneously, it must be tenable for efficient filtering through number crunching, logic, design rule and simulation tools. Finally, the document aspect should be easily mappable on to one or more display views, and be capable of modifying itself upon user interaction.

Discrete display surfaces and bitmaps

Display surfaces connected to computers come in various sizes and resolutions. CAD applications are mostly concerned with CRT type display surfaces, and sometimes printers, for obtaining hard copies. Almost all standard display surfaces may be viewed as a two-dimensional, discrete and finite rectangular grid of display 'spots', commonly known as *pixels* (from 'picture' 'cells'). An *image* or *bitmap*, the commonly used technical terms for a picture, is a two-dimensional matrix of pixels. A pixel may be monochrome (also called black-and-white) or it may be coloured.

In a typical situation with a CAD software, a commodity being designed is rendered as an image. To the user, the current rendering is the only representation of the commodity available. However, the user may request for a different rendering, for example, a view from a different angle. Performance of a CAD software for a given commodity may depend considerably upon whether the different views are internally represented as bitmaps or in a format different from the displayed image.

Let us consider the advantages and disadvantages of the bitmap as a viable internal representation.

Advantages of bitmaps in design representation

- Rendering can be done at the highest possible speed. This is because the bitmap structure has a one-to-one correspondence with the display surface and the mechanism that controls the surface is geared up to receive bitmaps and render them on the surface at the fastest possible speed.

- Certain primitive rendering operations like moving a bitmap from one part of the display to another, drawing copies of a bitmap and filling closed areas with an indicated colour may be done easily and speedily on bitmaps.

Disadvantages of bitmaps in design representation

- Bitmaps take too much space. For example, the bitmap of a 128 pixel by 128 pixel rectangle in black and white requires 16 KB (plus a few bytes for the header) of storage. The same rectangle can easily be represented in 4 bytes by storing only coordinates of the two diagonals.

- Bitmaps are too coarse-grained for a good representation. The accuracy of representation is limited by the inter-pixel distance.

- No information regarding the contents of the picture can be obtained easily.

As an illustration of the last point, consider a situation where a red circular disk is placed on a blue background material. An image for the scenario would have red pixels shaped like a circle (approximately) in the centre, the remaining pixels of the display rectangle being blue. While this bitmap can be moved, copied and even stored in the disk quite easily, to answer a simple question about the scenario it represents, viz., 'what is the diameter of the disk?' would require non-trivial search and count operations to be performed on the image.

Geometric Modelling in Interactive Presentation Graphics

The alternative to having bitmap representation of objects is to go for *Geometric Modelling*. Here, objects are assumed to be constituted of primitive geometric entities like lines, arcs, and well-defined curves (for example splines) for two-dimensional objects, and also planes, and spherical sections, for three-dimensional objects.

The advantage of geometric representation is economy of storage—every well-defined entity can be represented by a handful of parameters, accuracy of representation only dependent upon the internal numeric representation chosen (and hence left upto the designer's/programmer's choice), rather than on the rigidly defined inter-pixel distance for the display surface.

The disadvantage of the geometric representation scheme is that every time an object is to be rendered on the display surface, non-trivial operations are required to actually 'draw' the object. However, queries regarding the representation can be answered faster and with better accuracy.

Consider the earlier illustration of the red circular disk on a blue background. Here the information centre is the disk, which is basically a circle. It can be represented geometrically by specifying the diameter. Clearly, the answer to the question 'what is the diameter of the disk?' simply requires reporting the value of a parameter, in this case the diameter. However, rendering the scenario would require the centre coordinates of the position of the disk and its colour as parameters. The rendering operation should set all pixels that are on or inside the disk's perimeter to red and set other pixels blue. This takes considerably higher time than simply rendering a bitmap. If a copy of the scenario is required, the whole rendering process has to be repeated.

Geometric modelling is the preferred representation scheme for most CAD applications, not only because of the advantages listed above, but also because the model in most cases is a major part of the logical model (document) of the overall application. Consider a hypothetical design scenario where the commodity to be designed is a red disk of an appropriate diameter. The designer's job is to select the diameter, which is done by suitably altering the diameter till the drawing of four disks on a blue background appears aesthetically appealing. Clearly, the logical model of the commodity to be designed (the disk) contains only one variable—the diameter. The visual operation requires drawing the disk at four places of the display. As we have discussed above, the geometric model of the application requires the diameter of the disk as a document parameter.

View-Specific Parameters in the Document

The 'document' of an application using geometric modelling as the internal representation scheme may require to store parameters that are less relevant for other operations of the application except viewing. Let us augment our illustrative example to understand this fact.

Consider that the disk in our illustrative problem can be made of different materials and may have different thicknesses. The actual dimensions of the disks are much larger than the size of any realistic display surface. The user wants a two-dimensional rendering of the designed disk at any point of time, such that all the four renderings are fully visible and the colour of the drawn disks should reflect the material used for the disk as well as its thickness (for example, it could be the shade red for the material 'iron' with the depth of redness dependent upon the thickness of the disk).

In the above example, the thickness and material (code) parameters are basically logical ones, i.e. they have no direct view connotations. The document must, however, maintain an appropriate 'scale factor' parameter to achieve complete renderings of four copies of the disk. The scale factor, possibly, has no other connotation in the document. The document might also need to 'compute' the colour of the circles representing the disk. This can be done through some function of material (code) and thickness of the disk—two 'internal' document parameters.

The bitmap vs. geometric modelling dichotomy through an example

We have seen that the geometric model based on internal view parameters is not only economic and more accurate (than bitmaps), but also is the more natural choice. The bitmap is, however, quite often retained as a part of the view-specific parameter of the document in many CAD applications, usually for the benefit of fast rendering.

In the example taken up a little earlier, say, it takes time T to render the geometric model on view and time t to copy a bitmap from one point of screen to another and that $t<<T$. Consider the instant when the first of the four copies required is to be drawn. In absence of anything, the picture must be generated from the model, taking time T. However, for the three subsequent drawings, they can be copied as bitmaps from the first picture, thus requiring time $3t$. Thus, instead of requiring time $4T$ for drawing, only time $T+3t$ is necessary, provided the bitmap of the first rendering is retained in the document. The last three bitmaps are generated *in situ,* and need not be a part of the document.

Let us now augment the functionality of the system slightly in that the user can, even without changing the diameter or thickness of the disk, move around the four pictures of the disk on the display surface and/or draw more copies.

Now, so long as the diameter and the thickness of the disk is not changed, the pictures that are being moved about or created are copies of the original. If movement and creation is arbitrary, it may be difficult to create the bitmap of the original *in situ.* Under such circumstances, it may be necessary to attach a bitmap for each of the drawn bitmaps with the document. While this undoubtedly increases the memory requirement, it may be worthwhile in situations where fast rendering is important.

User Feedback in CAD Application

Another important aspect of a CAD tool is obtaining user's feedback. In the earlier generation of CAD tools, the user could interact with the software only through the keyboard. Nowadays however, more utilitarian devices are available like the mouse, digitizing tablet, and joy-stick (mostly used for games). The philosophy of user interface has greatly evolved over time. In the earlier CAD tools, 'commands' had to be typed in, sometimes in a specifically mentioned case —i.e. in upper or lower case. Modern CAD tools developed on GUIs (usually) on the other hand, use such GUI-specific artifacts like menus, sub-menus, and all type of control buttons, list boxes, edit boxes, and dialog boxes.

A CAD software translates user interaction through controls into manipulations on the document and/or modifications of the view. However, some amount of preliminary processing is sometimes necessary to translate user inputs into actual model/view manipulations. A majority of these preliminary processing methods are geometrical computations. Geometrical computations may also be necessary during other document manipulations. Indeed, there is currently, a specialization of theoretical computer science called Computational Geometry, that deals specially in geometrical computations.

An Example Problem Requiring Geometric Computation on User Input

Consider an older generation CAD application for designing boxes. The 'design' pertains to computing the width and height of the box, the length given as raw data. As visual output, the application displays either the top-view (length-width) or the front-view (length-height) of the designed box. At any one point of time, only one of the above views is provided. The user can enter the raw data (length of box here) by entering a number (at some prompt). The document part of the application designs the box and the application displays one of the views on view. If the user wants to see a different view, (s)he need only interact with the view since the designed box is not changed as a result. However, if (s)he re-enters a new length, the entire design process has to be repeated.

A more modern application might have the facility to enter the length of the box graphically. In a typical application, the user wanting to change the length of the box might simply use an interactive device like the mouse to 'click-and-drag' an edge (a width in top-view or a height in front-view) of the displayed picture to the desired position. What the view receives as input necessarily depends upon the view surface—input 'points' are necessarily points on the view surface. The view might then send the information about the user input(s) to the document and request the document for a re-display of the newly-designed box. The document on its part, must however, transform the user input(s) to its own representation scheme. Moreover, every time the view requests for some display operation, there must be a transformation from the document representation system back to output data relevant to the view surface.

The World and View Coordinate Systems

For a given view surface, there is usually a coordinate system defined for it. This coordinate system is the view's coordinate system. For example, for CRT-like view surfaces, the normal system assumes the origin to be at the top left corner, a one pixel per unit abscissa in a left to right direction, and a one line per unit ordinate in a top to bottom direction. The view coordinate system is, therefore, generally two-dimensional, may or may not be isotropic (i.e. the aspect ratio may or may not be unity) and is necessarily bounded.

The coordinate system on which the document is based is generally called the 'world' coordinate system. The dimension of the coordinate system is application specific. For example, it is three-dimensional in our application designing boxes. The document space may quite well be unbounded. For a seamless interaction between the document and its view, coordinate transformations have to be carried out somewhere.

Usually, the world to view transformation is required more often. However, where back flow of information from the view to document has to be catered for, the view to world transformation is also a necessity. The interrelationship between the document and its view should in such cases, be such that transformations in both the directions are possible. Finding such an 'invertible' transformations is quite often a considerably difficult job, and demands as high level of imagination and intuitive geometric sense on part of the designer, apart from sound knowledge of graphic techniques.

The Mouse Input Device

Modern computer terminals, especially those that cater for graphics-based CAD applications, are unthinkable without the mouse device. The mouse appears to be the most convenient and reasonably versatile device for obtaining positional feedback for the user. Let us briefly summarize the role of the mouse in an interactive GUI-based CAD application, where the mouse acts as a handy device through which the user can notify a number of wishes.

A mouse has several 'buttons', usually two or three, which the user may press (or release) at any point of time. A single press of a hitherto released button is called a 'click' of the button. Of multi-buttoned mice, the left button is given a special status because a right-handed person finds it most convenient to click this button. Unless otherwise mentioned, a 'mouse-click' is taken to be a click of the left mouse button. Nowadays, two rapid succession of mouse clicks, called 'double-clicks', is also considered as a popular method of notifying some user intention.

The user can also slide the mouse on an appropriate hard surface and by doing so, can indicate the point (or a neighbourhood of points) on the view on which (s)he is interested. A graphical user interface must provide an appropriate pictorial feedback of the 'mouse position' on the view clearly to the user. Usually, this is done by a small arrow shaped 'cursor' that transparently moves over the view surface. The tip of the arrow is the 'hot-point' of the mouse.

Sometimes, the mouse cursor may assume different shapes than the usual thick arrow, primarily to alert the user that either something special is happening, or the application is in some special 'state' or that the zone where the mouse cursor is at present, is different from ordinary view zones in certain respects. For example, many CAD applications display the mouse cursor as an hourglass (or a tiny clock face), when it is carrying out some computation that may be time consuming and during which it may not be able to cater to user interactions. In many applications, whenever the mouse cursor enters a view zone where textual input is expected from the user, the cursor is made to assume the shape of a vertical or triangular 'caret'.

A 'mouse status' is, therefore, clearly defined by its *position* and the *button status*. By position, we do not mean the actual position of the mouse device, but rather, the logical position of the (hot-point of the) mouse cursor on the view. Position is therefore a pair (mouseX, mouseY). Each button may be either *pressed* or *released* and can, therefore, be represented by a boolean number—TRUE for pressed and FALSE for released. Any *change* in the mouse status is known as a 'mouse event'. Thus, the user can generate mouse events by a combination of any of the following: a) moving the mouse, thus changing the *position*, b) pressing any unpressed button, and c) releasing a pressed button.

Note that while the mouse is being moved about, several of the buttons may remain pressed. Indeed, most 'click-and-drag' operations utilize such operations of the mouse—the user 'selects' the object to be dragged by moving the mouse cursor to the vicinity (application dependent) of the object to be dragged, 'drags' it by moving the mouse while keeping the button (the left button, since nothing was mentioned) pressed and finally, 'placing' the object at a new position by releasing the button. In between events, the mouse is said to be 'idle'.

The Mouse and GUIs

Almost every GUI ascribes speciality status to the mouse input device. The kernel of GUIs poll the mouse on behalf of all applications that may be currently running under it. It then identifies the 'window' that should receive the latest mouse notification, and sends it an appropriate message.

MS-Windows generates 10 messages for (client area) for mouse events—three each (button down, button up and button double-click) for each of the three possible mouse buttons (left, middle and right), and one message for mouse movement. We shall take up these messages again a little later. However, at this point, we can safely assume that the messages can be easily translated into mouse event functionalities of the view *class* as listed below:

- onMouseLeftButtonDown(int x, int y). This functionality caters for the situation when the user presses the left mouse button at location (x,y).

- onMouseRightButtonDown(int x, int y) and onMouseMiddleButtonDown(int x, int y). Same as above, except that they pertain to the right and middle mouse buttons, respectively.

- onMouseLeftButtonUp(int x, int y). This functionality caters for the condition when the user has released the hitherto pressed left mouse button, the position of the event being (x,y).

- onMouseRightButtonUp(int x, int y) and onMouseMiddleButtonUp(int x, int y). Same as above, except that they pertain to the right and middle mouse buttons, respectively.

- onMouseMove(int x, int y, int key). This functionality is invoked if the mouse has been moved, but there has been no change in the button status. The three least significant bits of the parameter key encode the status of the left, right and middle buttons, respectively. If the bit is '1', the corresponding button is pressed.

An Abstract Click and Drag

Consider the 'click-and-drag' situation introduced in an earlier example, i.e. the user clicks on some 'object' represented on the view, drags the mouse to a new position while keeping the button pressed, and finally releases it. The view of the application may achieve click and drag in the following abstract manner:

1. The application maintains a flag variable status (say) with possible values FREE and DRAG. Normally, the value of this variable is FREE, indicating that nothing is presently being dragged.

2. As user moves the mouse about, the functionality onMouseMove gets repeatedly invoked.

3. The function onMouseMove checks the flag status and exits immediately if it has a value FREE.

4. At some point, the user clicks the mouse on the object which is to be dragged. This causes the onMouseLeftButtonDown functionality to be invoked. Here, the application checks the coordinates to find out whether any valid object has been clicked upon, and if so, which one. If a valid object has been clicked upon, status is set to DRAG. If the object is an extended one, it may also be required to store the position of the mouse with respect to some local origin of the object.

5. As the user drags the object across the client area of the view while keeping the mouse button pressed, mouse position change events are regularly generated and the onMouseMove repeatedly invoked. However, now the function finds status to be in the DRAG state. What happens now may vary from application to application. In some applications, the entire object may be drawn on the view surface as dragging continues. Indeed, where the pictures of the objects that might be dragged are relatively small (with respect to the client area size) and not so complex to draw (and erase), such a 'complete' feedback is provided. Sometimes, to save upon drawing and erasing time, only the outline of the object is drawn and redrawn during dragging.

6. Finally, at some point of time, the user releases the mouse button that results in the onMouseLeftButtonUp being invoked. In this function, the application 'moves' the object to the final position (with appropriate validation, if any) and sets status back to FREE. The moved drawing usually retains the stored relative position of the original mouse click with respect to the object's local origin.

Document Interaction during Click and Drag

Although the click-and-drag scenario can be abstractly described as above, there may be considerable amount of application-specific tasks to be carried out in the process. In most cases, these tasks pertain to flow of information back and forth from the document. A few aspects are described here.

- The first click that selects the object should translate in a document interaction with a transformed point of the click position as a parameter.

- The document should respond to the interaction through a 'search' of its internally maintained list of objects. If the transformed point is found to belong to no object, it should be reported accordingly to view. Otherwise, the following should be done in the document.

- The object 'found' should be marked selected, and possibly connected to a temporary pointer for easy access in the future.

- Every new view drag position should be transformed and sent to the document which should respond as in the following three steps.

- A view object (usually a bitmap) *for erasing* should be generated corresponding to the selected object(s) and despatched to the view which results in the dragged object in the old position being erased.

- The selected object(s) should be logically 'moved' to its (their) new position(s). This could be done by simply altering the *key point(s)* (trivially, the local origin(s) of the selected object(s)).

- A view object *for drawing* should be generated corresponding to the selected object(s) and despatched to the view which results in the dragged object being drawn in the new position.

- The end of click and drag operation identified the view should signal the document to clear its (list of) selected object.

The `DragView` Class

The `DragView` class encapsulates automatic drag drop behaviour.

```
class DragView : public View {
protected:

    int                 dragOn;
    BitMap              *dragBitmap;
    int                 bitmapOffsetX, bitmapOffsetY,
                        moveStartX, moveStartY,
                        moveX, moveY;

friend class DragDocument; // See later.

    DragDocument *myDocument() { return (DragDocument *) theDocument; }

    virtual void unSelectPreviousSelect(int x, int y,
                                        DeviceContext *dc,
                                        BitmapDeviceContext *bdc)
    {
        if (dragBitmap) {
// An already selected bitmap exists, to be de-selected.
            bdc->bindBitmap(dragBitmap);
            bdc->bitmapUnSelect();
            bdc->drawBitmapOn(dc, oldMoveX, oldMoveY, SRCCOPY);
```

```
      delete dragBitmap;
      dragBitmap = 0;
    }
}

virtual void drawMovedNewAt(int x, int y)
{
    if ( dragBitMap && (x != moveX || y != moveY) ) {
    int oldMoveX = moveX, oldMoveY = moveY;
      moveX = x;
      moveY = y;
      DeviceContext dc(handle);
      BitmapDeviceContext bdc(&dc);
      bdc.bindBitmap(dragBitmap);
      bdc.drawBitmapOn( &dc,
                        oldMoveX - bitmapOffsetX,
                        oldMoveY - bitmapOffsetY,
                        drawROP()); // Erase.
      bdc.drawBitmapOn( &dc,
                        moveX - bitmapOffsetX, moveY - bitmapOffsetY,
                        drawROP()); & Re-draw

    }
  }

public:

    DragView( BaseWindow *pWindow, char *name = NULL,
                  DragDocument *doc)
       : View(pWindow, name, &GLOBAL_DragViewClass)
       {
         dragOn = 0;
         drawBitmap = NULL;
         setDocument( doc );
       }

    virtual ~DragView();

    virtual LONG leftMouseButtonDown(int x, int y)
    {
      if ( dragDropFlag && !dragOn ) { // Drag drop enabled.
        dragOn = 1;
        int oldMoveX = moveX, oldMoveY = moveY;
        moveStartX = moveX = x;
        moveStartY = moveY = y;
        int oldOffsetX = bitmapOffsetX, oldOffsetY = bitmapOffsetY;
        DeviceContext dc(handle);
        BitmapDeviceContext bdc(&dc);
        Bitmap *newDragBitMap =
        myDocument()->beginObjectDrag( dc,
                                       x, y,
                                       &bitmapOffsetX, &bitmapOffsetY);
        if (newDragBitmap && newDragBitmap != dragBitmap) {
            // Mouse click on valid object.
          if (dragBitmap) {
            // An already selected bitmap exists, to be de-selected.
```

```
                    unSelectPreviousSelect( oldMoveX - oldOffsetX,
                                            oldMoveY - oldOffsetY,
                                            &dc, &bdc);
              dragBitmap = newDragBitmap;
          }
          bdc.bindBitmap(dragBitmap);
          bdc.bitmapSelect();
          bdc.drawBitmapOn( &dc,
                            x - bitmapOffsetX,
                            y - bitmapOffsetY, SRCCOPY);
        }
        else if (!newDragBitmap)
            unSelectPreviousSelect( oldMoveX - oldOffsetX,
                                    oldMoveY - oldOffsetY,
                                    &dc, &bdc);
      }
      return TRUE;
    }

    virtual LONG leftMouseButtonUp(int x, int y)
    {
      dragOn = 0;
      myDocument()->endObjectDrag( dc,
                                   x, y,
                                   bitmapOffsetX, bitmapOffsetY);
      return TRUE;
    }

    virtual LONG mouseMove(int x, int y)
    {
      if ( dragDropFlag && dragOn ) { // Dragging continued
        drawMoveNewAt(x, y);
      }
      return TRUE;
    }

    virtual LONG onMouseLeftButtonDown(UINT, WPARAM, LPARAM l)
      { return leftMouseButtonDown(LOWORD(l), HIWORD(l)); }
    virtual LONG onMouseLeftButtonUp(UINT, WPARAM, LPARAM l);
      { return leftMouseButtonUp(LOWORD(l), HIWORD(l)); }
    virtual LONG onMouseMove(UINT, WPARAM w, LPARAM l);
      { return mouseMove(LOWORD(l), HIWORD(l), w); }

    DECLARE_MESSAGE(View)
};

DEFINE_MESSAGE(DragView, BaseWindow)
  ADD_MESSAGE(WM_LBUTTONDOWN, onMouseLeftButtonDown), //
  ADD_MESSAGE(WM_LBUTTONUP, onMouseLeftButtonUp), //
  ADD_MESSAGE(WM_MOUSEMOVE, onMouseMove) //
ENDMESSAGE(Drag view)
```

GEOMETRIC MODELLING

We have already discussed at length how to dissociate the internal representation of objects that are to be displayed and the process through which they are actually displayed. While representation is an essential aspect of the document, the display aspects are delegated to the view. The user primarily interacts with the view which might notify the document about changes in the internal representations that might have to be made. As a part of handling such user notifications, the document might reverse notify the view to alter what is currently being displayed.

A great deal of research has been carried out in the quest for finding the best representation model in the above context. While it has clearly been realized that no single model can be the best for every application, the one that has a distinct edge in terms of representational compactness is generally known as *geometric modelling*—representing objects that can be displayed as structures recursively built upon rudimentary geometric objects like lines, arcs, circles, and splines. An entire discipline of research going by the name *computational geometry* is devoted to development of algorithms in a geometric modelling environment.

Computational Geometry

The term *Computational Geometry* (CG) was first used by M.I. Shamos. In spite of being a relatively new research discipline, CG has managed to attract an enormous amount of research and application interest in the past decade. CG deals with the design and analysis of data structures and algorithms for inherently geometric problems. The algorithms perform logical manipulation of complex geometric objects that are represented by data structures of varied complexity.

Standard geometric entities

Computational geometry algorithms extensively use the concept *geometric entities*—certain well-understood primitives in the geometric sense. The standard geometric entities are point, line, line segments, rectangles, and polygons. The entities are defined in unbounded two- or three-dimensional real space that is identical to the 'world space' of the problem being solved. Usually, but not always, the Cartesian coordinate system is preferred over others.

Specialized geometric entities

Sometimes, certain entities are further specialized so as to capture certain aspects that necessarily reduce computational burden. In this respect, line segments, rectangles and parallelopipeds (in 3D) that are aligned in cardinal directions receive special attention. Such entities are described as being *isothetic*. While three or higher dimensional space are quite often very meaningful for solving the problems at hand, human knowledge of two-dimensional geometry is far more established and vast as compared to the geometry of higher dimensions.

Indeed, the number of good CG algorithms based on a two-dimensional solution space far exceed those that also cater for higher dimensions.

We will concentrate mostly on the two-dimensional world. An additional advantage of this assumption is that it becomes easier to find an invertible transformation between the document and the view, the latter being essentially a bounded two-dimensional space.

Size of a geometric problem

The earliest CG algorithms dealt with the answering of some simple geometrical queries. In many cases, there exist intuitive solutions for them. However, the intuitive solutions are, in most cases, quite inefficient when the problem 'size' increases.

There is no unambiguous definition of the 'size' of a geometric problem. The concept of size is different in different situations. In most cases, the 'size' is synonymous with the number of a relevant type of geometric entity that may be present in a particular instance of the problem. Almost invariably, the computation time (average or worst case) required to solve a particular problem in a given problem instance, increases with the problem size.

If the size is quite small, possibly any solution method, including the intuitive one, may be equally suitable. However, when problem size increases appreciably, solution methods with better time complexity clearly start performing better than other methods. Therefore, if a CAD software expects to encounter a large problem size quite frequently, it is worthwhile studying and implementing relevant geometric algorithms of better time complexity. Sometimes, space complexity, rather than time complexity, is the deciding factor.

Some common CG algorithms

Some commonly used CG methods in CAD for which reasonably efficient, and sometimes proved to be optimal, algorithms exist are now briefly explained.

Point near entity. The problem space consist of different geometric entities of different types, where the size of the problem is the number of entities present. The query is, given a point p, to locate that entity (or those entities), if any, that is near enough (i.e. whose 'distance' from the query point is less than a threshold) to the query point.

Point within rectangle/polygon. Here the problem space consists of rectangles or polygons, as the case may be. The number of rectangles or polygons determines the problem size. An interesting specialization of the problem that is extensively used in most CAD applications is when the problem space consists of isothetic rectangles only.

Line segments intersect (H-V lines only). Isothetic lines are specialities in themselves and have attracted special attention in CG research. The problem space consist of isothetic lines. There may be different variations of the query. One popular query is, given 'a' horizontal (resp. vertical) line segment, report all vertical (resp. horizontal) segments that intersect this segment. Here the problem size is the number of vertical (resp. horizontal) segments in the problem space. Another popular query is to report 'all' pairs of intersecting segments. Here, the problem size is the total number of segments.

Line segments intersect (lines of any inclination). Queries considered for isothetic segments are also relevant in some problems for non-isothetic lines. However, here the complexities encountered are much more, since no help of special properties of the segments may be taken.

The ray shooting problem. This problem is less universal than the ones described above. Indeed, many aspects of the general problem is still in research phase. Simply speaking, the problem is as follows: Given a collection of entities and a semi-infinite straight line emanating from a given point (called a ray which has been 'shot'), report those entities that intersect with the line.

Points in a cardinal direction of an isothetic line. This is one of the most encountered geometrical problems in CAD applications. The solution space consist of a collection of points, the number of which determines the problem size. Given a horizontal (resp. vertical) line, the problem is to report those points that are above or below (resp. left or right) of the line. We have considered this problem in more detail in the paragraphs below.

Reporting points in a cardinal direction of an isothetic line

As mentioned above, the job is that given a horizontal line, report those points that are above or below it. Conversely, given a vertical line, report all points to the left or right of the line. Apparently, it seems that there is no problem here. If we have an H-line $y = k$ (say), all points whose ordinates are above k are above the line.

The problem arises when we consider that the points of the problem space are included in the collection in a haphazard fashion. In the absence of any pre-processing during the time a point is added to the collection or a post-processing over the collection after all points have entered it, the ordinates of points in the collection are expected to bear no correlation.

The trivial solution that works without any pre- or post-processing, is to check every point's ordinate, requiring a linear complexity. Good CG algorithms would, on the other hand, propose special data structures to represent the point collection. It may require pre-processing to enter a new point into the collection, or the points may enter into a flat data structure which is then transformed by post-processing on to the proposed data structure. In either case, the complexity of the reporting phase should be better than linear. Also, the complexities of the pre- or post-processing phase should be as low as possible.

Some Standard Geometric Object Classes

In this section, we have described how some common geometric entities may be encapsulated. Our examples include the point, the infinite line, the (general) line segment, the isothetic (i.e. parallel to either of the coordinate axes), and the (isothetic) rectangle. Everywhere we have considered the digital integral plane where all coordinate values lie within the extreme limits of values of an int data type.

Geometric Entity—Abstract base class of geometric entities

The class GeometricEntity heads the hierarchy and encapsulates the abstract behaviour of all geometric entities. This abstract super-class of all geometric entities is derived from the archivable and containable class Object. There is only a single *pure* virtual function, namely, distFrom(Point), that calculates the distance of the parameter point from this geometric entity.

```
class GeometricEntity : public Object {

// Abstract super-class
// of all geometric entities.
// By inheriting from object, we permit geometric entities
// to be contained in other containers, as well as be serializable.

public:

    GeometricEntity() { } // Default metric is also mm.

  virtual float distFrom(Point *) = 0;
};
```

The Point geometric entity

The class Point encapsulates a point geometric entity. Apart from two distinct distance computing (from another point) member functions, this class includes a member function to check whether another point is greater than this point. A point *P* being greater than another point *Q* is defined as either *P* is to the right of *Q*, else if *P* and *Q* are on the same abscissa, *P* is above *Q*.

The class Point is a real class. It overloads the member function distFrom(Point) to return the Euclidean distance of the target point from this point.

```
class Point : public GeometricEntity {

long x, y;

public:

    Point(long initX, long initY) { x = initX; y = initY; }

    long    manhattanDist(Point p) { return abs(x-p.x)+abs(y-p.y); }
    float   euclidDist(Point p) { return sqrt( (x-p.x)*(x-p.x)+
                                               (y-p.y)*(y-p.y) ); }

    Point   offsetPoint(Point p) { return Point(x+p.x, y+p.y); }

    float   distFrom(Point p) { return euclidDist(p); }
```

```
long    xCoord() { return x; }
long    yCoord() { return y; }
void    setX(long newX) { x = newX; }
void    setY(long newY) { y = newY; }
int     greater(Point p) // Returns true if p is right of this else
                        // if this--p is vertical, if p is above this
        { return abs(x-p.xCoord()) <= CLOSE ? p.yCoord() > y :
p.xCoord() > x; }

int     sameAs(Point p) { return abs(x - p->xCoord()) +
                                abs(y - p->yCoord()) <= CLOSE; }


int     less(Point p) { returns !sameAs(p) && !greater(p); }

    friend class DrawPoint;
};
```

The infinite Line geometric entity

The class Line encapsulates an infinite line and is characterized by two data
members for the gradient and the intercept of the line, respectively. This class
is designed to be able to represent lines in a more fine-grained manner. Hence,
both the data members are floating point numbers.

```
class Line : public GeometricEntity {

// Class for infinite line.

protected:

  float grad, icpt;

public:

    Line() : GeometricEntity() { grad = icpt = 0; // X-axis }
    Line(float m, float c) : GeometricEntity() { grad = m; icpt = c; }
    Line(Point p1, Point p2) // Line from two points.
     : GeometricEntity()
    {
      if (p1.x==p2.x) { // Line is vertical.
        grad=INFINITY+INFINITY;
        icpt=p1.x;
      }
      else    if (p1.y==p2.y) { // Line is horizontal.
        grad=0;
        icpt=p1.y;
      }
      else {
        grad = ((float)p1.y-(float(p2.y))/((float)p1.x-(float(p2.x)));
        icpt = p1.y - grad*p1.x;
      }
    }

    Line(AbstractSegment s) // Infinite line of a segment.
     : GeometricEntity()
    {
```

```
        grad = s.gradient();
        icpt = s.intercept();
    }

float gradient() { return grad; }
float intercept() { return icpt; }

int   pointLine(Point p)
    // returns 0 if p sufficiently close to line,
    //         1 if p is on 'right' of line,
    //        -1 if p is on 'left' of line.
{
  float dist = distFrom(&p);
  return abs(dist) <= CLOSE ? 0 : dist<0 ? -1 : 1;
}


Point *intersection(Line l)
    // Returns closest grid point to intersection of this
    // line and l. NULL if l is parallel to this line.
{
  if ( abs(grad - l.grad) <= CLOSE ) return NULL;
  float fx = (icpt - l.icpt) / (l.grad - grad);
  return new Point(fx, grad *fx + icpt);
}

int   axisIntercepts(float *a, float *b)
    // Returns closest integral axis intercepts through a and b,
    // i.e., if x/a + y/b = 1 were the equation of the line,
    // return value is 0 if line is neither vertical nor horizontal,
    // -1 if vertical (*b=0) and 1 if horizontal (*a=0).
{
  if ( abs(grad) <= CLOSE ) { // line is (nearly H).
    *a=0; *b=icpt;
    return 1;
  }
  if (abs(grad) >= INFINITY) { // line is (nearly V).
    *a=icpt; *b=0;
    return -1;
  }
  // Line is neither H nor V.
  *a = -icpt/grad; *b = icpt;
  return 0;
}

float distFrom(Point *p)
    { return (p->y-grad*p->x-icpt)/sqrt(1+grad*grad); }
};
```

The **AbstractSegment** and **Segment** geometric entities

The class AbstractSegment is the abstract super-class of all finite length line segments. Pure virtual functions are provided to return the gradient and intercept of the infinite line, of which this segment is a part. In addition, pure virtual functions initiate abstract behaviours for returning the first point (the 'lesser' of the two end points of the segment) and the second point, respectively. A pure virtual member function initiates an abstract behaviour to check whether a given point is on the segment, while another one initiates the method to find the intersection point between this and a given abstract segment.

```
class AbstractSegment : public GeometricEntity {
// Common parent
// of Segment and Orthogonal Segment. Abstract class.

public:

    AbstractSegment() : GeometricEntity() {}

  virtual float gradient() = 0; // Pure.
  virtual float intercept() = 0; // Pure.

  virtual float doubleAreaSubtended(Point p)
     // Signed area*2 of triangle p- [p1-p2—this segment's ends].
  {
     return firstPoint().distFrom(&(secondPoint())) *
                 // Base multiplied by
            Line(firstPoint(), secondPoint()).distFrom(&p);
                // Altitude.
  }

  virtual int   pointOnSegment(Point p) = 0;

  virtual Point intersection(AbstractSegment s) = 0;
     // Returns closest grid point to intersection of this
     // segment and s. NULL if s is parallel to this segment
     // or not on this segment.

  virtual int isVertical() = 0;
  virtual int isHorizontal() = 0;

  virtual Point firstPoint() = 0;
  virtual Point secondPoint() = 0;

  Line    infiniteLine() { return Line(gradient(), intercept()); }

  float  distFrom(Point *p);
  {
     float d  = infiniteLine().distFrom(p),
           d1 = firstPoint().distFrom(p),
           d2 = secondPoint().distFrom(p);

     return min ( min(d,d1), min(d,d2) );
  }
};
```

The class Segment encapsulates a real line segment. This is done by maintaining two Point data members representing the first and the second points of the segment, respectively. All the pure virtuals are appropriately overloaded.

```
class Segment : public AbstractSegment {
protected:

  Point p1, p2;

  void checkDirection() // Ensures p2 >= p1.
        { Point p = p1; if (p2.greater(p1)) { p1 = p2; p2 = p; } }

public:

    Segment() : AbstractSegment()
      { p1.x = p2.x = p1.y = p2. y = 0; // Null segment}
    Segment(int x1, int y1, int x2, int y2) : AbstractSegment()
      { p1.x = x1, p1.y = y1; p2.x = x2; p2.y = y2; checkDirection();
}
    Segment(Point fPoint, Point sPoint) : AbstractSegment()
      { p1=fPoint; p2=sPoint); checkDirection(); }
    Segment(Line l, Point fPoint, float length) : AbstractSegment()
      // fPoint assumed to be on line l.
      {
        p1 = fPoint;
        float x2 =  abs(l.gradient()) >= INFINITY/2 ? p1.xCoord() :
                    abs(l.gradient()) <= CLOSE ? length + p1.xCoord() :
                    p1.xCoord + length / sqrt( 1 +
l.gradient()*l.gradient() );
        float y2 =  abs(l.gradient()) >= INFINITY/2 ? length +
p1.yCoord() :
                    abs(l.gradient()) <= CLOSE ? p1.yCoord() :
                    l.gradient() * x2 + l.intercept();
        p2 = Point( x2, y2);
        checkDirection();
      }

  float gradient() { return p1.x == p2.x ? INFINITY :
                        ( p1.y - p2.y ) / ( p1.x - p2.x ); }

  float intercept() { return p1.x == p2.x ? p1.x :
                        p1.y - p1.x*gradient(); }

  int   doubleAreaSubtended(Point p)
   // Signed area*2 of triangle p-p1-p2
        { return p.x*(p1.y-p2.y) +
                p1.x*(p2.y-p.y) +
                p2.x*(p.y-p1.y); }

  int  pointOnSegment(Point p)
  {
    if (isVertical() || isHorizontal()) {
      IsoSegment o1( intercept(),
                      isVertical() ? p1.y : p1.x,
                      isVertical() ? p2.y : p2.x,
                      isVertical() ? -1 : 1 );
    return o1.pointOnSegment(p); // Despatch to orthogonal case.
    }
    Line l(gradient(),intercept()); // Make infinite line.
```

```
  if (l.pointLine(p)) return 0; // p not sufficiently close to l,
  // otherwise, check if distance from p1 to p, plus the
  // distance from p to p2 is about the same as distance from p1 to p2.
  return
    abs( p1.euclidDist(p) + p.euclidDist(p2) - p1.euclidDist(p2))
      <= 2*CLOSE;
}

Point *intersection(AbstractSegment s)
    // Returns closest grid point to intersection of this
    // segment and s. NULL if s is parallel to this segment
    // or not on this segment.
{
  if ( (isVertical() || isHorizontal() ) &&
       (s.isVertical() || s.isHorizontal())) {
    IsoSegment o1( intercept(),
                   isVertical() ? p1.y : p1.x,
                   isVertical() ? p2.y : p2.x,
                   isVertical() ? -1 : 1 );
    return o1.intersection(s); // Despatch to orthogonal case.
  }
  Line l1(gradient(),intercept()),
       l2(s.gradient(),s.intercept());
  Point *p = l1.intersection(l2);
  if (pointOnSegment(*p) && s.pointOnSegment(*p)) return p;
  else {
    delete p;
    return NULL;
  }
}

int   isVertical() { return p1.x==p2.x; }
int   isHorizontal() = {return p1.y == p2.y; }
Point firstPoint() { return p1; }
Point secondPoint() { return p2; }
};
```

The `IsoSegment` geometric entity for isothetic segments

The class `IsoSegment` represents the specialized version of a segment, where the segment is either horizontal or vertical. In the integral coordinate system, four integer values are required to represent such a segment—a direction flag indicating whether the segment is horizontal (resp. vertical), the left (resp. bottom) and right (resp. top) values in the variable axis, and the fixed value of the fixed axis.

```
class IsoSegment : public AbstractSegment {
protected:
  int icpt, loVal, hiVal, dirFlag; // dirFlag = 1 for H and -1 for V.
public:
    IsoSegment() { icpt = loVal = hiVal = 0; dirFlag = 1; }
                    // NULL H segment through origin.
    IsoSegment(int offset, int a, int b, int dir) // offset assumed
positive.
      { icpt = offset, dirFlag = d; loVal = min(a,b); hiVal = max(a,b);
    }
```

```
int    lowValue() { return loVal;}
int    highValue() { return hiVal;}

float gradient()  { return dirFlag==1 ? 0 : INFINITY; }
float intercept() { return icpt; }

int    doubleAreaSubtended(Point p)
       { return (hiVal-loVal)*(icpt-dirFlag==1 ?p.y:p.x); }

int    pointOnSegment(Point p)
         { return dirFlag==1 ?
               icpt==p.y && loVal<=p.x && p.x<=hiVal :
               icpt==p.x && loVal<=p.y && p.y<=hiVal; }

Point *intersection(AbstractSegment s)
{
  int c;
  if (dirFlag==1) { // Line is horizontal.
   if (s.isHorizontal()) return NULL;
   if (s.isVertical()) {
     c = s.intercept();
     return loVal<=c && c<=hiVal ? new Point(c,icpt) : NULL;
   }
   // s is inclined. Create a segment out of this ortho-segment.
   Segment s1(loVal,icpt,hiVal,icpt);
   return s1.intersection(s);
  }
  else { // Line is vertical.
   if (s.isVerticalal()) return NULL;
   if (s.isHorizontal()) {
     c = s.intercept();
     return loVal<=c && c<=hiVal ? new Point(icpt,c) : NULL;
   }
   // s is inclined. Create a segment out of this ortho-segment.
   Segment s2(icpt,loVal,icpt,hiVal);
   return s2.intersection(s);
  }
}

int    isVertical() { return dirFlag == -1; }
int    isHorizontal() { return dirFlag == 1; }
Point firstPoint() { return dirFlag == 1 ? Point(loVal,icpt)
                                          : Point(icpt,loVal); }
Point secondPoint() { return dirFlag == 1 ? Point(hiVal,icpt)
                                          : Point(icpt,hiVal); }
};
```

The Rectangle geometric entity

The class Rectangle represents a rectangle by maintaining two points—the lesser or bottom left point and the greater or top right point. Member functions are provided to check whether a point is within the rectangle, to find the union or intersection of this rectangle with another rectangle.

```
class Rectangle : public GeometricEntity {
protected:
  Point  p1, p2;

  void checkDirection() // Ensures p2 >= p1.
        { Point p = p1; if (p2.greater(p1)) { p1 = p2; p2 = p; } }
public:
    Rectangle(Point bottomLeft, Point topRight)
            { p1 = bottomLeft; p2 = topRight; checkDirection(); }
    Rectangle(int x1, int y1, int x2, int y2)
            { p1 = Point(x1,y1); p2 = Point(x2,y2); checkDirection(); }

  Point bottomLeft() { return p1; }
  Point topRight() { return p2; }

  Rectangle offsetRect(Point p)
      { return Rectangle( p1.offsetPoint(p), p2.offsetPoint(p) ); }

  Rectangle setUnionRectangle(Rectangle *other); // Not implemented here.
  Rectangle setIntersectionRectangle(Rectangle *other); // - ditto -

  int within(Point p) { return (p1.greater(p) || p1.sameAs(p)) &&
                                (p2.less(p) || p2.sameAs(p)); }

friend class DrawRectangle;
};
```

Geometric Modelling in Document

In most applications where at least a part of the document consists of entities
that can be drawn on the screen as geometric figures, geometric modelling is
highly recommended as the approach to store document data. As already discussed
earlier, the advantage of geometric modelling is that the application need not
maintain memory hungry objects like bitmaps for all entities of the document
that can be drawn. The 'geometrically modelled' document receives information
from external agencies, usually a view, to draw one or more of its entities on
a display context supplied to it. The document responds by creating a bitmap
compatible to the display context for the entities to be drawn and returns it as
the result. The invoking agency, the view, can then take the necessary action
to draw the bitmap and destroy it after use.

To aid the designer, most object-based GUI libraries offer a hierarchy of
two-dimensional drawable geometric object classes. A drawable object has the
following properties:

- It is usually associated with either a small number of 'finite' geometric
  entities (usually only one) or 'contains' other drawable entities.

- It has a well-defined range box.

- It can draw itself on a given display context.

- It is characterized by a unique point, usually within its range box,
  called its 'hot-point.'

- It has an overloadable method called `entityAt()` that takes the coordinates of a point as a parameter. It returns true if the given point lies within the range box of the entity. For open-ended segment entities, it additionally checks if the point is sufficiently close to the entity.

The abstract `DrawGeometricEntity` class

The abstract base class `DrawGeometricEntity` can be declared as follows:

```
class DrawGeometricEntity : public Object {
// Abstract Base class for geometric entities that can be drawn.
public:
    DrawGeometricEntity() : Object() {}

    virtual void draw(DeviceContext *) = 0;
            // Draws the entity on the device supplied as parameter.
            // Drawing is on entity virtual co-ordinate system.

    virtual void Rectangle rangeBox() = 0;
    virtual Point hotPoint() = 0; // Returns the hot-point.
    virtual void setHotPoint(Point) = 0; // Changes the hot-point, thus
                                         // effectively shifting it.

    virtual DrawGeometricEntity *entityAt(int x, int y)
        { return rangeBox().within(Point(x,y)) ? this : NULL; }
};
```

The real drawable geometric entity classes

Real drawable geometric entities for a point, a line segment and a rectangle, can be declared as follows. (Note that each of the classes below includes an (pointer to an) object of an appropriate (abstract where applicable) geometric entity class.):

```
class DrawPoint : public DrawGeometricEntity {
protected:

    Point    *geoPoint;

public:

    DrawPoint(long initX, long initY) : DrawGeometricEntity()
    { geoPoint = new Point(initX, initY); }

    DrawPoint() : DrawGeometricEntity() { geoPoint = new Point; }

    ~DrawPoint() { delete geoPoint; }

    Point *thePoint() { return geoPoint; }

    void    draw(DeviceContext *d)
    { d->circle( 0, geoPoint->x, geoPoint->y); }
            // Draw a zero width circle at the point's position.

    void    Rectangle rangeBox() { return Rectangle(geoPoint, geoPoint); }
```

```
  Point hotPoint() { return *geoPoint; }
  void  setHotPoint(Point p)
    { geoPoint->setX(p.xCoord()); geoPoint.setY(p.yCoord()); }
};

class DrawSegment : public DrawGeometricEntity
protected:

  AbstractSegment *geoSegment;

public:

    DrawSegment() : DrawGeometricEntity()
        { geoSegment = new Segment;}   // Null segment.

    DrawSegment(int x1, int y1, int x2, int y2) : DrawGeometricEntity()
        { geoSegment = new Segment(x1, y1, x2, y2); }
        // Segment from coordinates of end points.

    DrawSegment(Point fPoint, Point sPoint) : DrawGeometricEntity()
        { geoSegment = new Segment(fPoint, sPoint); }
        // Segment from two points.

    DrawSegment(Line l, Point fPoint, float length) : DrawGeometricEntity()
        { geoSegment = new Segment(l, fPoint, length); }
        // Segment from infinite line, first point and length.
        // fPoint assumed on line. Other point
        // computed at 'length' offset in positive x-direction.

    DrawSegment(int offset, int a, int b) : DrawGeometricEntity()
        { geoSegment = new OrthoSegment(abs(offset), a, b,
offset/abs(offset)); }
        // Orthogonal segment. Sign of offset determines H or V [1=>H,
-1=>V].
        // abs(offset) is the length of segment.

    ~DrawSegment() { delete geoSegment; }

  AbstractSegment *theSegment() { return geoSegment; }

  void    draw(DeviceContext *d)
    { d->line( geoSegment->firstPoint()->xCoord(),
               geoSegment->firstPoint()->yCoord(),
               geoSegment->secondPoint()->xCoord(),
               geoSegment->secondPoint()->yCoord()); }
        // Draw a line on the device.

  void Rectangle rangeBox()
    { return Rectangle(geoSegment->firstPoint(), geoSegment-
>secondPoint()); }
  Point hotPoint() { return geoSegment->firstPoint(); }
  void setHotPoint(Point p)
    {
      Segment *newGeoSegment =
          new Segment(geoSegment->firstPoint(), geoSegment-
>secondPoint());
```

```
        delete geoSegment;
        geoSegment = newGeoSegment;
    }
    DrawGeometricEntity *entityAt(int x, int y)
    {
      if (!DrawGeometricEntity::entityAt(x, y)) return 0;
      // So, the given point is within the range box.
      // Check whether the point is sufficiently close to the line.
      return abs( geoSegment->distFrom(&(Point(x, y))) ) <= CLOSE;
};

class DrawRectangle : public DrawGeometricEntity {
protected:
  Rectangle *geoRect;

public:
    DrawRectangle(Point bottomLeft, Point topRight)
        { geoRect = new Rectangle(bottomLeft, topRight); }
    DrawRectangle(int x1, int y1, int x2, int y2)
        { geoRect = new Rectangle(x1, y1, x2, y2); }

    ~DrawRectangle() { delete geoRect; }

  Rectangle *theRectangle() { return geoRect; }

  void draw(DeviceContext *dc)
  {
    Point p1 = geoRect->p1, p2 = geoRect->p2;

    int x1 = p1.firstPoint(), y1 = p1.yCoord(),
        x2 = p1.firstPoint(), y2 = p1.yCoord();

    dc->line(x1, y1, x2, y1); // Left.
    dc->line(x2, y1, x2, y2); // Right.
    dc->line(x2, y2, x1, y2); // Top.
    dc->line(x1, y2, x1, y1); // Left.
  }

  void Rectangle rangeBox() { return *geoRect; }
  Point hotPoint() { return geoRect->bottomLeft(); }
  void setHotPoint(Point p)
  {
    Rectangle *newGeoRect =
      new Rectangle(geoRect->bottomLeft(), geoRect->topRight());
    delete geoRect;
    geoRect = newGeoRect;
  }
};
```

DrawList, an entity which is a collection of drawable entities

Our description of drawable entities can easily be extended logically to include a collection of such entities as a full-fledged entity itself. The class DrawList encapsulates such a collection. It maintains a List of DrawGeometricEntity-s. Observe that since DrawList is itself a

DrawGeometricEntity, it can be a member of another such list. The class DrawList naturally displays some collection class properties. Some of these collection properties relevant to DrawList as a drawable class may merit some discussion.

The draw() property of a drawable class is actually a group behaviour in DrawList. It simply iterates over the contents invoking the drawing property of each content.

The hot-point for a DrawList object is defined to be the hot-point of the first contained object if any, else the origin (0, 0) point. Setting the hot-point of a DrawList object is a non-trivial operation. The given new hot-point is to be the new hot-point of the first entity in the list, if any. Additionally, it would translate the hot-points of all other entities in the list by the same amount that the first entity got translated. In other words, setting the hot-point of a DrawList results in a translation of all its contained entities.

The entityAt() member is meaningful for the first time. It searches and returns the first contained entity within which the given point lies.

```
class DrawList : public DrawGeometricEntity {
protected:
  List itemList;

  void removeAll()
  // Protected method to remove and delete all contained entities.
  {
    ListIterator l(itemList);
    l.start();
    while (!l.endReached()) {
      delete l->current();
      l.next();
    }
  }

public:

    DrawList() { itemList = new List; }
    ~DrawList() { removeAll(); delete itemList; }

  void add(DrawGeometricEntity *e) { itemList->add(e); }

  void remove(DrawGeometricEntity *e) { itemList->detach(e, 1); }

  List *theList() { return itemList; }

  void draw(DeviceContext *dc) // Draw all contained entities.
  {
    ListIterator l(itemList);
    l.start();
    while (!l.endReached()) {
      ((DrawGeometricEntity *) l->current())->draw();
      l.next();
    }
  }
}
```

```
void Rectangle rangeBox()
// Returns the union of range boxes of all contained entities.
{
  ListIterator l(itemList);
  l.start();

  if (!l.current()) return Rectangle();
  // Return a null rectangle if list is empty.

 Rectangle r = ((DrawGeometricEntity *) l->current())->rangeBox();
  // Get range box of first item.

  l.next(); // And go ahead by one step.

  while (!l.endReached()) {
    r.setUnionRectangle(
          ((DrawGeometricEntity *) l->current())->rangeBox());
    l.next();
  }
}


virtual DrawGeometricEntity *entityAt(int x, int y)
{
  ListIterator l(itemList);
  l.start();
  while (!l.endReached()) {
    DrawGeometricEntity *e =
        ((DrawGeometricEntity *) l->current())->entityAt(x, y);
    if (e) return e;
    l.next();
  }
  return NULL;
}


Point hotPoint()
{
  ListIterator l(itemList);
  l.start();
  if (l->current())
    return ((DrawGeometricEntity *) l->current())->hotPoint();
  return Point(0, 0);
}

void setHotPoint(Point p)
{
  ListIterator l(itemList);
  l.start();
  if (!l->current()) return; // List is empty.

  Point oldP = ((DrawGeometricEntity *) l->current())->hotPoint(),
        oPoint =
  Point(p.xCoord()-oldP.xCoord(), p.yCoord()-oldP.yCoord());

  ((DrawGeometricEntity *) l->current())->setHotPoint(p);
  l.next();
```

```
    virtual void endObjectDrag( DeviceContext *dc,
                             int x, int y, // End of drag (mouse) point.
                             int bitmapOffsetX, int bitmapOffsetY
                                   // Previously obtained offsets).
  {
     if (!entityBitmapped) return; // No entity was bitmapped.

     x -= bitmapOffsetX; y -= bitmapOffsetY;
// Get left-bottom point of shifted

     dc->transform(&x, &y);
// entity's range box and transform it.

     entityBitMapped->setHotPoint(Point(x,y));
// Shift the entity previously held.
  }
};
```

References

[Aho74] Aho, A., Hopcroft, J. and Ullman, J. (1974): *The Design and Analysis of Computer Algorithms*, Addison-Wesley, Reading (Mass.).

[Anuff96] Anuff, E. (1996): *A Complete Guide to Creating Java Applets for the Web*, Wiley, New York.

[Bakker90] de Bakker, J.W., de Roever, W.P. and Rozenberg G., Eds. (1990): *Foundations of Object-Oriented Languages,* Springer LNCS 666, Springer-Verlag, New York.

[Ball89] Ball, H., Steiner and Tanenbaum, A. (1989): Programming languages for distributed systems, *ACM Computing Surveys*, **21**, 3, 262–322.

[Bergin94] Bergin, J. (1994): *Data Abstraction—The objected-oriented approach using C++*, McGraw-Hill, New York.

[Bob95] Bob, F. (1995): *A STL Hash Table Implementation*, Internet distribution, Feb. 16, 1995. **ftp://butler,hpl.hp.com/stl.**

[Booch86] Booch, G. (1986): Object-Oriented Development, *IEEE Transactions on Software Engineering,* **12**, 2, 211–221.

[Booch90] Booch, G. and Vilot, M. (1990): The Design of the C++ Booch components, *Proc. ECOOP/OOPSLA '90,* 1–11.

[Booch91] Booch, G. (1991): *Object-Oriented Design with Applications,* Benjamin Cummings.

[Booch94] Booch, G. (1994): *Object-Oriented Analysis and Design with Applications*, 2nd edn., Benjamin Cummings.

[Borland94a] (1991, 1994): Borland C++ (ver. 4.5) Class Library Reference. Borland International, Inc., 1994.

[Borland94b] (1991, 1994): Borland C++ (ver. 4.5) ObjectWindows Reference. Borland International, Inc., 1994.

[Budd91] Budd, T. (1991): *An Introduction to Object-Oriented Programming,* Addison-Wesley, Reading (Mass.).

[Budd94] Budd, T. (1994): *Classic Data Structures in C++*, Addison-Wesley, Reading (Mass.).

[Cardelli85] Cardelli, L. and Wegner, P. (1985): On understanding types, data abstraction and poliymosphism, *ACM Computing Surveys*, **17**, 4, 472–522.

[Caromel96] Caromel, D., Belloncle, F. and Roudier, Y. (1996): The C++ // system, in *Parallel Programming Using C++*, G. Wilson and P. Lu (Eds.), MIT Press, Cambridge (Mass.).

[Carrol91] Carrol, M. (1991): Using multiple inheritance to implement abstract data types, *The C++ Report*, April 1991.

[Carrol93] Carrol, M. (1993): Design the USL standard components, *The C++ Report*, June 1993.

[Cay95] Cay, H.S. (1995): Evaluating class libraries, *The C++ Report*, May 1995.

[Cline95] Cline, M.P. and Lomow, G.A. (1995): *C++ FAQs*. Addison-Wesley, Reading (Mass.).

[CNS91] (1990, 1991): *C++/Views User Guide (C++/Views for MSWindows)*, CNS, Inc.

[Coad91] Coad, P. and Yourdon, E. (1991): *Object-Oriented Analysis*, 2nd edn., Prentice Hall, Upper Saddle River, New Jersey.

[Coad93] Coad, P. and Nicola, J. (1993): *Object-Oriented Programming*, Yourdon Press.

[Coplien92] Coplien, J. (1992): *Advanced C++ Programming Styles and Idioms*. Addison-Wesley, Reading (Mass.).

[Cox86] Cox, B.J. (1986): *Object-Oriented Programming—An evolutionary approach*, Addison-Wesley, Reading (Mass.).

[Danforth88] Danforth, S. and Tolinson, C. (1988): Type theories and object-oriented programming, *ACM Computing Surveys*, **20**, 1, 30–72.

[Dijkstra76] Dijkstra, E.W. (1976): *A Discipline of Programming*, Prentice Hall, Englewood Cliffs, New Jersey.

[Dony92] Dony, C., Malenfant, J. and Cointe, P. (1992): Prototype-Based Language: From a new taxonomy to constructive proposals and their validation, *ACM OOPSLA-92*, **27**, 10, 201–217.

[Ellis90] Ellis, M. and Stroustrup, B. (1990): *The Annotated C++ Reference Manual*, Addison-Wesley, Reading (Mass.).

[Goldberg83] Goldberg, A. and Robson, D. (1983): *Smalltalk-80: The language and its implication*, Addison-Wesley, Reading (Mass.).

[Gorlen87] Gorlen, K.E. (1987): An Object-Oriented Class Library for C++ Programs, *Proc. USENIX C++ Conference,* Santa Fe, NM. Nov. 1987.

[Gorlen90] Gorlen, K.E., Orlow, S. and Plexico, P. (1990): *Data Abstraction and Object-Oriented Programming in C++,* Wiley, New York.

[Graham91] Graham, I. (1991): *Object-Oriented Methods,* Addison-Wesley, Reading (Mass.).

[Grien81] Gries, D. (1981): *The Science of Programming,* Springer-Verlag, New York.

[Henderson93] Henderson, P. (1993): *Object-Oriented Specification and Design with C++,* McGraw-Hill, New York.

[Hopcroft87] Hopcroft, J.E. (1987): *Introduction to Automata Theory, Languages and Computation.* Addison-Wesley, Reading (Mass.).

[Hu89] Hu, D. (1989): *C/C++ for Expert Systems.* MIT Press, Cambridge (Mass.).

[Ince91] Ince, D. (1991): *Object-Oriented Software Engineering with C++,* McGraw-Hill, New York.

[Javier95] Javier, B., et al. (1995): *Hash Tables for the Standard Template Library,* Internet distribution, January 30, 1995. **ftp://butler.hpl.hp.com/ stl.**

[Johnsonbaugh95] Johnsonbaugh, R. and Kalin, M. (1995): *Object-Oriented Programming in C++,* Prentice Hall, Upper Saddle River, New Jersey.

[Kernighan88] Kernighan, B.W. and Ritchie, D.M. (1988): *The C Programming Language (ANSI C Version),* 2nd edn, Prentice Hall of India, New Delhi.

[Knuth73a] Knuth, D.E (1973): *Fundamental Algorithms,* 2nd edn, Addison-Wesley, Reading (Mass.).

[Knuth73b] Knuth, D.E. (1973): *Sorting and Searching,* Addison-Wesley, Reading (Mass.).

[Koenig88] Koenig, A. (1988): Associative Arrays in C++, *Proc. USENIX Conference,* San Francisco, June 1988.

[Koenig89] Koenig, A. and Stroustrup, B. (1989): As close to C as possible— but no closer, *The C++ Report,* July 1989.

[Koenig90a] Koenig, A. and Stroustrup, B. (1990): Exception Handling for C++. *Proc. USENIX C++ Conference,* San Francisco, April 1990.

[Koenig90b] Koenig, A. (1990): Applicators, Manipulators and Function Objects, *C++ Journal,* **1,** 1990.

[Koenig92] Koenig, A. (1992): Space Efficient Trees in C++, *Proc. USENIX C++ Conference,* Portland (OR), August 1992.

[Knudsen88] Knudsen, J.L. and Madsen O.L. (1988): Teaching object-oriented programming is more than teaching object-oriented programming languages, *Proc. ECOOP'88,* Springer LNCS 276, Springer-Verlag, New York, 21–40.

[Krasner84] Krasner, G. (1984): *Smalltalk-80: Bits of history, words of advice,* Addison-Wesley, Reading (Mass.).

[Krasner88] Krasner, G.E. and Pope, S.T. (1988): A cookbook for using the Model-View-Controller user interface paradigm in Smalltalk-80, *Journal of OOP*, August, 26–49.

[Lea93] Lea, D. (1993): The GNU C++ Library, *The C++ Report,* June 1993.

[Lippman91] Lippman, S. (1991): *A C++ Primer,* 2nd edn., Addison-Wesley, Reading (Mass.).

[Locke94] Locke, N. (1994): C++ FTP libraries, *C++ Report,* **6,** 4, 61–65.

[Masini96] Masini, G. (1996): An Introduction to C++, Comparisons with Eiffel, *CRIN/CNRS-INRIA Lorraine ISA Project.*

[Meyer88] Meyer, B. (1988): *Object-Oriented Software Construction,* Prentice Hall, Englewood Cliffs, New Jersey.

[Meyer90] Meyer, B. (1990): Tools for the new culture: Lessons from the design of the Eiffel libraries, *Communications of the ACM,* **33,** 9, 69–88.

[Meyer92] Meyer, B. (1992): *Eiffel: The language*, Prentice Hall, Upper Saddle River, New Jersey.

[Microsoft92a] (1992): *Microsoft C++ Tutorial,* Microsoft Corp.

[Microsoft92b] (1992): *Microsoft Windows Guide to Programming*, Microsoft Corp.

[Microsoft95a] (1995): *Visual C++ 1.52: Class library user's guide,* Microsoft Corp.

[Microsoft95b] (1995): *Visual C++ 1.52: Class library reference,* Microsoft Corp.

[Microsoft95c] (1995): *Visual C++ 1.52: C++ language reference,* Microsoft Corp.

[Mullin89] Mullin M. (1989): *Object-Oriented Program Design with Examples in C++.* Addison-Wesley, Reading (Mass.).

[Musser94] Musser, D.R. and Stepanov, A.A. (1994): Algorithm-oriented generic libraries, *Software Practice and Experience,* **2,** 47.

[Pohl89] Pohl, I. (1989): *C++ for C Programmers,* Benjamin Cummings.

[Rumbaugh91] Rumbaugh, J., Blaha M., Premerlani, W., Eddy, F. and Lorensen, W. (1991): *Object-Oriented Modeling and Design,* Prentice-Hall, Upper Saddle River, New Jersey.

[Saunders89] Saunders, J. (1989): A survey of object-oriented programming languages, *Journal of OOP*, March/April 1989, 5–11.

[Sedgewick92] Sedgewick, R. (1992): *Algorithms in C++*, Addison-Wesley, Reading (Mass.).

[Stepanov94] Stepanov, A.A. and Lee, M. (1994): The Standard Template Library, *Technical Report HPL-94-34*, Hewlett-Packard Laboratories.

[Stepanov95] Stepanov, A. and Lee, M. (1995): *The Standard Template Library*. Internet distribution, July 7, 1995. **ftp://butler.hpl.hp.com/stl.**

[Stroustrup82a] Stroustrup, B. (1982): Classes: An abstract data type facility the C Language. *ACM SIGPLAN Notices*, January 1982.

[Stroustrup82b] Stroustrup, B. (1982): *Adding Classes to C: An exercise in language evolution*, AT&T Bell Laboratories Computer Science Internal Document.

[Stroustrup84a] Stroustrup, B. (1984): *The C++ Reference Manual*, AT&T Bell Laboratories Computer Science Technical Report No. 108.

[Stroustrup84b] Stroustrup, B. (1984): Operator overloading in C++, *Proc. IFIP WG2.4 Conference on System Implementation Languages: Experience and assessment*, Sept. 1994.

[Stroustrup84c] Stroustrup, B. (1984): Data abstraction in C, *Bell Labs Technical Journal*, **63**, 8, Oct. 1994.

[Stroustrup85] Stroustrup, B. (1985): An extensible I/O facility for C++, *Proc. Summer 1995 USENIX Conference*, June 1995.

[Stroustrup86] Stroustrup, B. (1986): What is object-oriented programming? *Proc. 14th ASU Conference*, August 1996.

[Stroustrup87] Stroustrup, B. (1987): Multiple inheritance for C++, *Proc. EUUG Spring Conference*, May 1987. USENIX Computer Systems, **2**, 4, 1989.

[Stroustrup88] Stroustrup, B. (1988): What is object-oriented programming? *IEEE Software*, **5**, 3, 10–20.

[Stroustrup91] Stroustrup, B. (1991): *The C++ Programming Language*, 2nd edn., Addison-Wesley, Reading (Mass.).

[Stroustrup94] Stroustrup, B. (1994) *The Design and Evolution of C++*. Addison-Wesley, Reading (Mass.).

[Stubbs87] Stubbs, D. and Webre, N. (1987): *Data Structures with Abstract Data Types and Modula-2*, Brooks-Cole.

[Taivalsaari93] Taivalsaari, A. (1993): On the notion of object, *Journal of Systems Software*, **21**, 3–16.

[Tello89] Tello, E.R. (1989): *Object-Oriented Programming for Artificial Intelligence*, Addison-Wesley, Reading (Mass.).

[Weiner88] Weiner, R. and Pinson L. (1988): *An Introduction to Object-Oriented Programming and C++*, Addison-Wesley, Reading (Mass.).

[Weiss93] Weiss, M.A. (1993): *Data Structures and Algorithm Analysis in C++*, Addison-Wesley, Reading (Mass.).

[Wilkie93] Wilkie, G. (1993): *Object-Oriented Software Engineering—The professional developers guide,* Addison-Wesley, Reading (Mass.).

[WirfsBrock89] Wirfs-Brock, R. (1989): Object-oriented design: A responsibility-driven approach, *Proc. OOPSLA'89,* 71–75.

[WirfsBrock90] Wirfs-Brock, R., Wilkerson, B. and Wiener, L. (1990): *Designing Object-Oriented Software,* Prentice Hall, Upper Saddle River, New Jersey.

[Wirth76] Wirth, N. (1976): *Algorithms + Data Structures = Programs*, Prentice Hall of India, New Delhi.

[Wirth83] Wirth, N. (1983): *Programming in Modula-2*, Springer-Verlag, New York.

Index